WOMAN AND CHILD

WOMAN AND CHILD

MOHINDER SINGH

PUBLICATIONS
KALPAZ PUBLICATIONS
DELHI-110052

Woman and Child

Rs. 690

ISBN: 81-7835-543-4

Published in 2007 in India by
Kalpaz Publications
C-30, Satyawati Nagar,
Delhi-110052
E-mail: kalpaz@hotmail.com

Lasser Type Setting by: Rudra Computer Graphics, Delhi
Printed at : Salasar Imaging System, Delhi

Contents

Preface

The book consists of 15 chapters.

The first five deal with marriage; choosing a marriage mate, what makes for a happy marriage, marital troubles, sex in marriage, and other marriage-related factors. These include the trend towards successful men looking for 'trophy' wives, some tips on pepping up your marriage, marital sulk and nagging, the sex life of dual-career couples, spousal infidelity, money in marriage, and the phenomenon of retirement tuming out a 'second marriage'.

The next three chapters relate to family life. Here one dwells on the family eating together, sibling rivalry, discipling children, teenager troubles, more so in drinking and driving, the role of grandparents, and the influence of peers versus parents on adolescents. And there is talk of the latest trend whereas more and more of adult children, even married ones, are continuing to stay with parents, or retuming to the parental' empty nest'.

Chapters nine, ten and eleven spe.11 out the problems of working women, such as sexual harassment in workplace, hassles of women business travelers, and working wives under pressure of time. Some aspects of workplace romance are highlighted, such as being 'more than friends, less than lovers' with a male colleague. And there is the piquant position where a wife outshines her husband in professional career or business -putting a bit of strain on the traditional patriarchal primacy.

Chapters twelve to fifteen spell out the man-woman equation, as it evolved over time. And discusses how alike or different are men and women. Surely they differ in the way they shop, they drive, they laugh, and they converse, or even when they watch TV. One chapter makes out how things work out unfair to women, such as the compulsion to go for tube atomy than the husband going for the simpler vasectomy, longer wait at cinema urinals, and sexism in sports.

Yet the book comes up with an increasingly satisfying scenario for women in the 21st century.

1

Choosing Marriage Partner

Marrying Someone Like Yourself!

A new trend can be discerned in the marriage market; upcoming professional men wanting to marry "someone like yourself".

Achievers themselves, they look more for women with educational and professional achievements than the customary plus-points of good looks, family background or even money. "I am not interested in someone who doesn't have as much to offer as I have to offer her," says one youngish head of an ads agency.

Traditionally, successful doctors, lawyers, bankers, businessmen or members of Civil Services sought wives who were beautiful and well-bred. Now not a few seek wives who are doing similarly well in their callings/careers. One commonly comes across couples where both are architects, or doctors, or dentists. Thriving professionals, on their own, they are going in for career women. That way a higher degree of parity is evident today between go-getter marital partners.

Providentially, the number of women available in this category is witnessing a rapid rise. More and more women figure in higher education and professional courses. These vibrant women are registering marked success in business, professions, media, fashion, even sports—-the last bastion of male superiority. And the same is ringing in an attitudinal sea change in gender equation.

It was feared that achiever-women may put off men marrying them. But this isn't happening. Successful men are looking for trophy brides. It seems we may be experiencing a historic change in the things people want out of marriage.

Once, men were a good catch because they were high earners. It now seems to be applying to women, too.

A fellow mated to a beauty used to evoke envy. Currently someone married to a successful career woman is often the subject of greater peer envy. In a way a woman's success makes her sexy.

Indeed a wife with no achievements or distinctions to her credit is becoming a bit of turn-off among upwardly-mobile circles. It's no longer enough to be beautiful and a good hostess.

Some observers of social scene were apprehensive that such women may not find mates coming up to their expectation. Surely successful career women are behaving increasingly picky in their selection of mates. It's more like a proposed business merger than merely love. Any potential husband is carefully sized up and passed through a string of scoring points,

How does it effect a husband's masculinity or male ego where his mate is no inferior to him in qualifications and earning capacity? Or, she's even enjoying an edge at times.

It was different when man was the sole breadwinner in a family. His headship stood unquestioned. Now, with dual-income couples becoming a common norm, men are learning to live with the new situation of an equal economic partnership.

As an offshoot, it can also mean lower age differential between career-oriented partners. Once a gap of 6 to 7 years was usual; typically a man of 26 marrying a woman of 20. Now he could well marry someone of the same age. They could be classmates in a professional course or colleagues. She could even be a year or two older. Happily, modern women manage to keep their looks and figure into ripe years.

The trophy wife, with all its benefits in money and companionship, comes with a price. These wives are more demanding emotionally, being less dependent economically. And they have their own views on childbearing. Often it means children coming late, and far fewer.

Difficulties arise, not because the man feels emasculated, but because the woman grows disappointed with her partner.

Men truly want bright, smart wives who do well in the world. And most men aren't worried about their male ego in relation to their wife's success. Indeed they are quite happy to enjoy the material benefits of the double income. But they do wish such wives to be more wifely, less aggressive at home. And they certainly don't fancy a situation where they are ever under pressure from ambitious wives to reach their potential in income and achievement.

Some have likened it to driving a Ferrari. It can be uncomfortable and dangerous, but it's ultimately more rewarding than owning a Maruti Esteem, which is serviceable but boring.

Arranged or Love Marriage!

What works better; an arranged marriage or love marriage? A question often asked, yet begging an assured answer.

I am the product of an arranged marriage. My parents hadn't even seen each other before their wedding day. They certainly weren't in love on that fateful evening. And they did stay married for sixty-five years—ostensibly happy with each other—till the demise of one.

What to say of India, arranged marriages were quite common in the West until the 19th century. Marriages were a way of forging alliances, ensuring inheritance, and stitching social and religious needs of a community. Love had nothing to do with it, says historian E.J. Graff in *What is Marriage For?: The Strange Social History of Our Most Intimate Institution*.

In time, there developed the concept of romantic love—first love, then marriage. To its votaries, the very notion of an arranged marriage offended the ideas both of love and liberty; the act of choosing, whom to love and marry, representing the very essence of freedom.

In a way, a love marriage can also be construed as an arranged marriage; arranged by fate, or coincidence. The major reason why people find themselves involved with somebody else is proximity and physical attraction.

Both these factors, say the advocates of arranged marriages, are terrible predictors of long-term happiness in marital relationship. The myth of "love at first sight" gets so many into trouble. When people marry blinded by passion, they are virtually incapable of making a sound decision. As the heat of passion wears off—and it always does—you are left with really nothing.

Indeed sociologists blame the prevailing high divorce rate in the West (the incidence as high as 50 percent in USA) on love marriages. Even couples who marry after a live-in period aren't doing significantly better.

Andrew Hacker, the distinguished social scientist of Queens College, New York, in his book *Mismatch: The Growing*

Gulf Between Women and Men, talks of another dimension. Based on a wealth of statistics and surveys, he finds more psychological separation between American spouses than was there a few decades back. And he attributes it to women's expectation of "full equality" and rising receipt of higher education and jobs. A woman now wants much more from marriage than her mother or grandmother did. And she does express her disappointment when she doesn't get it.

All in all, the marital scene looms far more volatile.

No wonder, people are getting more selective, if not exactly picky, in choosing marriage partners. And this, in turn, has triggered a quest for wider selection than that offered by the typical love marriage, born out of proximity and sex appeal.

One offshoot is the growing reliance on matrimonial ads in newspapers and magazines. These are clearly designed to obtain a wider selection than available through family-and-friend contacts, and in the obvious absence or rejection of love leading to marriage. Some ads go to the extent of spelling out that their sole purpose is to seek a wider choice—notwithstanding existing options.

And of late, there has been a sharp increase in the number of professional matchmakers (as distinct from the traditional ones). Yet the most explosive growth has been of online dating services. Sites like Match.com and Yahoo Personals attracted some 20 million people in USA alone last year. Now Web sites' search engines play the role of fathers and grandfathers, searching for good matches based on any criterion that you select.

Dr. Alvin Cooper, the director of the San Jose Marital Services and Sexuality Centre, and author of *Sex and the Internet* (Routledge, 2002), says that because online interaction tends to downplay proximity, physical attraction, and face-to-face interaction, people are more likely to take risks and disclose significant things about themselves. The result is that they attain a higher level of psychological and emotional intimacy than if they dated right away. The protected (cyber) space encourages self-revelation while maintaining personal boundaries.

Matrimonial ads in papers are necessarily sketchy—loquacity costs money. To pack maximum meaning in less than fifty words, a sort of telegraphic language has emerged.

In comparison, online dating, besides being inexpensive—giving more information doesn't cost more—has a much higher likelihood of finding "the one" due to the computer's capacity to sort through thousands of potential mates. That's what computers are all about—efficiency in sorting information.

Admittedly a fair number of people continue to feel a stigma about online match-making, as too technical, too businesslike. Yet the general prejudice against it is on the decline, the way it has waned with matrimonial ads in papers.

The dating Web sites allot a page to each client. And these profiles are works in progress, continually edited, fortified with newer, more flattering pictures and descriptions. Many online daters maintain more than one profile, sometimes on the same Web site.

Two people who have read each other's profiles may know not only facts of income, possessions. tastes, attitude to children but a lot about each other's hobbies, religious affiliations, political views, and so on.

Small lies are understandable; dropping a year of age or adding half an inch to height. But outright lying is counterproductive. The lie will be discovered when some interested person eventually agrees to meet you.

While women are generally more comfortable approaching men online than face to face, men tend to go for physical meeting at the earliest. An attractive woman posting her photograph and good credentials may receive scores of responses before accepting a physical meeting.

With expanding Internet use in the country, online search for a suitable mate is sure to go up. Even with our limitations about religion and caste, language and community, online dating should be able to offer a much wider selection. It means less reliance on chance, surprise or coincidence of a love marriage. Online dating that way opens up possibilities, which in turn could emphasize factors that are more conducive to a successful marriage.

Love marriages will remain, and so also those arranged by families. Yet online dating opens up a unique new window in the search for suitable marriage partners.

This Matter of Matrimonial Ads

Glancing through matrimonial columns of Sunday papers can be a revealing reading, even if you aren't in the marriage market. Possibly nothing rivals matrimonial ads in reflecting the values and aspirations of the middle classes. Some of the ads are no less illuminating than passages from Varma's book *The Great Indian Middle Class*.

Marriage continues to be a serious, solemn commitment with us; not only for the individuals involved but for their respective families, too. No wonder, most matrimonial ads are formalized as offers of "alliance" between families. The prospective groom, whether he happens to be a 34-year-old MD (Ophth) or a 37-year-old NRI engineer, is still a "boy". And the bride whether a lawyer of 29 or a teacher of 35 is still a "girl".

The idealized bride-to-be! Who's she? And how has her image changed over the years?

Some things stay unchanged: she should be young, beautiful, tall, slim, fair, homely, well educated. And, of course, hailing from a respectable, cultured family—the word "respectable" steadily giving way to "status" and "reputed".

Thirty years back the optimum age was 20 or just below—the age at which beauty queens get selected. With the emerging demand for brides with higher education, preferably professional, the same has moved up by a few years. But anyone pushing 30 has to do some explaining, such as "looking younger than she is". That's the irony. Young men and women climbing up the career ladder through their late twenties face an altogether differing prospect; while men keep on notching gains, women start losing in the marriage market—most successful men go for younger mates.

Beauty is the common denominator, both asked for as well as offered.

There is almost an obsessive concern with height. With the ideal around 5ft 4, many girls are still failing to make it—better nutrition is taking its time to make impact on girls' height.

It's rather intriguing why slimness is so much in demand. Perhaps the term is popular because "slim" is such a nice-sounding word. After all who can vouchsafe, today's slim won't be tomorrow's plump? An obese condition that's apt to attract unwelcome attention is euphemistically described as "healthy".

In our colour-conscious setting, the skin pigment is paramount. Everyone wants a fair bride; irrespective whether the man himself is brown or black. The ads give umpteen gradations of fair: very fair, most fair, extremely fair, milky white. On the other hand, "wheatish" alone is there to accommodate all shades of the less-fair. It's a pity, the Queen's English is not inclined to incorporate this picturesque word.

It is still a sexist world where a girl's physical attributes undergo a far closer scrutiny than that of the boy. Any female infirmity, such as a stammer or squint or even spectacles, has to be listed out bravely while "boys" rarely bother to mention their bodily imperfections. And that's when males, on average, are heir to more body infirmities than females.

One significant development, however, has occurred. Instead of keeping mostly mum over the boy's personality, his looks increasingly find a mention. But it mostly remains confined to the word "handsome" or "very handsome". Indeed, if what's advertised about "boys" and "girls" turns out to be true, we should we one of the most beautiful people on the planet.

The most popular epithet used for girls is "homely", both demanded—and offered. Surely other aspects of her good nature get listed, such as amiable, affectionate, simple natured, sweet natured, soft-spoken, cooperative, cheerful, or perfect. Yet the adjective "homely" takes the cake. "Homely" in the Concise Oxford Dictionary means simple, primitive, unpretending. Americans are far harsher; the New Webster defines it as plain in appearance, unattractive.

Yet, to us, the word "homely" (taken as home-loving) symbolizes the very quintessence of what an Indian male and his family would want of the new bride, a *bahu* for the whole family. At the minimum, it denotes a good homemaker, a devoted housewife, an obedient daughter-in-law, and a would-be doting mother; in short, a giver, not a taker. And the homely part not to be pared down, irrespective of her being required to work outside to augment the family income.

Close on the heels of beauty comes education; the higher the better, preferably professional or technical with its surer potential for earning. Yet the Open Sesame is still Convent education—popularly associated with a flare in social mixing, and getting children admitted into the coveted English-medium schools. Many bride-seekers specify it as eminently desirable whereas some others make it an obligatory requirement.

Similarly, on the girl's side, such education is invariably highlighted. As even a brief spell of convent schooling could qualify for being "convented", some have started putting forth phrases like "throughout convent education".

At certain levels, a girl's job and salary become as crucial to her marriage prospects as her looks and family. Of course, some people are seeking career women as wives for more equal partnership—let alone women themselves finding work satisfaction as the prime consideration. With the growing consumer culture and inflation, the attractions of a double-income are obvious.

Indeed, an increasing number of men are picking brides for brains. And this trend is almost worldwide, especially in consumerist societies. It marks a novel departure from the age-old male approach to accord primacy to looks in choosing life-long partners. Of course, if someone combines both—brains and beauty—so much the better.

What strikes one most while reading today's matrimonial ads is the growing thrust on money power. Parents of girls enumerate their wealth. And so do the parents of boys. At one time the only-child was thought to be somewhat unfortunate, having missed the fun of siblings. Now the fact of someone being the only child is boldly advertised for its property potential.

Many an ad proclaims: Dowry not wanted. This really means nothing. If someone actually wastes space and money on these words, it is because they want something.

The groom's side seems to have an easier job framing ads. You list your requirements of the bride and then mainly concentrate on detailing the groom's income—often mentioned in terms of five figures or six figures or seven figures—and the family property, more so if it includes a house in South Delhi. Grooms don't have to spell out they are caring or that they would be a help at home. At best, it is made out on their behalf that they have "clean habits".

Composing a concise matrimonial ad for a near one is not such a simple affair. You have to compress a complex human equation in some 50 words—loquacity costs money. To pack maximum meaning into minimum words, a sort of telegraphic language has emerged that calls for some skill in deciphering. "Decent marriage", for one, is a meaning-laden term.

In our matrimonial ads (increasingly backed by technological advances like E-mail address) the concept of an ideal husband has remained largely unchanged over the years. But the concept of an ideal wife has undergone a sea-change in the last few decades—the added imperative of being an actual or potential earner, without compromising any of her traditional prerequisites.

2

For a Happy Marriage

What Matters More is Small Stuff

There are a lot more marital arguments over a wink than a mink.

Sanjiv is an early riser while Meena gets her best sleep in the morning hours between 6 and 8. Before he goes to bed at night, Sanjiv hangs his next day's clothing in the bathroom, so he doesn't have to disturb his partner again and again by opening doors and drawers. On getting up, he doesn't switch on any light in the bedroom, and takes care to move noiselessly to the bathroom, and then out to the car.

When Meena woke up this morning, one of the first things she noticed was the empty hanger hooked to the tub curtain railing. Remembering Sanjiv's obvious efforts not to wake her made Meena smile and think, "He's so thoughtful."

Last night Deepa, sitting in the double bed, kept watching an old Raj Kapur movie late into the night. Ranjit had a long day at work and was fagged out. Inwardly he wished Deepa could step out and see her favourite movie on the living room TV. Deepa, however, prefers the comfort of her bed and the bigger television set in the bedroom. Ranjit buried himself under the bedclothes, but still had a hard time falling asleep. "Why does she have to be so selfish?" mulls Ranjit.

In the realm of love and marriage, there's nothing too small to be unimportant. Every single issue can have certain impact, every single gesture carries some weight. The marital world provides a constant stream of "small stuff" where every piece makes a difference. These small pieces, when they are negative, soon accumulate into large problems. "Small annoyances in marriage adding up as particles of sediments build great deltas," says James Thurber, the noted American humorist. On the other hand, an ongoing supply of small positive moments helps a couple feel loved and loving.

Far too many husbands and wives have a "grand gesture" approach to their relationship. They worry about the larger relationship moments: birthday presents, special dinners, or the big fights. That's when they pay attention to what's taking place. All the in-between time isn't considered vital or important, often not considered at all.

Indeed, for the most part, people handle the serious parts of life with courage and dignity—things like sickness of a child or a death in the family. But then, much of the life doesn't consist of really big stuff.

The truth is that a vast part of our life is consumed with day-today, moment-to-moment small stuff—dealing with minor hassles and frustrations, disagreements, lost items, noise, gestures, and so forth. It therefore becomes so important to learn to deal with the small stuff. In fact if we've learned to deal with the small stuff with equanimity and amity, we handle the bigger things better as well.

Bulk of the working marital relationship is taking place in quieter moments in small, minute doses. Keeping the phone line open when you know he's expecting a call. Helping your wife make the bed. The man lifting the toilet seat on urinating and then putting it back. She picking up his dirty socks without a reproachful look. These are classic examples of the absolutely small kind of stuff that can have a disproportionately large effect on the day-to-day experience of love and regard in marriage.

Why is it so? Because every one of these small moments tells your partner, "I care about you."

How to work on the small stuff? How to stay on track day after day, month after month, year after year? It isn't as complicated as it sounds.

Pay attention to your partner's preferences, concerns, and anxieties, howsoever small or inconsequential they may seem. It isn't enough to rest on your laurels if you have managed the big stuff, such as gifting a pair of diamond earrings; small stuff is serious stuff.

Tune in to your partner's habits and schedules. Pay special attention to common areas where small conflicts might arise, such as the use of telephone or the temperature in the bedroom.

The key to working out the small stuff is active, quick processing—immediate action as each piece of stuff surfaces. Don't postpone action for some later opportunity, as there is no "good time" to deal with uncomfortable stuff.

Small-stuff problems need small-stuff solutions: an acknowledgement, a gesture, a brief conversation, a simple compromise, an apology, a loving touch. Don't turn every issue into a larger-than-life drama. As long as it hasn't been accumulating, small stuff shouldn't be hard to manage.

On the other hand, taking care of small stuff can keep your marital relationship lively and loving.

Pepping Up Your Marriage

Marriage is a case of two people agreeing to change each other's habits.

Kapurs, Hari a surgeon and Mohini a beautician, began a dream marriage 15 years back. But by now much of the mutual adoration has evaporated. What exactly went wrong?

Is it because Mohini got more and more into the habit of 'correcting' Hari in things big (how he managed finances or handled the growing son) and small (how he drove the car or put away his shoes)? Evidently it stemmed from her intense desire to run a model home, wherein Hari's imperfections may well be ironed out. But instead of the anticipated improvement, Hari is behaving increasingly aloof, withdrawn. Mohini would love to pep up her marriage but is at wits' end how to go about it?

There is a new batch of self-help books on the subject, mainly from women writers advising troubled wives—hardly any books on what husbands should do. Prominent among these publications: *The Surrendered Wife* by Laura Doyle (Simon & Schuster), *Surrendering to Marriage* by Iris Krasnow (Talk Miramax), and *The Marriage Sabbatical: The Journey That Brings You Home* by Cheryl Jarvis (Perseus).

After 25 years of marriage, two children, and a journalistic career, Jarvis became firm in her notion that a sabbatical from marriage would give her room to escape for a while without renouncing marriage. She quotes the Mosaic law which required land to lie fallow every seven years "as a Sabbath to the Lord".

At 48 Jarvis moved to a writers' colony for 3 months and felt much better—a room of her own, no cooking, no daily interaction with the husband. And she discovered that her absence from home had pepped up the marriage.

Jarvis has interviewed fifty-five marital partners who did just that: one going to India for yoga, another doing a couple of years in Namibia with the Peace Corps, another taking to mountains for months with a trunkload of books. And almost all her interviewees expressed satisfaction with the same, as it helped their personal growth as well as invigorated their marriage.

Jarvis's diagnosis: marriage—even the strongest of marriages—is predicted upon wifely confinement, saddled with the usual household chores. And she thinks the institution of marriage is in serious trouble. "How do we stay married to one person for a long time when the only constant in life is change," she asks. "If married women are going to fulfill their dreams, they will sometimes have to say, 'I can't take care of you right now.' Saying no to others is saying yes to something deeper within ourselves."

The practicality of managing a fairly long sabbatical from marriage, especially in our typical conditions, is no simple matter.

In *Surrendering to Marriage*, Krasnow has in mind mutual submission to the institution, as "a commitment we made, a spiritual promise larger than our own selfish desires". Surrendering means deciding to stand by marriage vows even when boredom becomes the dominant theme; learning to live with less than great sex, or with no sex at all. She cites several instances of husbands who are derelict in their conjugal duties.

Krasnow concedes that marriage does not provide happiness (though it can often provide an environment in which to experience happiness), and that it is not an exhilarating journey of self-discovery but a mode of living in the social world. It is actually the most sensible, practical way of living in the world that has thus far been devised. And so her counsel, especially to her American sisters: instead of breaking up a less-than-satisfactory union, better make all efforts to "surrender" to the institution of marriage. Nobody is perfect, so you may as well love the one you're with.

Laura Doyle's *The Surrendered Wife*, a best-seller by now, is the most provocative of them all. And it bears a cover endorsement as "practical and valuable" by John Gray, the author of *Men Are From Mars, Women Are From Venus.*

"When I was newly married at twenty-two, I had no idea I would ever call myself a surrendered wife. At that time, the very phrase (coined by her later) would have repulsed me. . . .

At first our marriage was blissful. Then, I started to see John's imperfections more glaringly, and I began *correcting* him. It was my way of helping him to improve. From my point of view, if he could just be more ambitious at work, more romantic at home, and clean up after himself, everything would be fine. I told him as much.

He didn't respond well. . . The harder I pushed, the more he resisted, and we both grew irritable and frustrated. While my intentions were good, I was clearly on the road to marital hell. In no time I was exhausted from trying to run my life and his. Even worse, I became estranged from the man who had once made me happy. Our marriage was in serious trouble and it had only been four years since we'd taken our vows."

This is how Doyle starts her book, and it has been quoted at length, because the book grew out of her own marital experience. When none of her agitation produced the marital bliss she had assumed, Doyle stopped trying to change her husband and instead changed herself, becoming a "surrendered wife". The book is shaped as an instruction manual. Doyle also runs a Web site, Surrenderdwife.com, and offers one-to-one "relationship training".

The basic theme of Doyle's message: a wife not to exert inappropriate control over her husband. Most importantly, to resist the temptation of finding fault—"some people find fault as if it were buried treasure". She ceased "correcting" John about his driving—conceding he had been driving all right for years before marriage without outside advice. She stopped buying clothes for him (yes, even his underwear), even when she was worried that he wouldn't buy any for himself. She stopped bossing him, giving him advice. And John began reciprocating with appreciation reminiscent of their early marriage days. Instead of bickering all the time, they were laughing together, holding hands, and enjoying an electrifying closeness that they hadn't had for years.

Doyle's recipe for a wife wanting to be "treasured, pampered, protected and adored": leave most decision-making to the husband; express gratitude for everything he does; give him charge of the family finances; respect his thinking; and receive his gifts graciously. She goes as far to advocate no denying of sex to him, at least join in once a week, whether she likes it or not.

And Doyle wants wives listen to husbands, instead of voicing the usual complaint, he isn't listening. Her advice: On some evenings, make a point of really hearing everything he says. Demonstrate you're listening rather than plotting your next sentence, or jumping up to talk to a toddler or answering the phone. Even if you disagree, don't dismiss his ideas, or laugh at him or make fun of him. Smile and invite him to say more. He'll love it and can be very forthcoming. "A man is already halfway in love with any woman who listens to him," says Brendan Francis.

What to say of correcting the husband, a wife should resist giving him guidance even when he asks for it, says Doyle. In the interest of allowing him to develop his natural dominance, she could respond with a deflective "Whatever you think" or "That's a good question". All in all, wives not condescending to their husbands by treating them like children.

Doyle does concede that the "surrender" she advocates won't be easy to attain for many a wife. There'll be the ever-present temptation to revert to the earlier bossing mode. But then, it isn't impossible to manage if a sustained effort is made. And, whenever there's a slip up, an instant apology should be forthcoming.

Of course, Doyle doesn't recommend surrender to a husband who is guilty of verbal or physical violence, given to grievous addiction like drugs, or chronically unfaithful. According to her, any attempt by a wife to "control" a normal husband whom she adored and respected enough to marry in the first place, proves counterproductive; makes him resentful, even drives him away from her in favour of work or golf.

The surprisingly appeal of *The Surrendered Wife* may have something to do with disillusionment with the kind of feminism which urged women to take control in marriage. It often led to bickering and disappointment, with a marked deterioration in the quality of marriage. "The Surrendered Wife" is no simple solution for marital harmony, but it does elaborate a point of certain validity: most husbands are inclined to please their lives and stay loving, if they aren't put off by spousal bossing or what's called 'mothering'. In any event, a majority of husbands show little improvement in their behaviour under pressure from their wives.

"When a man does not feel loved just the way he is, he will either consciously or unconsciously repeat the behaviour that is not being accepted," says John Gary.

One Secret of Happy Marriage:Separate Bathrooms

When Charles Watts of Rolling Stones was asked the secret of his happy marriage, he replied "separate bathrooms".

Indeed a husband can do better by using a separate room for keeping his clothes and dressing up. If nothing else, he can press the spare guestroom into service—perforce to be shared with the guest when there's one. In effect, he uses the master-bedroom (still carrying the sexist nomenclature) strictly as "bedroom". And he restricts his use of the attached bathroom to "emergencies".

That way he leaves his mate an almost autonomous zone for bathing, dressing, and various other intimate matters women are supposed to attend to. Such personal space is all the more welcome to her if she's seeing too much of him otherwise, like his happening to work at home.

A well-appointed bathroom all to oneself is a real luxury. You don't have to "adjust" to the convenience of anyone else. A place where you're with yourself, undisturbed, unhurried. You can spread out all your stuff, and there's none to pry into or interfere with the arrangement. And whether you clean it immediately after use or leave it in a mess is entirely your own business.

Bathrooms that way are a private world. Well, if you want to know the truth about other people, their bathroom possibly gives out better clues than the living room—of their habits and hopes, illnesses and hang-ups, even bits of sex life stand revealed in that small room.

One common source of contention between couples sharing a bathroom: the one gone before had left it messier. Husbands generally labour under a genuine belief their use of the bathroom is tidier, based on the premise their ablutions are seemingly simpler. Even otherwise many a man rates himself tidier than his mate in matters of hygiene. One fellow claims he washes the soap after taking his bath.

Wives routinely complain it falls to their lot to wipe things clean—the tub, the washbasin, the toilet seat, even the floor after their man has been through. And mostly it's the man who is the first user of a shared bathroom—possibly not a bad arrangement otherwise, with men averaging less time in bathrooms than women. And, of course, there's the perennial complaint of husbands neglecting to lift the seat every time they urinate. In Sweden some feminist groups have started advocating, men should adapt the practice of urinating sitting down.

The scene at the breakfast table should spell far more harmonious where a working couple assembles after having used separate bathrooms—and separate dressing places—for getting ready. "The critical period in matrimony is breakfast," says A.P.Herbert, a noted writer. Similarly, with separate bathrooms and dressing places, one can visualize a less contentious scenario when a couple is getting ready for an evening party.

Admittedly this arrangement of separate bathrooms calls for some sacrifice on the part of the hubby; forsaking the dwelling's best bathroom for something less elegant. Yet the gains in spousal goodwill could far outweigh the foregone comfort and convenience.

A Recipe of Happy Marriage

Joan Erikson, the wife of the famous pyschoanalyst Erik Erikson and a scholar in her own right, was once asked what could be the secret of their celebrated marriage. Eriksons had been happily married for sixty years and were known for radiating mutual love and respect in each other's company.

"Well, that's easy," she said without hesitation. "A sense of humour. Humour is what keeps everything in balance."

Over and over again, it has been observed that shared laughter happens to be an important bond between happy couples. Not laughter in the sense of jokes making the rounds but something deeper. It's a state of marriage where the partners continue to find each other interesting, almost "funny".

Happily married couples have an intimate way of relating to each other. And this connection they are often seen to be keeping through a mild sort of spontaneous bantering. A majority of happily married couples are to a degree playful. Light-hearted attitude towards each other keeps them from acting defensive, combative or argumentative.

The same factor, it seems, was operating between my parents. They enjoyed an enviably happy marriage extending over sixty-five years. As children we would hear father's marital banter, sometimes we also joining in the fun. If mother got upset misplacing her bunch of keys, he would banter about the manner she kept the bunch, while helping in the search. Father also had a knack of relating petty office incidents in their comic context. In later years when mother gained in self-confidence and education, she bantered in her own inimitable style. And she learnt to laugh over little household mishaps.

Right into their old age, you could see them teasing each other with light-hearted banter. Even under umpteen illnesses, they retained a capacity for amusement over each other's good-humoured remarks; their banter poking fun at the ups and downs of everyday life.

Good marriage that way is not a business partnership, or a form of friendship, or just a support system. The distinctiveness of a good and happy marriage lies in its electricity.

I remember when I was a kid, Mahatma Gandhi had visited our town. In the crowded public meeting my father got his purse picked, with rupees fifty in it. In the 1940s that was some money.

Anguished over the loss, father was saying, "Gandhiji was raising a fund. I wanted to contribute rupees ten. To my dismay, when I put my hand into my trousers' pocket for the purse, it was gone. Some rogue making merry with it."

"Gandhiji would have welcomed all of rupees fifty," says mother. "This is what happens when you defy a Mahatma."

And her banter lightened the mood all round.

Here are a few allied do's and don'ts for a happy marriage.

Learn to laugh at yourself.

Stay away from ultimatums.

Learn to deflect occasional uncalled-for comments.

Accept apologies gracefully.

Allow your partner a few eccentricities.

Stay away from comparisons.

And don't let your children come between you.

6-Point Programme for Happy Marriage

Nobody, I hasten to admit, has asked me to draw up a programme for the perpetuation of marital bliss.

My qualifications for the job; seventy-five years of warily watching marriages—happy, unhappy, mixed. I have sat like a fly on marriage walls, even meddled as a middleman in marital disputes. And I have nearly fifty years of running a marriage myself—again (confidentially) mixed.

Axioms and admonitions on the subject are galore. "Don't date your secretary, or for that matter, anyone else's wife." "Praise her cooking and sometimes her clothes if inexpensive." ..."Be a sweetheart as well as a wife." "Share his hobbies and be seen enjoying his jokes." He to "earn more", she to "talk less'~ Seems, these time-tested teachings to hold the sacred knot are somewhat wearing thin.

Here is my 6-point-programme for keeping a marriage happy.

Point One: A wife's dressing table is inviolable: the one place in the house you should stay away from. Curb your curiosity. Don't ever disturb the contents. If you've cracked a nail, you can't go rummaging there for a file. You are supposed to approach the owner.

Point Two: Better receive—without fuss if you can—her relatives and friends at airport, railway stations and bus-stands at all times of the day or night. Excuses like being tired or weak eyesight for night driving won't help. Hire a taxi if you can't drive.

Point Three: Bridle your urge to be humorous at her relatives' expense, especially elderly aunts. Extending further, no aspersions, insinuations, or plain cracks on the character, looks or intelligence of her former friends (of either sex). She can, however, regale your men friends with hilarious accounts of your blunderings (an egg rolling off the kitchen table when you set out to make an omelette).

Point Four (Point One for Wives): Keep in some check your normal female inclination to interrupt your man when reading. One can appreciate your concern—he should not be idling like this, when some house help is needed. But then, this creature yearns to idle in the comfort of his home. If perchance he's reading aloud to you—his favourite health tips—sit quiet and relaxed. At least pretend to be attentive; not take out your tweezers and mirror set or start swapping at a fly. Needn't break in to correct his pronunciation or draw attention to a graying strand in his hair. Now and then you may even concede to his request—not that he should be reading all the time—to switch off the TV sound while you are viewing it. Your loss in viewing may turn out marginal.

Point Five: That reminds me, could you be gracious enough not to puncture the bubble of his male superiority in matters of traditional manly competence: luggage packing, house shifting, involved finance planning, what to say of combating a seedy stranger or a suspect stray dog. Once the other head on your pillow begins to feel inferior and that also in mundane matters like these, the body below that head may get less effective in bed.

Point Six: Men are contrary creatures. Their hobbies, tastes and amusements often border on the bizarre. As long as he isn't knocking holes into the family budget or wrecking the marriage morale, give him a long leash. His evening drink (without turning alcoholic), golfing on weekends (without your being turned into a golf widow), ogling at shapely figures (without the follow-up of dating), or peeping at pornographic stuff (without being a collector). Glancing back over the 6-points, I do concede, a number of loose ends are left untied. Somebody else, with a better track record, needs delve deeper into the mysteries of modern marriage: what's popularly termed as the RUNNING FEUD.

3

Marital Troubles

The Longest War in History:Between Women and their Husbands' Mothers

At Unisinos, a university in Sao Leopoldo, Brazil, they are running courses on mother-in-law/daughter-in-law conflict. There they analyse What Can Go Wrong and What Can Be Done.

The standard 15-hour course with 40 participants (mothers-in-law and daughters-in-law roughly equal in number) is proving popular. Dr Fetter, the course director when asked whether there was any tension among participants, said jokingly, "The only fighting that goes on is to find a place on the course." The course for women is so successful, the university is planning a similar one for male in-laws.

In cultures all over the world, mothers-in-law—with their No-One-Is-Good-Enough-For-My—Boy belief—have a dodgy reputation. In Italy, for example, the Supreme Court has ruled that being forced to live with a mother-in-law is grounds for a woman to ask for divorce. A plant with long, sharp-edged leaves has been given the name of Mother-in-law's Tongue.

This adverse image, however, is gradually undergoing a change. Previously it was always a live-in mother-in-law. Now, more often, it's a visiting mother-in-law. Anyway the mother-in-law jokes are no longer in favour.

Admittedly the mother-in-law/daughter-in-law relationship is far more complex and sensitive than, say, of mother and daughter. A mother and daughter can be forthright with each other, even be furious with each other—and then make up. Any confrontation between a mother-in-law and daughter-in-law is rarely such a simple, straightforward affair.

To a daughter-in-law the initial reception from her mother-in-law is rather crucial (a point whose importance some mothers-in-law underestimate, with the hope of making amends later on). If she isn't made to feel welcome, the younger woman may take it as being found wanting. This perceived rebuff may affect her relationship with her mother-in-law for a long time, even leave permanent scars. And it comes harder to a daughter-in-law whose background occupies a lower rung on the socio-economic ladder.

Where a daughter-in-law's socio-economic background is well above that of her mother-in-law, differences in lifestyle could add stress on both sides, particularly if the newcomer tries to wean her husband away from the customs of the family. The in-laws may feel rejected.

To have a daughterless mother-in-law can well be a disadvantage. A daughterless mother-in-law may not know how to relate to a younger woman. Or, she may hope that her daughter-in-law will be the dreamed-of perfect daughter she never had.

Various surveys reveal that the younger the mother-in-law, the better the relationship between the two women. And, where both of them work, full time or part-time, their relationship gets an added plus. Working mothers-in-law and daughters-in-law know what it means to juggle a job, home and children.

Even mothers-in-law who have retired but worked once, display a greater tendency of non-interference with their children's lives. And, of course, where the live-in mother-in-law is there to share the housekeeping and childcare burden of the working housewife, she's doubly welcome.

What often causes maximum trouble between a mother—n-law and daughter-in-law is the rendering of "advice" by the senior woman; the younger woman interpreting it as criticism. Many a mother-in-law sincerely believes she gives advice only when necessary. But who's to judge what's "necessary"? Actually, a certain amount of advice-giving is a part of our daily conversations; we all dole it out to others, and a mother-in-law is no exception to this condition. But such advice can only be tolerated in small doses, with the tone and manner of handing it out being just right. Otherwise it puts the young daughter-in-law, still unsure of herself, on the defensive. Once she has matured and acquired the necessary self-confidence, she can cope much better with the advice coming from the senior woman, even appreciating it.

Ideally, a "good" mother-in-law ought not to make critical remarks about the way her grandchildren are being brought up—that's primarily the responsibility of parents. But this is easier said than done. At certain moments, a mother-in-law may be unable to control her accumulated feelings about what she believes good or bad for a child, and blurt out her suggestions. This is commonly construed by a daughter-in-law as meddling in the upbringing of children—in things like whether the baby be left to cry or be picked up, the strict enforcement of bedtime, the amount of TV viewing to be allowed, and so on. Grandparents are often charged with "spoiling" grandchildren with their indulgent approach.

For a mother-in-law, it is wise and helpful to think of her son and his wife as a couple from the very beginning. Any serious discussion with her son over family matters should include the daughter-in-law.

The wife who can think of her mother-in-law as her husband's mother instead of associating her with the stereotyped mother-in-law of myths and jokes, will be starting off well. Her husband may occasionally complain of his mother, but if the wife joins him in attacking the mother, he'll eventually come to resent it.

One of the deepest gratification of a mother-in-law is to feel wanted and needed. It's therefore a good strategy for a daughter—in-law to keep on asking for her help or advice in day-to-day matters. And a widowed mother-in-law is to be extended greater consideration; widowhood magnifies the need for feeling wanted, more so if she lacks other satisfactions such as work, friends or hobbies.

By and large, with the education and advancement of women, coupled with a growing democratisation of our family life, the relationship between mothers-in-law and daughters-in-law is assuming a more sophisticated, appreciative shape. Still the longest war in history, one that ruined many a marriage, is far from over. Anything that helps defuse the tension is welcome. And, in this context, the sort of courses started by the Brazilian university.

The Nag or Not to Nag?

The unflattering stereotype of a nagging wife has persisted through centuries. She's a figure of fun whose one preoccupation is to correct and improve the husband.

Women, men make out, remain engaged in persistent, petty faultfinding as if they are under some compulsion to treat their husbands as kids. "Use your hankie, not the napkin, to blow your nose." "Again you left your book open upside down." "At yesterday's dinner you started nibbling at your food before all the ladies had been served." "You're overtaking from the wrong side." And it goes on endlessly.

To feminists, nagging is a male word and a way of debasing female speech. Women, being conditioned to be effective in matters of detail, can't help pointing out when their men are found wanting.

A nagging wife is often an indication that the man of the house is inconsiderate or lousy. Hasn't it been rightly said that a man who has faults he doesn't know about probably doesn't listen to his wife—because she is the person who knows him best in the world.

Conceded, women may be doing more than their fair share of nagging but men nag too; in their case it's more like bullying or teasing. Conceited men actually prove to be the worst naggers.

Indeed, the popular notion that women are natural naggers is more of a myth. Just because wives keep reminding husbands of what they should be doing, their talk is construed as nagging. Feminists anyway make out that nagging isn't natural to women; it's a consequence of women's subordinate position in society. Having less power than men, women at times have to nag out of necessity.

Nagging as a way of self-assertion by either party can remain a light-hearted affair if indulged in private. The problems start when it's done in front of others, and that includes one's own children.

To nag or not to nag? That's the question on which the final word has still to be said.

In Defence of Marital Sulk

One of the most gratifying options in ventilating a marital grievance is to sulk, a sort of Satyagraha in the wedded world. And Satyagraha, as Gandhi Ji its fountainhead postulated, "may be offered to one's nearest and dearest".

You can actually nurture a sulk with dignity. And the best part; you can slip out of it when you wish. You don't have to await an apology from the guilty party; you simply stop moping, behave like a normal spouse again.

You don't have to be a wife to sulk; husbands can sulk as well.

Yet wives, one imagines, must be experiencing far more occasions to sulk: the hubby turning up unduly late from work without the courtesy of a phone call, or bringing along somebody for dinner without as much as prior notice. But wives have this problem; it's their lot to ensure that the wheels of the household run smoothly. That sometimes makes them forget they're in the midst of a well-deserved sulk.

A sulk can be anything from a half-hour affair to a full Forty-Eight-Hour Sulk. It's akin to emotional strike action; you still function as a spouse but you work to rule. The underlying message in sulking is the hurt you feel because the other party has acted so selfishly or thoughtlessly.

Retiring to another room or staying out of sight does no good to a sulk; the other party might forget you're nursing one. However it's important to avoid eye contact. An inadvertent smile can damage a sulk irreparably. That's the ironclad rule of sulk: once you've unsulked you can't resulk.

What's better for marital peace; silence or speech? Not an easy question to answer.

"Communication" is the buzzword these days. To its devotees, every problem—political, social, marital—arises out of poor communication among the participants. Marriage counsellers are extolling the rewards of communication and marriage manuals sing its virtues.

Yet one is not sure whether the communication mantra—good for the boardroom—is always productive in the bedroom.

Couples highly tuned to communication are often seen making use of verbal weapons camouflaged as "reasonable discussions". Phrases seemingly polite but actually barbed are apt to be employed. "Forgive me if I say" is one. "I've my faults but you..." is another. Such verbal game-play can end up more in frayed tempers than increased understanding of each other's point of view.

Sulking, with its studied silence, may well have an edge over instant speech in many a marital situation. "If you don't talk you don't fight" is an old adage. "Silence is one of the hardiest arguments to refute," says John Billings. So if speech is silver, silence is sometimes gold.

A sulk anyway gives a couple time enough to develop an altered perspective and an opportunity to separate what is vital from what is not, before words fly out like arrows—missiles that can't be recalled. In the meantime, the routine of daily living should begin to soften the hurt that gave rise to the sulk.

In defence of the marital sulk; the offending party gets the message while no harsh words are bandied about. The only risk; a sulker starting to enjoy the attention the sulk evokes from the sulkee—-things like little acts of help, even an admission of guilt or selfishness.

Staying Incompatible for Fifty Years

If compatibility is a necessary condition of happy marriage, then ours would rate as a serious mistake made forty-five years ago. Theoretically, marriage is all about Two persons becoming One. But that sort of fusion has made precious little headway in ours.

As I try to figure out areas of compatibility, I actually end up with a long list of incompatibilities. How the marriage survives—in fact, it fares surprisingly well, at least to me—is somewhat of a mystery.

I finish a shower in five minutes. Indeed I'm through all the morning ablutions in less than half an hour. She seems to spend an age in the bathroom; it's a first-class crisis if she happens to go in there first.

I am an early riser, often out for a long walk before 6. She never wakes before 7; says, her best sleep happens between 5 and 7. Perforce, I've to sneak out of bedroom without putting on a light, hoping not to hit my shins against a piece of furniture. She's a night person, often watches TV or reads newspapers into the night. I usually put on eye shades, courtesy an airline.

I eat like a dog: fast, heaping everything on one plate, gorging myself till hunger pangs subside. She eats like a cat: slow and picky. Often I finish the main course when she's only half through, and then wait impatiently for the dessert, drumming the table with my fingers.

Television we watch differently. I prefer to watch attentively in relative silence. She can easily combine it with ironing, telephoning, and conversation.

My main watching is sports—cricket, football, golf; she favours romantic serials and tear-jerkers. At times, I have to move to the living-room TV set for a prolonged sports viewing, as she takes over the main one.

She loves parties, birthdays, and fun-shopping. I have a hearty distaste of shopping. Having known prices prevalent in the 1930-40s, to me everything appears atrociously priced. And birthdays don't excite me, anyway not my own.

The list of incompatibilities goes on endlessly. Yet I can't imagine being married to anyone else. We're together, but it's not because of compatibility.

Household Mess and Marriage

There is a theory that the tidiness of your home reflects the state of your marital relationship. A neat household, it's argued, is a sign of marital harmony whereas a messy one signals an uneasy relationship.

Possibly real trouble arises if one of the partners happens to be either obsessively tidy or hopelessly slovenly.

My uncle, Mohan is ever on the lookout for specks of dust whether settled on the TV set or the wall pictures. He even moves sofa chairs to find it; dust that's sitting nicely underneath without doing anybody any harm. Apparently it hasn't occurred to him, chasing dust is such a frustrating pursuit, with precious little to show for all the effort that goes into it.

Mohan promptly rubs away dirty finger marks on light switches if he espies any. And he frowns at anything which isn't in its ordered place. His own bottles of bath oils, lotions and after-shave are seen ranged in the their order of height—with labels pointing the same way. He's the family "neatnik", runs a standing joke.

And I know of a neighbouring housewife who is a virtual clutter bug. Hers isn't the old-time clutter confined to the family box-room or stowed under raised beds but present-day clutter pervading the whole house—the almirah tops, the lofts, the basement, the garage, even to the point of squeezing their Maruti out. The crammed pantry contains items that haven't been used for years. And so many curios and knick-knacks are crowding the centre and side tables, there's hardly room to put down one's tea cup. Indeed Kanta has a few sob stories where, to her regret, a favourite object was given away by her hubby against her wishes.

Another complicating factor in her case is the presence of three small kids. Children are great producers of clutter in the shape of toys and clothes that they outgrow or they no longer want. Even otherwise Kanta sees no point in tidying up till the super-active kids have gone to bed.

Happily, most people are neither compulsively fastidious nor inordinately messy; they figure somewhere in-between. Actually a majority of us rate ourselves as fairly tidy. Yet in real life, people tend to behave in a manner that's both tidy and messy. They are often immaculate in things that matter to them and seemingly slovenly in things they deem inconsequential. Sportsmen, for example, are often obsessively neat with their play implements while astonishingly messy with their rooms.

I, for one, am quite particular about order in my study. The wall-to-wall carpet is vacuum-cleaned every Sunday morning in my presence. The computer and the printer stay in their plastic covers when not in use. Books are stacked height-wise, and all private papers neatly filed away. I even don't allow a cup of coffee to be put on the teak writing desk without a coaster underneath.

Yet the good wife stays critical of how I use the bathroom or eat at the dining table. I'm often accused of leaving the tub dirty, splashing too much water around the wash basin while shaving, even letting urine drops on the toilet seat. At meals I'm blamed for soiling napkins too fast by wiping my fingers on them—I believe that's what napkins are meant for.

The wife, in turn, is running a tidy kitchen. That's what I presume as I rarely go in there. And she keeps the rest of the home commendably clean.

But then she has her own pockets of chaos. The spare room has been turned into a virtual dump. And her dressing room is mostly in a mess—at least that's the way it seems to me. Clothes lie heaped everywhere or just shoved into half-open shelves. At times the whole place looks as if ransacked by burglars.

Maybe she has collected far too many clothes and accessories, and is unable to make up her mind what to discard. I have been advocating a large "indecision" box or closet where clothes not worn for some years could be just thrown in. And periodically, items thrown in there given away unless reclaimed for use.

Husband Seen Neglecting His Health

What should a wife do when she sees her husband neglecting his health? This is the predicament of Poonam, a trim forty-eight. Her husband, fifty-four, drinks, smokes, overeats and does no regular exercise. He even skips the nightly teeth brushing, content with rinsing his mouth with water. Little wonder he's developing a pronounced paunch.

Keshav Misra, a senior bank manager, takes immense care about the health of his bank. And he is otherwise well-informed, well-read. But when it comes to taking care of his own health, to Poonam he seems quite remiss.

When she tells Keshav to quit smoking or restrict his alcohol intake to no more than 21 drinks a week (so says the US Surgeon General), or heap smaller helpings of dessert on his plate, he takes it more as nagging than friendly advice. "I'm healthy for my 54 years. Why should I change my lifestyle? Why lower the quality of my life for some fancy health fads?" he retorts back. "Anyway we have long lives in our family; you know papa is going strong at 85."

Yes, Keshav is all right at 54. But will he healthy at 60 or 65? That's what Poonam can't help worrying.

And she is not alone in such worries. Countless wives of smokers, drinkers, overeaters and under-exercisers ask the same question. Why do blokes, otherwise smart and successful, behave so dumb when it comes to taking care of themselves?

One possible explanation lies in the differing perceptions men and women have about their bodies. Men are brought up to take risks—it's a macho thing to take risks—and that includes taking risks with one's own body. Men by nature are exuberant creatures: loving dangerous sports, drinking heavily, driving fast.

A new book *The Adonis Complex* (Simon & Schuster) by three of the world's leading authorities in psychiatry—Harvard's Harrison Pope and Dr Robert Olivardia, and Professor Katharine Phillips of Brown University—has pulled together all the evidence from a multitude of studies to make an irrefutable case that highlights the dangerous relationship between men and their bodies and the impact this has on their relationships.

Admittedly, compared to the female body, the male one is a low-maintenance proposition: trim the finger nails every 10 days, a haircut once a month, and that daily chore of shaving. A man's body does not betray its tenant as rapidly as a woman's. Never as fine and lovely, it has less distance to fall. "The male body skims the surface of nature's deeps, wherein the blood and pain and mysterious cravings of women perpetuate the species. Participating less than the female body in nature's processes, the male body gives the impression—false—of being exempt from time," says John Updike, the noted novelist.

Again men aren't that concerned as to how they look (admittedly the same could be fast changing with trendy young males). A few pounds of flab on the belly do not bother many a man. In fact, when they look in the mirror, men, unlike women, generally like what they see and feel no serious compulsion to take cumbersome remedial measures. Being less critical, men have a whole lot less motivation to change their ways. Far fewer worry about their weight as compared to women.

And when things go wrong, they're less inclined to do anything about it, much less to consult a doctor. On average, men go to doctors half as many times as women do. Indeed, many men visit a doctor only when their wives make them do so.

Men are supposed to tough it out. Even when it becomes imperative to see a doctor, men often don't do it properly. They tend to skip on case history or otherwise belittle the problem—both male patients and doctors have absorbed lessons in being strong and silent. One survey of UK's National Health Service revealed that a consultation between a woman GP and a woman patient will last four times as long as one between a male doctor and a male patient.

What's a wife supposed to do when she feels convinced that her hubby wasn't taking good care of himself? Doing nothing about it would virtually amount to colluding with him. And yet her telling has to be tactful, not to be construed as nagging. A bit of humour in the telling always helps.

Possibly her most effective strategy is to set an example. She can take to indoor exercise or vigorous walks/jogging. Chances are he would join in at some stage. And she could cut down the calories in home cooking. Here she will do well to take him into confidence, lest he undo all her good work by gorging on sweats and snacks outside.

And if still he continues blithely negligent about his health, she better persuade him to take a higher life insurance policy.

Forgetful Husbands

"Do pick up my shawl from Snowhite on your way back from office," says Neelam.

"Sure," replies Narendra, watching cricket on TV.

But when he returns home next day, he has forgotten to collect the shawl.

"Don't forget it tomorrow," says Neelam in an irritated vein.

And, lo, next day again Narendra forgot to bring it, busy with unexpected business visitors. He's genuinely sorry for the lapse.

Neelam is exasperated. She just can't understand how Narendra, a considerate husband otherwise, forgets such a simple errand when he can remember and follow up numerous minute details of his managerial job.

To wives, this phenomenon of forgetful husbands is well-nigh baffling. Why men forget while women remember? It can't be all the pressure of work. Working women, operating under similar pressure, rarely forget any of the umpteen household chores.

One explanation is that in the male instinctual priority, household tasks figure far lower than work. And there again things that aren't instinctually male get missed more often. Collecting the laundry or picking some foodstuff run a greater chance of getting forgotten than, say, repairs to the family car or fixing a leaky faucet.

Men, it seems, are mainly focussed on their work, despite a growing inclination on their part to be of help at home. And the more focussed a man is on his work or more stressed with it, his tendency to forget the domestic details increases.

This tendency is most evident in married men. Apparently as the wife begins to remember more and more of household details, the husband starts remembering less and less of them. The more she worries, the less he worries. Surely the wife can't be blamed for this development but her behaviour does have an impact on what the man forgets.

How to make him remember? Nagging or getting angry over his memory lapses proves rather unproductive. And so also the oft-repeated charge: "You weren't listening". That may actually be incorrect; he did listen but forgot. The more a woman nags, the more he's apt to forget what he was asked to do.

Marriage counsellors and psychiatrics have been putting forth a flurry of suggestions. But possibly the best advice for wives comes from John Gray in his book *What your mother couldn't tell you and your father didn't know* (Vermillion).

According to Gray, a man forgets a request when it is conveyed in a negative way. The forgotten request, however, is not completely lost. It is just stored in a different place. With a little help from his mate, he can automatically remember what he normally forgets.

Gray advocates advanced relationship skills for wives, which carried over a period of time, can reap them enormous benefits. And here he puts emphasis on two particular points.

Every time you ask your man to do a thing, ask as if for the first time. The tone of your voice is very important. Behave as if you have completely overlooked his earlier omissions to do the thing despite being asked twice or thrice. Such behaviour comes most pleasing to the man. It's a refreshing change for one who was apprehending a whining complaint or an angry argument.

Each time a man forgets to do something, and his wife reacts in a non-demanding way, he will suddenly remember all the times he has forgotten. It is amazing. If she does not remind him of how many times she had to ask, then he remembers all on his own. His memory for doing the little day-to-day things is strengthened when he's getting reminded without having to feel guilty.

Gray's recipe looks clearly irksome, especially to start with. It calls for much self-control and patience, to be practiced over months or longer till it becomes a part of her marital skills. But then she is only extending it to her loved one. And the gains in his goodwill and cooperation are enormous.

The other point he makes out is the man's perennial hunger for appreciation. The secret of getting more from a man is to appreciate what he is already doing and then ask for more in small increments.

So it makes an excellent strategy for the wife to show her appreciation, by word or smile, whenever her mate does anything in the house, big or small. She should always behave as if he has done a favour, though it may well be expected of him. Over time as a man experiences that his doing small things is so well appreciated by his mate and brings her happiness, he remembers to do more and more of them.

Violence Against Wives

Wife beating, the most common form of family violence, poses a threat to the quality of women's lives in nearly every culture and society on earth. It occurs with regularity in nearly 85 percent of all cultures.

And there's the common tendency to trivialize violence against wives, relegating it to domestic sphere. Actually, it's one of the most under-reported crimes.

56 percent of the women interviewed in the National Family Health Survey, 2000 supported the use of force to "discipline" wives in certain circumstances: suspected infidelity, showing disrespect to her in-laws, going out without telling her husband, neglecting house or children, or cooking food improperly. Even working women as well as younger women (age group 15 to 19) condoned some wife-beating—"to keep her in line".

Recently Oxfam, the reputed international NGO, conducted a study on domestic violence covering metros, small towns and rural areas, and encompassing men and women from all socio-economic segments and income groups. According to its findings, people across income-groups, age groups, and geographical areas consider domestic violence acceptable. Others despise violence but do not stand against it.

If what these surveys point out is truly representative of popular opinion, then we have a long way to go to rid ourselves of the barbaric practice of wife beating.

Police and courts can, at best, play a supportive role. Specific legislation in the shape of Section 498A was added in the Indian Penal Code, mainly to protect women from being ill-treated by the husband or his relatives for reasons linked to dowry or otherwise.

Even in cultures and countries where by now public opinion against wife beating is fully firmed up and punitive legislation backed by administrative measures in place, its eradication is proving no easy task. Take England and Wales. 63,000 women and children spend at least one night in a refuge each year. One in four is a victim of domestic violence at some point in her life.

Seized with the gravity of the situation, the UK authorities have set up dedicated courts as a part of government clampdown on men who beat their wives or girlfriends. The government's latest message to men, "enough is enough," and there will be no more tolerance to wife-beating. Magistrates have been told to hand out the harshest possible sentences to wife-beaters while treating with scepticism claims by men that they were provoked by "nagging" partners.

How helpful are the courts? Many a woman fears that dragging a violent husband through the courts can simply provoke further attacks. Even when she has obtained protective orders, there's no guarantee against being beaten by an enraged spouse. And many husbands, especially those in the lower socio-economic group, do not take kindly to court-mandated counselling sessions; they tend to take it as punishment, not corrective therapy.

No wonder, women have been showing scant faith in the criminal justice system. They fear that in most cases men will be let off with a fine (which eventually becomes a fine on the household) or conditional discharge that leaves men more enraged and vicious. It's a rare fellow who gets really punished for wife beating; most complaints don't mature into court cases and very few cases end in conviction.

Immediate arrest of the wife-battering husband by police is seen to have a salutary effect. One American survey showed that such arrest resulted in a reduced chance of new violence within the next six months. These findings are encouraging some states to institute mandatory arrest in battering cases.

Police, however, have their own difficulties. Often when they reach the domestic scene in response to a desperate call, they find the parties have patched up. Or later, the wife goes back on her statement when in court.

An American Task Force on Family Violence recommended a "no-drop" policy, making it impossible for a defendant to pressurise a victim to drop charges. A no-drop policy signifies that the prosecution is committed to acting against wife-bashing. Others argue that a no-drop policy disempowers victims who may be able to use the possibility of dropping charges to negotiate self-protective arrangements. The jury is still out whether the no-drop policy wherever adopted has been effective in deterring wife beating.

A particular problem with marital violence is that it mostly takes place in private. And is generally over by the time someone intervenes. Our joint-family living could be operating as a bit of brake against vicious acts of violence.

Violent partners beating down their wives with threats or blows often justify their savageries as provoked by women themselves. It makes many a wife wonder whether she would be beaten less if she stayed more submissive. Germaine Greer, the noted feminist, goes as far as to say that "men bash women because they enjoy it; they torture women as they might torture an animal or pull the wings off flies".

The Indian scene has another complicating dimension; dowry demands keep persisting for years after marriage—possibly nowhere else in the world it features in this particular form. And such demands can trigger violence if unmet.

Whether eve-teasing commonly indulged in by many of our youth makes them more prone to wife-beating later in life is something that merits a special study.

Studies of marital violence in UK (the most studied in the world) have revealed a few interesting findings. Most women being beaten are relatively young, 35 and below. Nearly 60 percent of the frequently beaten ones were hit within a year of their marriage. With many, the beatings started with their first pregnancy or with the birth of the first child.

Battered women are more at risk of having miscarriages. Indeed, many battered women report intentional changes in the pattern of beating during pregnancy. While their upper body parts were the most frequent targets prior to pregnancy, after pregnancy blows are directed toward the stomach or genitals.

Sex was one of the weapons used in marital violence. The most common marital rape was the "battering" one, where sex used to degrade the wife; even anal rape, the "quintessential sexual act by which to humiliate a woman".

Wife-beating is said to happen more frequently where the male possess no superior skill or talent or resources which are supposed to legitimize his superior status. "Men simply have no culturally approved ways of coping with 'uppity' women." If their yelling or sulking fails, "there is an almost overwhelming temptation to use a resource men have to a greater degree than women—physical force".

One of our National Family Health Surveys showed a widespread belief among responding wives that working women are more vulnerable. This is because working women defy stereotypes of domesticity, and demand equality, something that goes against the patriarchal mindset.

What does a typical wife do faced with recurring beatings? The first reaction is generally of shame and failure. She feels too embarrassed to take anybody into confidence. If the beatings continue, she seeks informal support from relatives and friends. In case of injuries needing medical attention, she may perhaps confide in the family doctor (it's often less awkward to confide in doctors). But when things go beyond bearing, it's police and courts, separation and divorce.

Women who have nowhere to go seem to put up with a lot of "shit". A husband taunting his beaten wife, "Where can you go? What can you do?" Rubbing in her helplessness and dependence on him; the power of his hand and the power of his purse. And ironically, without his "protection", she could risk sexual harassment from rowdies and strangers in unsafe areas.

Those with a place to go or an income to fall back, display a lower threshold of endurance. But many are held back because they would be depriving their children of their father—perhaps not such a bad father. It becomes a kind of "moth and candle" situation—getting hurt but still hovering around. And then "some husbands seem to have a fantastic facility for saying they are sorry". In India a beaten woman usually finds "refuge" at her parents' home—though at immense cost to her self-respect and mortification to her parents.

"Women of each and every class, of every age, all religions, educated and uneducated, employed or unemployed, suffer from it," has been made out in deliberations of various Workshops on Family Violence Against Females.

Surveys by the International Centre for Research on Women (ICRW) estimate that 60 percent Indian women face violence at some point in their marriage.

One is, however, not sure whether the incidence of marital violence is on the increase. It has always been high; only the idealized view of the family prevented us from seeing it until recently. The incidence may actually be declining slightly in most places, because of being less tolerated.

Alcohol—involved in a majority of violent incidents at home—adds an extra chemical dimension to the organic damage, and alcohol use is on rapid rise in the country. Many a wife puts up with alcohol-induced violence, "He's OK, when he's sober".

Many feminist writers have suggested that pornography encourages objectification of women. Both laboratory research and field surveys lend support to the view that heavy exposure to pornography tends to increase men's aggression towards women, particularly when a male is provoked by a woman.

Violence against wives is a complex problem, defying simple off-the-cuff solutions. It calls for extensive, in-depth studies and surveys. There's a good case for creating a national lead agency that could promote and co-ordinate research studies in the country. Even set up an Institute, with government aid and private funding. Such an Institute could also train researchers, as research in marital violence involves skills of a high order.

Grieving over the death of a spouse

"Well, everyone can master a grief but he that has it."
Shakespeare "Much Ado about Nothing"

The loss of a husband or wife is one of the most traumatic events of a person's life. Yet it is one that many of us can expect to undergo at some point of time.

The unpleasant thought may well prompt us to shrug off the whole nasty subject. Yet, the grief, particularly the grief of a bereaved widow or widower, is a harsh fact of life.

The grieving spouse stands in need of sympathy, reassurance and time to recoup. A little help given at this time of transition will often be more effective than help given at other times and, in the long run, it will be appreciated more.

The grief of the newly bereaved can be likened to an illness; society treating him in much the same way as a sick person. Employers expect him to miss work, he stays at home, and relatives visit and talk in hushed tones. For a time others take over his routine responsibilities.

On the whole, grief resembles a physical injury more closely than any other type of illness—of course, without the physical pain. The loss is often spoken of as a "blow", and like a physical injury the "wound" heals gradually. Occasionally complications set in and the healing is delayed, or a further injury reopens a healing wound. In rare cases the outcome is fatal.

But doctors don't treat grief, you may say. In fact they do. Many people go to their doctor for help after a bereavement, and a large proportion of their complaints—loss of appetite or sleep, headaches, muscular pains, palpitation and digestive disturbances—are a consequence of grief.

Yet there is an important difference between the two. Grief is a process and not a state with a set of symptoms like disease.

Grief has stages: the initial numbness, the subsequent pining, then depression, and thereafter the start of recovery. And each of these stages of grieving has its own characteristics. And there are considerable differences from one person to another as regards both the duration and the form of each stage.

Apart from grief, two other factors play. A part in determining the overall reaction to a bereavement: stigma and deprivation.

By stigma is meant the change in attitude that takes place in society when a person is bereaved. Every widow discovers that people who were previously friendly and approachable become embarrassed and strained in her presence. Expressions of sympathy often have a hollow ring and offers of help are rarely followed up. It is as if the widow has been tainted with the death. We do not now burn widows, we still pity them, even tend to avoid them.

Deprivation—as distinct from grief over the loss—implies the discontinuance of those essential "supplies" that were previously provided by the lost person such as security and status, company and emotional support, money, sex and other things. A marriage has come to perform many functions, and these aren't adequately carried out after its dissolution.

And for widows, the death of a spouse can also mean a loss of identity. She's no longer a wife, she's a widow. Suddenly, somewhat unaccustomedly, "we" has become "I", "ours" has become "mine". Decisions have now to be made mostly alone, not by a committee of two. Considerate children may treat her well but her most precious prop is gone.

Can one die of a "broken heart"? You wouldn't find grief on a death certificate. Yet studies reveal that there is increasing mortality among the widowed population. Widowers over 55 show a significantly higher death rate during the first six months of their bereavement. Older widows however seem to take it better.

The most characteristic feature of grief is not prolonged depression but acute and episodic pangs. Pangs of grief begin within a few hours or days of bereavement and usually reach a peak of severity in five to fifteen days. At first they are more frequent and spontaneous. As time passes they become less frequent and take place only when something occurs that brings the loss to mind, like finding a photograph in a drawer or waking up alone in the marital bed.

Pining is actually the persistent and obtrusive wish for the person who is gone; the way an animal anxiously searches for its disappeared mate. The bereaved adult human is likely to be well aware that there is no point in searching for a dead person but this does not prevent him from experiencing a strong impulse to search or imagine the reappearance of the deceased.

Crying is a frequent feature of grief. This crying isn't always necessarily for the deceased. It may well be an expression of one's own helplessness and a plea for sympathy. Some are seen suppressing their urge to cry. But the suppressed cry again is a sort of social signal for help.

Even when pining is at its most intense, there are things that mitigate the pain of grief. "We shall meet again in the after-life"; this widely held belief based on our philosophy and religion is a source of some consolation. Again disbelief in the fact of loss is seldom complete. The inconsolable Uttara, the widow of the slain warrior Abhimanyu, can't believe that her husband is dead; she's wanting to wake him up for the battlefield. This tendency to disbelieve the true situation is even evident prior to death, say during a terminal illness. A wife may well know that her husband in the hospital bed was dying. And yet she may continue to think and to some extent act, as if he was not.

Till the cremation "brings home" the reality of what had happened. In a way cremation spells more of an air of finality than a burial.

Studies indicate that irritability and anger are a common feature of the early phase of grief. Relatives and friends who try to induce a widow to stop grieving before she is ready for it, are surprised at her indignant response. She may personalize the death as something that has been done to her: "Why did he leave me?" she may burst out. God and the doctors come in for a lot of angry criticism since both are seen as having power over life and death. Such anger is often accompanied by a feeling of guilt or self-reproach; some act or omission on her part which might have harmed her dying spouse or in some way disturbed his peace of mind. In agonizing again and again over the events leading to the demise, she's looking for a chance to castigate herself as if by accepting blame she could somehow reverse the course of events and get back the missing spouse.

Retrospective distortion, especially idealization of the dead person, is so common that it is hard to know of the widow's real relationship with the husband. However it is surmised that widows experiencing the largest amount of guilt were generally those who had quarreled the most with their husbands.

A proportion, albeit a small one, of the bereaved people "break down" in bereavement. They are in need of psychiatric help for their depression, alcoholism, hypochondriac symptoms or other phobic symptoms. Some seem to suffer from what may be termed "chronic grief". Perhaps a few of them regard unlimited mourning as a duty to the dead and are not truly grieving though they continue mourning.

Age of the deceased is obviously an important factor in determining the intensity of grief. Whereas it's easier to reconcile oneself to the demise of an elderly person, untimely death is a cause of intense grief. And also a death that is sudden or unexpected, for which the survivor has had no time to prepare. A more gradual death, say from cancer instead of from a stroke or heart attack, is less traumatic. It is even sometimes possible for a husband and wife to work together towards an acceptance of the approaching death—besides attending to practical affairs over that contingency. Despite the sadness which is an inevitable component of such anticipatory grieving, couples who choose to face the future in this way often manage to win through to a more peaceful end, and to a more balanced bereavement.

Granting we believe that the rituals attending a bereavement have no value to the dead, they have a value to the living. In fact some psychiatrists are worried over the decline in ritual observation of mourning today. They think, this may be responsible for much mental ill health among bereaved people. Our death rituals, that way, are as elaborate as any, and are still being largely observed. With all those relatives and friends gathered, the bereaved is made to feel that he is not alone. The social support, more so of the colleagues of the deceased, is viewed positively.

Those whose religious beliefs help them to place the bereavement in a meaningful perspective cope better with the bereavement than those who have no such faith. But that implies genuine faith, not an activity merely limited to religious rites. Orthodox Sunni Muslims, with their pronounced fatalist approach and being enjoined not to mourn too visibly, seem to suffer less. When there is a prescribed period for mourning, a time is prescribed for its ending too. (The term quarantine comes from quarantina, the Italian for "forty", which was the number of days of sequestration expected of the widow.) Thus an accepted mourning period provides social sanction for ending grief, and it is likely to have psychological value for the bereaved. An absence of the same could leave a bereaved person somewhat confused and insecure in his grief.

The person who is most valued in bereavement is not the one who expresses the most sympathy, but the one who "sticks around", and quietly gets on with day-to-day tasks and makes few demands on the bereaved. The helper should neither "pluck at the heartstrings" nor connive with the bereaved in endless attempts to avoid the grief. Both probing and "jollying along" are unhelpful. The bereaved person has a painful and difficult task to perform; it cannot be avoided or rushed.

While a conventional expression of sympathy can probably not be avoided when visiting a newly bereaved person, pity is the last thing the bereaved person wants. So it is best to get conventional verbal expressions of sympathy over as quickly as possible and to speak from the heart or not at all. Trite formulas serve only to widen the gap between bereaved and non-bereaved. Bereaved people, however, do appreciate the visits and expressions of sympathy paid to them by others. These are seen as a tribute to the dead and a regard for the bereaved.

Since pain in grief is inevitable, helpers must be prepared to share the pain, to accept it as their contribution to friendship. Help derives from the quiet communication of affectionate understanding and this can be conveyed as well by a squeeze of the hand as by speech.

Sometimes an outsider can render more effective help than family members. Families, with their own hierarchy and elements of rivalry and competition, frequently distort the natural expression of feeling. If one member of the family cries more, or less than another, this is noticed and conclusions are drawn. A widow may well feel obliged to curtail the expression of her own feeling after witnessing what she takes to be insincere grief in her in-laws.

People who themselves experienced a major bereavement may be particularly well qualified to help the bereaved. They really do understand what the other person is going through and know that bereavement is not the end of life.

4

Sex in Marriage

Sex Life of Dual-Career Couples

Pran and Prabha are a career-couple in their forties, he a leading lawyer, she heading a large travel agency.

They have everything one commonly wants: money, health, work satisfaction, a loving relationship, and two nice kids, a girl of 10 and a boy of 7. But sometimes a whole month passes without an episode of sex between them.

Pran and Prabha may well be relieved to learn that, even in the most stellar dual-career marriages, months can go by without "action". Almost everything in the contemporary dual-career couple's life operates against marital sex. No wonder this group of people has earned the acronym DINS—double income, no sex. It's essentially a lifestyle problem, not a sexual problem.

Some career-couples make a laugh of their "pathetic" sex life—no spunk remaining to invest in it after the exhausting demands of work life. Many a professional woman admits to having hardly anything left over at the end of the day after working aggressively all day in what's largely a man's world. On top so many careers these days involve a lot of travelling.

Pran starts his workday around seven in the morning, labouring over his briefs. And he starts seeing clients by 8. After a full day at the courts, he's again at his home office till nearly 9, preparing briefs and talking to his clients. "It's work, work, all the time. I've let my physical, sensual side go, and when you do that your sex drive just shrivels up. And then you start fearing your own performance and so avoid sex," he confides.

After a quick bath, a large whisky, dinner and a little rap with kids, it's time for the 10.30pm news. "Give a man the option of watching late news or having sex with his mate, and he'll almost always choose the former," says a wit.

Prabha's work hours—9 to 6—are relatively shorter. But then she keeps receiving oversees calls at all odd hours. And has to undertake a hectic travel schedule. Over and above, the unending business of running an elaborate household, the upkeep of her wardrobe, and finding time for kids.

Only on rare occasions are the two partners free at the same time, and suitably "relaxed" for sex. Women, sexologists say, usually need to feel relaxed before they are in a mood for sex, while men often need to have sex before they can feel relaxed. This quirk of nature can exacerbate the "Not Now" syndrome in an already complex sex situation obtaining within a career-couple.

And quite a few hurdles go like this:

Does she have to get up early for work?

Is any family member in the midst of a crisis?

Any significant aches or pains she had in the last thirty minutes?

As children enter the picture, sex takes a back seat for some time—many parents going into a sexual hiatus that could last a year with every childbirth. Parental fatigue mounts up. In our conditions, the presence of servants or some live-in relative does help but then these generate their own problems. The demands of kids, coupled with all the other pressures of life, don't exactly turn a career woman into a sex kitten.

And when kids grow up—these days they hang around into adulthood, some refusing to leave home altogether—privacy is a big factor. You feel the way you used to feel trying to do it at other people's houses.

What keeps most career-couples going through the dry spells is that they pay much attention to connecting on a daily basis. Touching each other now and then is a common tactic, even if no sex is wanted. "I can't imagine not being entwined in his arms when we start sleeping," says one woman. "I can't imagine going without the day-to-day physicality, the hugs, the kisses, the emotional intimacy. It is this consistency that's comforting." Anyway couples mostly tend to make no big deal about the frequency of sex, if the relationship is otherwise cruising along nicely.

Two-career couples, say some experts, may have to fall back on appointment-book sex if their sex lives are going out of whack. Where a couple finds that sex was getting pushed off the schedule by other commitments, it's time to get out their appointment books and mark each other in, better with indelible ink. Setting aside, say every week, a block of time—two to three hours—for each other, to crawl into bed and cuddle. Occasionally this could be afternoons; the time men are known to get more horny. Actually the levels of testosterone in men and progesterone in women are significantly higher in the morning hours than at any other time. That way the best time for lovemaking may well be morning.

A couple is advised to keep its appointments with each other. Don't let fatigue or other put-offs (guests in the house, an unexpected engagement, a particular TV programme or sports fixture) keep you from this primary tryst. Every put-off is a put-down. It sends a signal you don't deem your partner as important as some other activity.

The video revolution has been a blessing for many couples confronting the problems of flagging desire. Couples have been reporting a far livelier love scene as they watched an erotic film together. Admittedly, for a majority of women porn is still a problem but, of late, the porn industry has been cleaning its act to attract women viewers.

What possibly produces the best results is a respite from home and work. No wonder, long-weekend trips or short holiday excursions are the in-thing these days. If you can manage one—-possibly dumping your small kids with their grandparents—nothing equals a nice holiday for boosting a couple's sex life. Better still if you keep your cellular phones deactivated for most of the holiday time.

Spicing Marital Sex: Go Beyond 50-50

Many modern couples have come to believe that sexual intimacy between spouses is best attained through a "50-50" ideal of equality. But then some of them are discovering to their dismay that such equality, by itself, is not making for passionate relationship.

Wives commonly complain that their men are behaving less sexy; seemingly lost in their work life. Women often ask why men are such "wimps" these days.

Husbands complain that wives are becoming hardened, more resistive, and independent to the point that they no longer attract sexually. In short, men often ask why women are becoming such "ballbreakers" these days.

So where do we go from here?

Intimate love life between men and women began with "dependence relationships".

The modern ideal is of two independent people, whole into themselves, coming together as equals, and evenly splitting the responsibilities of the household—what's called the "50-50 relationship".

Nobody would disagree that the 50-50 relationship is a positive step over the dependency stage.

The trouble is, many a modern woman has to cloak her natural expression of feminine radiance in order to succeed in today's masculine-oriented world of work. And many a modern man, stuck in a vague transition between old models of the masculine and new identities, is unable to be fully present and confident in relationship.

Inadvertently, men and women have become more and more sexually neutralized, unable to give to each other what they really want in intimacy. Rather than celebrating the attractive differences between the masculine and feminine qualities in each of us, some people have begun to deny that there is even a difference in gender (except the obvious physical difference).

Feminists have accomplished major improvements in women's lives in many ways. And there's all that emphasis on egalitarian and respectful marital sex.

Esther Perel, a noted American psychotherapist, writing in Psychotherapy Networker (May/June 2003) however makes out that belief in equality, consensus-building, fairness and tolerance (very desirable features otherwise in marriage or elsewhere) can, in the bedroom, result in very boring sex. Sexual excitement often thrives on power plays, role reversals, imperious demand, and seductive manipulations. It's the complementarity—the appeal of difference—rather than strict gender equality that makes couples more erotic.

"It amazes me how willing people are to experiment sexually outside marriage, yet how tame and puritanical they are with their spouses," says Perel. "Many of my patients describe their domestic sex lives as devoid of excitement and eroticism, yet they are consumed by a richly imaginative sex life beyond domesticity—affairs, pornography, prostitutes, cybersex, or feverish daydreams. Having denied themselves freedom of imagination at home, they go outside to re-imagine themselves."

And unlike therapists who typically encourage patients "to know" their partners, Perel wants them to stay a bit ambiguous; most couples already exchange enough direct talk in the course of daily life. Eroticism can draw its powerful pleasure from fascination with the hidden, the mysterious, and the suggestive.

Intimacy and trust between partners is surely desirable. Yet too much of familiarity could actually sabotage sexual desire.

Couples, she says, should recover their curiosity, hone their senses to see the invisible and hear the inaudible.

Inventive, Carefree, Joyous Sex!

The doctor who propagated inventive, carefree and joyous sex has passed away at the age of eighty.

Today's sexual scene is vastly different from that of the early 1970s when Alex Comfort, M.B. Ph.D. came up editing an inhibition-breaking book *The Joy of Sex.* Yet his rather refreshing approach to sex as something un-anxious and playful did contribute in no small measure in moulding prevailing mores about lovemaking and sex.

The Joy of Sex—dubbed by some as the Kama Sutra brought up to date—turned out a smashing hit, a record-breaking international bestseller. It was everywhere, in bookshops, in homes, even in libraries. While many read it openly, a lot more read it surreptitiously. And to many others the most enticing part of the book were its illustrations; explicit photographs and drawings of a naked young couple—a man with a bushy beard and a woman with bushy armpits—in umpteen forms of lovemaking. It was said that at one time the two books most stolen were the Bible and *The Joy of Sex*.

Dr Comfort's (the name itself no less appropriate) fame now rests entirely on this "sex manual"—originally intended as a text for medical students. Yet he was a man of many parts: physician, a prominent British medical biologist, novelist and poet. In all, he authored some fifty books.

Presumably many of us have read *The Joy of Sex*. But if you haven't, the book can come as an interesting read, though it was written nearly 30 years back.

The Joy of Sex or *A Gourmet Guide to Lovemaking*, is structured like a cookery book: Starters, Main Courses, Sauces and Pickles. Starters deal with things such as beds, deodorants, body parts especially genitals, and the appeal of nakedness. The main dish is loving, unselfconscious intercourse—long, frequent, varied, ending with both parties satisfied. Sauces and pickles speak of a few sexual deviations and the use of various objects for sexual titillation. To Comfort, there are only two "rules" in good sex: One is "don't do anything you don't really enjoy", and the other is "find out your partner's needs and don't balk them if you can help it".

And he has some suggestions for long-term loving couples on how to get the best out of the book. "Read through or dip into this book together and separately. These are all techniques which straight people need and use to fill out their sex lives, or simply enjoy as play and relaxation. . . . Go by your own needs and your partner's. Do note anything which turns one or both of you on to the point of saying 'I'd like to try that'. If you're shy of talking about sexual needs, make a list of page numbers you'd like your partner to read, and exchange lists. Then take it mutually from there. You will find out things about each other you didn't know, and all of them will be rewarding."

Now this isn't any obsolescent advice: many of today's couples stay shy of signalling to each other their sexual needs, urges, or arousal. Anything that could help them overcome this awkwardness should be welcome. "The aim of *The Joy of Sex* is to stimulate your creative imagination," says Comfort.

Hundreds of books on sex counselling have come out since *The Joy of Sex*. Of late particularly, there's a rash of "straight books" and "counselling" magazines. Yet none has been able to rival Comfort's book in style, substance, and popularity. He still carries the title, the doctor of love, or Dr Sex.

Sexual Liveliness in Long Marriages

"We've had an active sex life for over forty years. Of course it isn't the same what was in the beginning. It's more affectionate and friendly than passionate these days, and nowhere as frequent, but a great source of love and comfort to both of us." —A man of 65

Is sex in long relationships really as bad as it's joked about? Obviously it is for some couples. There is a lot of dysfunctional, unsatisfying sex in many long marriages. One reason, of course, is that most of these marriages themselves leave a lot to be desired.

The main factor operating against good sex in the long run is what's called the Coolidge Effect, based on a story about the American President Coolidge. The president and his wife had been given separate tours while visiting a farm. Mrs

Coolidge saw a rooster mounting a hen and asked how often this happened. The answer was; many times each day. "Please tell that to the president," she said. When the president was informed of the rooster's performance, he inquired whether it was with the same hen. "Oh, no," was the answer, "a different one each time." "Tell that to Mrs Coolidge," replied the president.

No doubt, fresh flesh turns us on, especially men. And it's mostly the man who determines how much sex there is in a marriage.

A number of surveys, however, strongly suggest that married men and women have more and better sex than anyone else. If we look at subjective satisfaction, studies indicate that both men and women are more satisfied with marital sex than with outside flings.

What keeps the sexual spark alive in a long relationship?

Experts have a few explanations to offer as well as some words of advice.

One way to have better sex life over time with the same partner is to do whatever is necessary to combat the taking-her-for-granted syndrome. Admittedly the thrill of chase is not there; you can have her when you want. Yet men are advised to bring an element of courting to enliven the proceedings.

Couples managing good sex over time put sex high on the list of priorities. They are willing to do what it takes, to take time for it. It could mean arranging vacations just for the two of them, without children or friends. It could mean turning down the requests of relatives to stay at their place for extended periods. It may also mean that you keep track of how sex is doing.

Good sex flourishes only when there is time for it. In many marriages the partners spend little quality time together. When they are together, they're mostly dealing with money matters, children, and other household work. When they go out, they often go with others. They spend little time together, free of distractions.

A majority of couples, when questioned, make out that they had more and better sex on vacations than at other times. So one way to keep sex lively in a marriage is to plan numerous vacations, at least some of them just for the two of them.

Timing means two things, seemingly contradictory things. First is that you plan for being together and for sex. Second is that you seize the times that come up spontaneously. Couples enjoying good sex are known to take advantage of both.

One characteristic of satisfied couples is that although they disagree and argue and have periods when they can't talk to each other, as do all couples, they recover quickly. They tend not to sulk or carry around anger for long periods. Emotional distance at midlife can increase sexual distance, when you and your partner misinterpret each other's actions and intentions.

Midlife change comes in many forms, some of which can affect you sexually, such as financial anxiety, problems with adolescent or adult children, or ageing parents who suddenly need help.

People who have good sex over time tend to be sensual. They understand the importance of hand-holding, hugs, kisses or just touching for touching sake. And this touching is not done in a perfunctory manner. It is unhurried, gentle touching that conveys love and closeness. Women routinely complain that men are too hurried and too rough in touching. Not that a quick, firm touch isn't appropriate at times, but mostly these have to be soft and slow.

Sexy couples believe in romancing. They know the importance of surprise, tenderness, compliments, and all those special little things. They comment on how sexy or lovely the partner looks; they occasionally arrange romantic dinners; they remember special days and come up with surprise presents.

And couples who have good sex over the years learn to play at it rather than work at it. They have fun with it. Playing at sex also means not having any rigid rules about it, being tolerant of what it is and what it can give. This is especially important for older people, with age and illness taking a toll. These couples don't go into a hysterical overdrive when they aren't functioning perfectly but instead they use what they have to enjoy themselves.

It is important to remind your partner periodically of what you need, such as more foreplay. Just because you told your partner several years ago, doesn't mean he'll remember. In fact, if it's physically important to you but not to him, it's normal for him to forget.

Tell your partner what feels good and what doesn't. Be positive, but don't hesitate to guide your partner's hand when necessary.

Children are hazardous to good sex unless you are aware of the difficulties and prepared to deal with them. Parents who have good sex have found it necessary to carve out and protect private time for themselves. They make it clear from the outset that, barring emergencies, there are times when they are not to be disturbed. One couple was putting up a "Do Not Disturb" sign. It meant that their three kids were not to knock on the door, make loud noises near it, or get into fights when the sign was up.

The TV Hug

William Cane has written a book *The Art of Hugging* (St Martin's Press, 1996). Cane is already the author of a book *The Art of Kissing.*

In his latest one on hugging, the American writer provides "precise how-to instruction for more than twenty-five different hugs," including the long hug, the platonic hug, and the comforting hug.

Here are a few of the points made out by him in the Item on "The Television Hug".

When they're at home, 62 percent of American men and women enjoy television hugs more than just about any other kind. "We like to sit side by side on the love seat, sometimes with my arm around her or hers around me. Or we watch a show lying on the couch, with her in front of me," says a husband.

Women sometimes like you to stroke their hair and groom them during the television hug. Another thing a woman likes is to sit on your lap. She'll appreciate if you allow her to do so for a good while without interruption. This doesn't mean you have to let her cut off your circulation. Make it easy on yourself and take a break during commercials to stretch your legs.

Sometimes a woman is happy just to be able to lean against you while you're watching television. Tell her to rest her head on your shoulder. Stroke her hair now and then. Snake an arm around if you can. Or place your hand on her knee or thigh.

Men like it when women spoon with them on the couch or bed while watching television. This usually involves the two of you lying on your sides close together, like a couple of spoons, both of you facing the television so that you can see the show.

The most important thing to remember about the television hug is to stay focussed on your partner's needs. One woman says she gets annoyed when hugging her mate if he gets too engrossed in the programme and seems less interested in her.

When the Husband has a Headache

"Not tonight, I've a headache"; a wife's standard excuse when she wasn't in the mood for it. There's the stock image of men as persistent and shameless seekers of sexual gratification and wives as off-putting.

The reality may well be quite different. Various surveys on the subject, especially among urban upper classes, have revealed that increasingly it's the husband, not the wife, who's fizzling out. Appropriately Janet Wolfe, Ph.D., a psychotherapist, has come out with a self-help book *When* He *Has* a *Headache* (Hyperion). The book is not addressed to "ailing" husbands but to the "deprived" wives. The latter are guided as to how a little more joy can return to the bedroom.

Several explanations have been advanced for this role reversal.

Educated, modern women are becoming more aware of their capacity for sexual fulfillment. The age-old sexual inhibitions are wearing thin. Even older women, those into their forties and fifties, have come to expect regular marital sex. When a spouse does not come up to this expectation and desire, the wife can justifiably feel deprived. "He's more interested in nudes on paper or screen than in real life," was the wry comment of one wife.

Men, in turn, feel increasing pressure to perform. And the more pressure someone feels in this regard, the less well he performs. Many men respond to the situation by avoiding sex altogether, than risk a failure or flop. Anatomy as it is, there's a limit to which a man can simulate passion. And then there are husbands who can be quite horny with other women but are rendered rather dysfunctional with their own wives.

To make matters worse, many men find themselves fagged out at the end of a long working day, with all the tensions of work and the tiresome commuting to office and back. Some have barely the stamina left to sit and watch TV. TV itself can be a great killer of conversation and sex. And it's no help if he has downed a few large drinks. Kafka, the noted writer, deemed sex as dirty and degrading. He went as far as saying, "Coitus is the punishment for the happiness of being together".

Men anyway, contrary to the common notion of being strong and hardy, are actually delicate creatures. They are seized by obsessions, tormented by ambitions, and easily depressed by failures. They drink, they put on weight, they die early. Of course, they lie a lot about their sexual prowess but that doesn't alter the reality, more so of ageing men.

With performance anxiety on the rise, sex becomes another chore, another responsibility. Husbands look for excuses to avoid it. A minor tiff or even an uncomplimentary remark from the wife is considered a good enough pretext to put off sex for the evening. Others employ the tactic of going to bed much before their spouse does. By the time she joins after the obligatory winding up for the night, they are asleep or feigning sleep, all curled up on their side of the bed.

And if nothing else, the good old fallback, "I've a headache".

Janet Wolfe suggests that men need to be reintroduced to non-sexual contact, such as handholding. And be made aware how pleasing and powerful it can be—and how easy. And it just might act as a non-threatening invitation to more full-bodied contact.

Wives are enjoined not to neglect some of the obvious things, such as high standard of personal hygiene and grooming, good care of her health and weight, attractive night clothes and a bedroom that's a private and pleasant.

Incidentally headache, one of the most acceptable excuses not to have sex, is under assault from another source. Recently a neurology professor at Southern Illinois University reports that sex is one of the best cures for relieving a headache, especially if the sex takes place within the first thirty minutes after the onset of the headache. "Hurry up, dear," a wife may well respond when her husband complains of a headache.

Matters of Marital Sex

Few fields of human activity happen to be attracting as much advice as marital sex. Here's some more on the same subject, apparently an inexhaustible subject.

A wife getting up to wash immediately after sex may well be sending a wrong signal. The husband is likely to interpret it as his wife's desire to literally wash him away. Men think, accepting their semen is accepting them. Jumping up after sex does convey a message of distaste, thus dampening the male afterglow.

One simple solution is to keep a towel or some tissues by the bed. It's worth postponing your cleanup if it means preserving the intimacy between you and your husband. Anyway make sure he understands that you never intended to hurt him; you just wanted to avoid the drippy discomfort.

The syndrome of Inhibited Sex Drive, or ISD, is known to mar many a marriage. A partner suffering from ISD can take to avoiding sex. A standard tactic is to go to bed long before your spouse does—to be asleep, or feign sleep, when the partner joins up. Or, in reverse, a wife disinclined to sex may linger on inordinately over her household chores and nightly preparations. The ardour of the waiting husband usually cools off in the process.

Of course, even the most loving couples occasionally experience dry spells—the desire disappearing altogether for days or weeks through crisis or stress or overwork. This phenomenon particularly surfaces up with today's career-oriented couples. However such phases pass away.

ISD is a more worrying matter. In one of its variations, a person is put off all sex by some hormonal imbalance, or deep-seated depression, or emotional conflicts. In the other, more common form of ISD, you continue to harbour sexual fantasies and longings with respect to some others, but cease to feel sexy towards your own marriage partner.

In fact, without realizing that you are doing so, you may be engaging in negative feelings or "anti-fantasies" about your spouse. A husband may picture his wife to be sloppy or her voice disagreeably squeaky, or having the knack of bringing up unpleasant issues during sex. A wife imagining her hubby to be sweaty or uncouth, or has come to hate his beery breath. Feelings of anger or disappointment towards one's mate play havoc with sexual desire. Once such negative feelings come to be nursed, your sexual appetite for your spouse plummets dramatically.

A good strategy in marital sex is to focus on the pleasant attributes of one's spouse; things like his muscular chest or her beautiful feet. Couples should be able to discuss their ISD problem in calm, loving manner. If this does not work, then perhaps they should consult a professional sex therapist.

Marital sex: use it or lose it. That's the phrase making the rounds these days, as if sexual activity was like any other physical workout. "The less sex you have, the less you want it," say the experts.

But too much emphasis on frequency of marital sex can also hurt a relationship. Why should a couple who average lovemaking once a fortnight and are content with it, start worrying because surveys have shown similar couples making love twice a week? Again you don't have to compete with the sort of love life depicted in some paperback novels; the latter rarely reflect reality.

However if you do feel that your marital sex is sluggish, there are ways of pepping it up. Sexual experimentation is one. The reason why some couples can experiment sexually is that they know failures won't make them look foolish. They've learned to laugh at flops.

Partners who enjoy good sex don't let their bodies go. They take care of their health, watch their weight, and maintain high standards of personal hygiene and grooming. They keep their bodies clean, hair neat and toenails trimmed. Teeth are brushed before getting into bed. They sport attractive nightclothes, and their bedroom is a private, pleasant place. One mother of a four-year old and a six-year-old encourages her kids to manage their own breakfast on Sunday mornings so she and her husband can linger on in bed and then take a shower together.

And loving couples never withhold sex to get back at each other for real or imagined grievances.

Sex After Sixty

Here are a few myths about sex and aging.

Intercourse and emission of semen are debilitating in old age and tend to hasten death.

Most older men lose their ability and desire to have sex. Coital satisfaction decreases considerably after menopause.

Older women who still enjoy sex were probably nymphomaniacs when they were younger.

Sexual desire and sexual ability of the old (conveniently classified as men and women over 60 or even over 65) has been the subject of much public misconceptions and conflicting opinions. There is the image of the aged male as an asexual, impotent being. Others assume sexual perversions as common in old age, especially indecent familiarity with children.

While some decline in sexual interest and activity does accompany the aging process, current studies seem to indicate that a person's sex drive remains fairly constant well into advanced age.

The pioneering Kinsey studies on women (1953) reported little evidence of any ageing in the sexual capacities of women. Masters and Johnson (1966) concluded: "there is no time limit drawn by the advancing years to female sexuality". Elderly persons in reasonably good health are known to have continued sexually active into their seventies, eighties, and even nineties. Pfeiffer's survey in 1972 of 62 men and women between the ages of 66-71 (of Americans selected at random) showed that 48% were having intercourse once a month, and 28% once a week or more. Only 24% had given it up. This also indicated a dramatic shift in attitudes from procreative sex to recreational sex.

The decline in sexual activity in older people is ascribed not so much to a decline in desire; there may be other inhibiting factors like the lack of a partner, physical disability, negative societal attitudes or psychological scars of retirement and powerlessness. For instance sex may cease for an older woman with the death of her husband (widowed old men seem sexually more active than elderly widows), or her husband's inability to perform or his loss of interest in sex with her. Here women labour under a double disadvantage; they are generally married to men older to them. So they cease having intercourse approximately 6-7 years before men. A large majority of older women attribute responsibility for cessation of intercourse to their partners, and older males often own the same.

Of course there are women "who never been too happy about sex during most of their lives find in menopause or in their advancing years a respectable reason for ending a duty that has always been onerous or distasteful to them".

Studies and surveys on human sexuality have proliferated in the last fifty years. Sexual research is no longer considered "so mysterious and spiritual". And even older people—long neglected in this field are receiving increasing attention. "Human Sexual Response" of Masters and Johnson devotes nearly 50 pages to it. With the life expectancy going up there will be a lot more people living beyond 65, and healthier too with the improving health standards.

Ageing brings certain physical changes. Overall, the age-related changes in the male reproduction system include (1) decrease in the size and firmness of testes, (2) decline in seminal production though sperm formation continues into eighties, (3) slow development of excitement and erection, and (4) lengthened refractory (recovery) period. The stage immediately preceding orgasm in younger men—the anticipatory feeling of orgasmic inevitability—is mostly missing. Again the contractions of the rectal sphincter, which in younger men occur regularly during orgasmic experience, decrease in frequency with aging. A smaller quantity of fluid is ejected with less force. While the refractory period in young men may be a matter of minutes, a man of sixty five may take about 12 to 24 hours to have another orgasm.

In females, besides sterility, ageing brings in a shrinkage of the external genitalia and a decrease in public hair. Uterus shortens in size too. The physiological counterpart of the male erection is vaginal lubrication. While young women experience vaginal lubrication within 10 to 30 seconds, women in their sixties take from one to three minutes. There is also much less of it. All this can cause irritation especially as the vaginal walls become thinner. A good deal of the difficulty can however be remedied through use of an artificial lubricant.

Some of the health disorders that interfere with sexual activity in old age are alcoholism, heavy smoking, stroke, arthritis, diabetes, cardiac weaknesses and prostate problems. Obesity and excessive consumption of food also have a tendency to repress sexual feelings.

The dangers of sexual intercourse to the damaged heart have been long exaggerated. The average heart rate during coitus is 120 beats per minute which is about the same level reached in light jogging. The oxygen supply used in sexual activity is similar to that required for a brisk walk. Death from a heart attack during coitus is highly unlikely.

The treatment of impotence is based on the premise that the impotent male is self-conscious, in effect watching himself from outside. He is unduly worried about his inability to achieve or retain erection, and in the process fails to have erection or loses it. Modern treatments focus rather on the couple than on him. A good deal of relaxed foreplay is usually recommended. Underlying causes like depression or marital discord are separately dealt with.

A failure in bed, once or twice at crucial moments, can set in motion an unfortunate train of events. The husband may altogether withdraw from lovemaking for fear of failure -the fear of failure itself paralysing. Men are rather too proud *or* reticent in these matters and just prefer to throw in the towel. She may misinterpret it all as being no longer attractive to him, or "too old for that sort of thing".

Some older people are also weighed down under sexual misinformation. For example many women harbour deep-seated fears of what will happen after the menopause. Men who are aged today grew up at a time when the concept of entropy was popular, i.e., you were born with a fixed quota of everything including sexual acts. Aged men who encounter difficulties in achieving or maintaining an erection may erroneously conclude that they have "used up" all their allotted ejaculations. Others may well believe that sex after 65 or 70 is positively ruinous to health and longevity.

Leave aside the physical problems accompanying age, societal factors also inhibit sexual activity in older people. If society insists that sex is inappropriate for the aged, the people themselves internalize this belief and give it up. The phenomenon is known as "socio-genic ageing", imaginary or imposed aging with little physical basis. Grandmothers, for instance, are supposed to have banished all thoughts of sex. Older couples are routinely denied the privacy extended to the young. The love life of old people attracts many a joke and mockery, or even resentment with some young of the family. These negative social attitudes towards physical love among older people in various cultures and societies (ours as negative as any) do operate as a serious deterrent—till such times these undergo a change.

Yet the factors inhibiting sexual activity in older couples may be more psychological than physiological or social. For men who have equated their work roles with their masculine sex roles, the end of jobs or retirement comes as a blow to their perceptions of maleness. It is particularly stressful for men whose younger wives are still employed. This means coping with the reversal of roles, besides other crisis like the trauma of powerlessness and the likely fall in living standard.

Sex: Shape of Things To Come

In another 25 years, sex should be healthier and safer. There could be less shame, and less violence.

For one, sexual activity will become widely accepted as an important aspect of healthy ageing. Studies have shown that the vast majority of seniors, both men and women, think about sex regularly. And people can have sex in advanced age if the body isn't stunted by illness or obesity. The next generation of elderly will have been raised with a more open attitude towards healthy sex.

Never in history has there been so much communication on all types of sexual subjects.

Censors have been relaxing on cinema and television.

Teenagers with Internet access can easily find free sexual material. Future generations will come of age, reach sexual maturity, with access to as much erotic material as they want. Viewers could download adult movies at home instead of facing the embarrassment of renting or borrowing videos. For the first time, you'll be only a click away from erotic material.

The Internet is fast becoming a place to connect for sex, courtship, and marriage. This affords its users a far wider choice, backed by much openness.

People will be more forthcoming about their sexual problems, particularly erectile dysfunction. And medication would help medicalize sexual problems, much in the same way as the treatment of depression.

IVF (*in vitro fertilization*) and technology will revolutionize marriage, sex and reproduction in the 21st century, says Dr. Carl Djerassi, Professor of Chemistry at Stanford University, California. He's the famous "father of the Pill" who synthesised the first oral contraceptive in 1951. As the Pill gave us the freedom to enjoy sex without the risk of conception, IVF technologies may make sexual intercourse as unnecessary for the creation of life, says he.

Djerassi envisages a world, especially in affluent societies, where most of us will only have "recreational sex". And we would be opting for IVF, using our own stores of frozen eggs and sperms when we want children. He's convinced this will become an accepted norm or at least a viable option with increasing numbers—a sort of separation of sex in bed from reproduction in the lab. Whereas IVF is now made use of by infertile couples, eventually it will be extended routinely to fertile couples.

With no dramatic advances in sight for a Male Pill and many more women reluctant to take the Pill, the most realistic option, he claims, will be for young women and men to have banks of their eggs and sperms deep-frozen and stored for future use, and then get themselves sterilized. Of course, in the process, the Pill and other contraceptives would become obsolete.

Women, he concedes, have a problem. It's not possible to avoid the necessary intensive hormone treatment to produce 20 to 40 eggs, although the cultivation of ovarian tissue may soon be possible. But then a woman stores her best eggs (harvested at youth) for future use. She can get on with her career until the time is right to have a child without worrying about eventual problems in late conceiving.

Djerassi vigorously defends that test tube conception won't hurt love and commitment in marriage. In fact it will strengthen than destroy all the good aspects of the traditional family. The decision to have a child, which is now not always made jointly, would be a completely voluntary, mutually consultative procedure, based not on lust but on love, tempered by responsibility and serious reflection. One partner could not coerce or blackmail the other to have a child. You couldn't have a woman pretending to be on the Pill and then getting pregnant.

It is a highly futuristic scenario he's picturing. Yet his ideas are evoking lively interest and debate in social and scientific circles.

Like all things pertaining to sex, this avalanche of new trends will mean different things to different people. Yet one can visualize a few positive aspects.

Less guilt, less shame, and more communication.

Greater acceptability of sex as a regular part of healthy ageing.

Husband Having an Affair

A husband should tell his wife everything he thinks she'll find out.

A lie detector without wires; it's called a wife.

That's the paradox: in an age of greater sexual freedom, couples are getting more intolerant of infidelity. People may have had a range of sexual experiences before marriage—the penalty for the same on the decline—but modern marriage has come to expect sexual exclusivity, plus satisfying marital sex.

Philandering—having repeated affairs—is predominantly a male activity. There is one thing we know about men: that they feel a tension between monogamy and promiscuity, with the balance of that tension different in different men. And this tension changes as the men age, sometimes from monogamy towards promiscuity and sometimes from promiscuity to monogamy.

If we accept as fact this one thing about men, then any marriage contains some seeds of instability, while at the same time marriage as an institution operates as a valuable social check upon the chaos of promiscuity. That way fidelity, more than anything else, is the signifier of marriage.

The poet Lord Byron argues a married man's case for infidelity like this. A man goes to sluts when wife nice! With all the splendour his to command at home? Because, of course, it is not his to command. It is his to indulge but in a chosen direction. Men have often sought justification for their philandering on the "frugality" and "restrictiveness" of the home-fare.

But then many happily married men who enjoy good sex at home don't turn down an opportunity for extramarital sex. It isn't a question of not getting enough sex at home—in general, monogamous couples have a lot more sex than people who are screwing around—but of variety and the adrenaline surge of a new conquest.

Another myth is the hydraulic pump theory—that you only have limited energy for something. If the man was having sex outside, he wouldn't be wanting that much at home, and his wife would get to know of it. Actually some men become more passionate at home when having extramarital sex; they stay sexually aroused by an ongoing affair.

Anyway it's hard to generalize about affairs. Every affair is different; the way it begins, the way it proceeds, and the way it would end.

Now modern workplaces offer umpteen opportunities for affairs. Women in increasing numbers work in daily proximity with men. And workplaces are sexy places; you dress up, you try to look your best, and there's often the stimulation of shared work. Today's work in many offices entails late hours, non-office settings, and the greater intimacy of business travel. An executive may well be seeing more of his female secretary—a woman who defers to his commands—than his wife.

Technology is having its own impact on affairs. Clandestine meetings are easier to fix up, aided by cell phones, answering machines, faxes and e-mail. On the other hand, these technological marvels leave their own electronic trail.

Quite a few people have discovered their partner's affair by looking at the cellular phone bill that listed the numbers dialled.

To catch their cheating husbands, Japanese women are said to be seeking the aid of forensic science. Using chemicals, anyway, works out cheaper than the old-fashioned method of hiring a detective to tail a straying hubby.

One detective technique employs two chemicals supplied in aerosol cans. Each of these is spread on the suspect underwear in turn. If traces of seminal fluid are present, the second spray turns the spots bright green. It's the same common test employed in forensic labs to detect presence of semen in rape cases.

The Japanese test relies on the fact that semen is secreted from the urinary tract for up to two hours after ejaculation. One detective agency claims that their "S-check" spray can detect semen for up to two weeks if the underwear is not washed.

Another detective agency is employing a gel which a wife rubs discretely on her husband's back before he goes to work.

If he has a shower during the day—commonly indulged in by Japanese men after an office affair—the gel reacts with water to form a blister which the wife can look out for when he undresses for the night.

What happens after an affair gets exposed? Psychiatrists are agreed that an affair creates a loss of innocence and is sure to leave some scars. Things will never be the same again. And a sound relationship cannot be rebuilt unless the unfaithful partner shows empathy for the pain caused.

Repair work only starts when the unfaithful one comes with a clean confession, besides ending the adulterous affair.

Accomplished liars deny, deny indignantly, when confronted with suspicion. "You must be mad," is one phrase used with effect. "How can you even think of such a thing about me?" is another one. Some let out a peal of laughter to disarm the suspecting wife.

There is no safety in denial against overwhelming evidence, while there is hope in admission. In fact, the continued lying and denial is the more unforgivable aspect of infidelity.

This Game of Hide and Seek

Most women believe that if the partners love each other, they won't be interested in an affair. And this is commonly true of women. A wife's infidelity is often a consequence of her continuing unhappiness with marriage. Men's behaviour works out differently. Many a happily married man who loves his partner and enjoys good sex at home, isn't averse to an extramarital fling.

It's usually the wife who keeps a watch over her husband going astray than the other way around. In this game of hide and seek, men mostly hide and women mostly seek.

If the "seeking" techniques are being honed, the "hiding" strategies are also getting refined.

In UK a company calling itself the Alibi Agency Ltd, aids straying husbands through providing an alibi.

"We offer a full and professional alibi service. We'll send invitations for corporate events, seminars, or sporting events to your home, then telephone you or your wife to confirm bookings. If someone tries to contact you, our receptionists will take the call as a hotel receptionist, for example, or a golf-club secretary. We will let the caller hear us try to page you, then offer to take a message when you can't be found. If we know where you are, we can even ring you while the caller is on hold, then patch the call through as if it were to your "room". We also take care of payments for hotels, meals, or gifts, then bill your credit card for car repairs or software purchases."

The alibi company justifies its work on the ground that most sexual affairs are inconsequential to long-term marriages. And so marriage and children should better be protected against the disruptive effect of a brief sexual encounter getting exposed. The company donates a portion of its profits to charities benefitting children from broken marriages.

The Latest on the Female Orgasm

Much ink has been spilled on the subject of the female orgasm. And yet information about the phenomenon remains conflicting. Women are spending more time thinking about their orgasms than actually having them. And somehow they've gotten men obsessed with these too.

For millions of years nobody knew there was such a thing as female orgasm (many languages including ours had no specific word for it). And ideas about where exactly the female orgasm was centred have been changing from time to time.

Initially it was presumed that the vagina would be its natural centre. Later clitoris was tipped as the seat (many African cultures have this custom of cutting off the clitoris to suppress female desire). Freud declared that a truly "mature" woman should be satisfied with orgasms born of penile thrusting. And when Freud said something, it was given due weight.

When the feminists came along, penis-vagina sex was passe. We don't need men to help us come anymore, cried the feminists. We'll manage with our own multi-speed vibrators.

The 1980s saw the emergence of interest in the G spot. The German gynaecologist Ernst Grafenberg had actually discovered the G spot (aptly named after him) in the 1940s. This was an identifiable erogenous region on the anterior wall of the vagina. Psychologists Alice Ladas and John Perry in their book *The G Spot* claimed that 100 percent of their four hundred female volunteers could locate the G spot. And the authors made out that if properly massaged by a thrusting male member, the G spot could blow up to the size of a small coin and trigger an orgasm.

Kinsey in 1953 and Masters and Johnson in 1968, however, did not accept such a thing as the G spot.

The current state of knowledge about the female orgasm may well be summarized like this.

For most women, orgasms take place in a contest of intimacy and love and are likeliest to occur in a stable relationship like marriage, and not during a one-night stand.

The average length of time it takes a woman to reach orgasm is from ten to thirty minutes, though even 40 minutes is not unusual. This can be a terribly long time for a man doing his thrusts. Male biological makeup, designed to ensure survival of the human race, gives guys the ability to achieve orgasm almost instantly. Such ability was vitally important millions of years ago, when primitive humans lived in a hostile environment. Back then, a guy could not afford to engage in a lot of time-wasting foreplay. He had to achieve immediate orgasm with the female, so that he'd ready to fight off predators or rivals.

The modern guy, to please his woman, employs all sorts of tricks to delay his ejaculation. When the guy is just to climax, he starts thinking of something really non-appealing, such as a mathematical problem. A lot of guys are making a tremendous and sometimes painful effort to be more effective at satisfying their mates, and yet they fail to stay in unison with their partners.

Researchers have found that a majority of women depend on clitoral stimulation from something other than a penis. Only a small percentage can get off from the friction of intercourse.

Between 5 to 10 percent American women (probably a much larger percentage of Indian women) never have an orgasm. Besides cultural and social conditioning, a good deal depends on a woman's state of mind, health, energy and age.

The female orgasm typically lasts from six to ten seconds. And many women claim they have more intense orgasms by masturbating than they do during sex.

Since women started making so much fuss about equal rights, many a man has taken on the female orgasm as *his* responsibility. "I blame myself if she doesn't come," says one. "I must not be doing something tight. It's the flip side of male performance anxiety."

While men may think a woman's orgasm is their achievement, it's really not. Her orgasm is a physiological event, and often a temperamental one. No man can "give" a woman an orgasm—he can certainly facilitate one. If a woman's mind is not in it, all the male tinkering in the world won't get her an orgasm. Indeed some women have started complaining that men are now paying too much attention to it, to the point of becoming tiresome.

And women hate to be asked if they've come. They hate it more than not coming. A woman particularly gets annoyed with a guy who clocks her orgasm, grilling her every five minutes about whether she's come yet, as if he's her coach for the Orgasm Olympics.

Some independent women have found a thoroughly modern way around the did-you-come-yet? problem by taking matters in their own hands. Since they have practice at making themselves come, they simply play with themselves during the proceedings, or they let the guy go first, and then finish with themselves. This reduces the pressure all round; the parties can relax and abandon themselves to some first-rate sex.

And there are other women who fake an orgasm to boost the ego of their man or to put an end to his clumsy efforts at getting them an orgasm.

Since these are strange times, it should come as no surprise that men are faking orgasms too. Sometimes men fake orgasms because they go on and on but just don't come. This is called retarded ejaculation and is not uncommon in older men. One who never comes may be novelty for a woman for a while but sooner or later the novelty wears off. The guy knows this, so he fakes it.

5

More in Marriage

Money in Marriage

The word "money" comes from the Latin word *moneta*, as the first Roman coins were struck at the temple of the goddess Juno Moneta. She was worshipped for her wise counsel—-somewhat akin to our goddess Lakshmi.

Yet many people lose their judgment and discrimination when it comes to money matters. Each of us seems to be endowed with a Money Complex-—an intertwined group of psychical "weak spots" that, in various circumstances, erupt into seemingly irrational behaviour. And this complex is formed, layer by layer, from infancy through adulthood.

Actually our money attitudes are not isolated psychic phenomena but an integral part of what we are. Someone who is withholding money may also be withholding affection. Another one who is perennially anxious about financial status may be lacking in self-assurance. Someone who is ever impoverishing himself financially may be harbouring self-destructive behaviour.

What money measures at the grocery store is relatively simple but what it measures in mind is not. Money's meaning differs from person to person, the way beauty differs in beholders' eyes. Money may be experienced as a weapon or a shield, a sedative or a stimulant, a talisman or an aphrodisiac. Having money may bring on feelings of fullness, pride, sexual attractiveness, even immortality.

Yet money has earned a reputation as the root of all evil. It drives mankind to fraud, forgery, theft and murder. It corrupts the young and bribes those in official positions. In some ways, it undermines every form of human decency.

The rising consumer culture and globalization have given rise to an almost obsessive concern with money. People are judged by the cars they keep, the gadgets they use, the houses they live in, the holidays they take, and the healthcare services they employ. Professional success and status have their importance but what currently matters most is the acquisition of money. With the steady decline in other forms of distinction, money is now the chief maker and marker of status and power.

What about money in marital relationship!

Between marriage partners, money is always a partner, too. And money issues are relatively harder to resolve, as couples often fail to explore each other's money beliefs.

Commonly, one finds couples polarized over money matters. If one is a spender the other is a hoarder. If one is a worrier about money, the other tends to overlook financial problems. A husband not believing in spending much money on gifts to family and friends is usually mated to a woman who believes in giving good gifts as tokens of affection.

In marriage, couples engage in this balancing dance of opposites. Where at the start, both happen to be spenders, one eventually assumes the role of super-spender, the other the role of a super-saver. A spender when not spending feels deprived. A saver when not spending feels virtuous. Evidently few marriages can survive two super-spenders. Sooner or later, couples start operating a system of checks and balances. Similarly if both happen to be hoarders, one often blossoms into a free spender while the other hardens in the worrier role; their living could turn pretty nasty if both stayed super-misers.

Ironically, the longer couples are married, the more they lock into polarized roles. And the confrontation game goes on; each side sticking to its own beliefs on money matters.

Among couples where both are independent earners, there often creeps up another curious phenomenon; that of staying rather secretive about their earnings. Take Mohan and Malti; he a leading lawyer, she a doctor in successful private practice. They are a loving, open-minded, imaginative couple. They have been together for nearly 20 years. They tend to keep few secrets between them, except of money. They aren't exactly forthcoming to each other about their earnings and bank balances. This might seem unusual, yet something similar may well be obtaining in many marriages. That way money is the last taboo. Among friends again, we may be happy to confide our innermost secrets, but when it comes to revealing how much we earn or save, most of us stay reticent.

Otherwise too, there are male-female differences in the approach to money. For example, in evolutionary terms, men evolved as hunters, women as gatherers. Men often display the hunter's approach: they go out, buy a pair of shoes, wear it out. When it dies, they go out and get another pair. Women, in contrast, gather things. Many times they buy things, not for immediate use but to store these for future occasions.

Despite advances in gender equality and the rising number of women with independent incomes, men are still bred to believe they are better at handling money. Women are mostly raised to believe they won't be good at it but, with luck, they may get a man who will take care of the money and its investing.

Another important difference between men and women concerns their approach to merging money as marriage partners. Typically, men want to merge all the couple's money, on which they hope to retain primary decision-making power. Women want at least some separate money. This they want as an expression of their prized autonomy.

A common strategy employed by two-income couples is to merge a portion of their income for joint expenses—the ratio of contribution, whether 50-50 or anything else depending on what each of them earns. The balance of income is kept separate where your partner doesn't have much say how you spend it. This can avert quite a few money conflicts. Indeed the best way to manage money issues in marriage is to put oneself in one's partner's place.

Men and Women Changing in Marriage

Men and women change in marriage. They often change in ways that make the romance go out of their marriage. Indeed, sometimes the woman wonders whether this is the same man she was once married to, while her husband wonders where is the woman he was once smitten with.

Wives have quite a few complaints to make. Husbands stop touching them except for sex. The male approach is understandable. Becoming privy to full sexual favours—the ultimate in touching—his impulse for affectionate touching grows fainter. By instinct, a male is tuned to touch only as a prelude to sex.

Yet non-sexual touch retains its prime importance for a woman. It boosts her self—esteem; experts claim a woman touched several times a day experiences high self-esteem. An affectionate touch is something her body actually craves for. No wonder a woman's skin is ten times more sensitive to touch than a man's.

Once a husband is aware of his mate's sensual need for non-sexual touching, he could be more motivated to please her with the same. She, on her part, should show evident appreciation whenever he touches her in affection; even encourage him in doing so in non-demanding ways.

Incidentally wives often complain that men are too hurried and too rough in their touching. This is not to say that there aren't times when a quick or firm touch isn't appropriate, but most of the time, touching has to be soft and slow.

Another complaint: husbands stop giving compliments. "He no longer compliments me on a nice dress or a new hairdo; not even an admiring glance when I look my best," rues a wife. A woman, whose body alters noticeably with years, needs lots of reassurance that her partner still finds her appealing.

To a lot of men this doesn't make much sense. A typical response: "I married her because she was beautiful. And she knows my feelings. But what's the point of my reminding her repeatedly of it." The shift does not take place because he doesn't love her, but because he doesn't realize that the action of noticing her and paying compliments means so much to her.

The situation possibly calls for some initiative on the part of wives, too. They should keep on asking husbands how they look, and remind them to say complimentary things. In course of time, their men may get tuned to giving admiring looks and compliments without any prodding.

And then the complaint: husbands stop pursuing them. "Kanwal used to find me when he came home from office," says Uma. "Now straightway he heads for TV or plays with the kids. I don't feel wanted as before." Kanwal, like many men, has attained his goal with marriage and so stopped pursuing—the automatic hunter reflex to stop pursuing when you have bagged the quarry.

It seems a good idea to give your wife your first attention on return from work, before settling down to other things. Of course there are days when one is under considerable stress from work and needs some time alone to recover, yet this practice of giving the first fifteen minutes—the golden minutes—to your mate can reap you rich dividends of her goodwill.

Wives voice a common lament: husbands stop talking to them, even stop listening to them. On their part, men usually make out they remain silent because there is nothing important to say.

With women it's different. The calm men achieve through silence, women usually achieve through talking. To women the very process of conversation with their partners boosts rapport. They experience greater intimacy by sharing thoughts and feelings.

Men have their own side of the story. Women also change over the course of a marriage. But mostly they remain unaware of how they have changed and how it was contributing to the problems of the marriage. Many women honestly believe it was only their husbands who had changed.

Wives stop appreciating the little things their husbands do. If a woman yearns for communication, a man thrives on appreciation, more so feminine appreciation. "Men would rather a woman "do" less for him and appreciate more what he "does" for her," says one marriage counsellor.

And then those wives who start giving a lot of unsolicited advice. When a woman tells her man, "Slow down, the road is wet", he hears her say, "You could be careless. Drive carefully."

In the beginning of marriage, a woman generally lets the man do things the way he is accustomed to do. But over time, she sees him doing things differently from the way she believes he should and so starts giving him unasked for advice.

The woman thinks she is helping her man by giving advice. But in reality she is sending him the message that he can't do things on his own. And this mothering he often comes to resent.

Who needs another boss at home? Enough of them in the office.

Retirement, a Second Marriage

What happens to a marriage when a husband and wife find themselves together 24 hours a day, maybe for the first time in their lives?

Prior to his retirement the man went out to work. The evening might be spent discussing the day's events and other people's problems; the couple's own getting side-stepped. Unfilled parts of a marriage can be masked by being busy.

But what happens when the work life ceases? The supportive job routine is gone. The network of colleagues is virtually cut off. The only outlet left is often the marriage partner; grown-up children may have also departed by this time.

Retirement has been likened to described as a second marriage. And it can be quite a difficult marriage to start with—till the parties adjust themselves anew to the enforced togetherness. Some couples discover to their distress that they have little in common.

A retirement is seen to be accompanied by four fearful demons: isolation, boredom, reduced income (plus poorer housing, loss of help and facilities), and fall in self-esteem. All the more damaging to one's self-esteem if retired at the relatively early age of mandatory retirement (58 or 55), with the physical and mental faculties intact. No wonder, people are at such pains to prolong their employment or clutch at any alternative avenue. It's here that the self-employed like lawyers and doctors are the subject of most envy.

Let's face it, we live in a society where our work defines us; well-nigh justifies us. In such a scenario, retirement can be tantamount to a near total loss of identity, another word for defeat. Unless, through some spirited activity, one can achieve the more acceptable status termed "keeping busy".

What about the one, who frankly admits, "I'm doing nothing?, or quips", "I'm killing time till time comes to kill me." Hearing a sorry response like this, his questioners look puzzled for an instant, then startled as the words sink in; and finally they stare at him in silent embarrassment. Plainly he is withering away before their very eyes.

Admiration these days is reserved for elders who successfully challenge their biological clocks with prodigious feats of energy and accomplishments.

After retirement, home becomes the central focus. A retiree is apt to cling to its resources. But here again he may discover to his dismay that the two of them—he and his wife—are one too many in the house, more so if it's a small house.

Howsoever circumspect he may be, he still prowls on his mate's turf. And interlopers arouse hostility. How would he have reacted if his wife had hung around his office all day?

A wife, with a husband all day at home, may feel herself maddeningly in a bind like the Siamese twins. No privacy for little things. If she's sorting out her clothes he comments. When she talks on telephone he's listening or even butting in. Any minor household mishap, such as the breakage of a china cup, gets known to him immediately.

Housewives commonly complain of overwork with a husband at home when it should be other way around.

Here's a handyman; available all time to fix up things, to tend the garden patch, to answer the doorbell. The last chore he possibly welcomes. Callers bring some excitement to his life even if it's an unwanted salesman or a suspicious mendicant.

But there is something worse for her than sharing the same turf. A sense of sadness floats in the air. She comes to hate her husband's retirement because it makes her feel old. You are diminished in an unexpected way, being married to a pensioner.

There is a plethora of guidebooks for the retiree; with statistics giving him dire warnings of death rates jumping markedly in the third and fourth years after retirement.

If you can't live comfortably on your pension, plus rent if any, better pocket your pride and take to paid work. Nothing is worse for marital harmony than the combination of enforced togetherness and the paucity of purse.

Things look a bit brighter if your wife still has her job—presumably younger to you by several years. But then you have to lay the welcome mat on her return (and no cribbing if she's late). Run a comb through what's left of your hair. Usher her in, give her the best seat. And don't pester her forthwith as to what transpired at her office. She will talk of these things in her own good time. What she hates is a the routine interrogation on return.

Your own distress stories: the sweeper woman not turning up for the day or the bananas going bad, can wait till she has time to settle down. And, by the way, when you are alone at home, don't wander too much in the neighbourhood—keep the shame of your unemployment to yourself.

When both the partners are grounded home, a fine balance has to be struck between togetherness and aloneness. Regular spells of reading in a separate room—you can call it your study—are a help; nobody minds even if you doze off there. It may not be a bad idea to be shaved and dressed up before breakfast time. This brings back some semblance of your former work life. Continuing clad in crumpled pyjamas and dragging a newspaper through half the day is a sorry sight.

Time-consuming games like golf and bridge can get you out of her hair. And, if both share these hobbies, you can play golf in separate foursomes and bridge on different club tables.

With enforced togetherness, little irritations and resentments build up in daily living, and these are no good for sex. Another fact: sadly at this stage of life men are the weaker sex. A couple of awkward failures in bed, and some throw in the towel. And older husbands, it seems, get put off too easily.

It would help if she behaves a bit cuddly instead of always brisk, busy and efficient. A particular evening could be planned to proceed without a jarring note, or it could even be daytime. Men are often hornier in the afternoon than after dinnertime.

A final word. Don't be unduly exercised over your wife's growing assertiveness. Researchers report that over time women become more assertive and men yielding, women more sure of themselves and men more dependent. Not that they lose their old traits but new ones get added; the older men and women respectively developing supplementary qualities that are customarily defined as appropriate to the opposite sex. A grandfather can be as tender to children as a woman was to infants when she was young.

All this doesn't mean, "the second marriage" of retirement is devoid of fun. But it calls for care and consideration, perhaps far in excess of what you brought in "the first".

Dynamics of the Double Bed

Theoretically, marriage is all about Two persons becoming One. But in the real world, they aren't one; they're two, and there's only so much two persons can conceivably blend.

Take the double bed, the quintessential mark of marriage. It's a real challenge when you have four arms and legs to find homes for. Arms and legs that didn't bother you all day are suddenly a burden.

One endearing model is to have her head on your chest, your arm around her shoulder. Another fetching variation is to face each other, with one of you wrapping your upper leg around the other's legs. But these postures aren't well suited for lengthy, sleep-oriented couplings.

And most challenging of all are the complications of a common cover. Eventually you slip back to your accustomed position, fix your pillow, and arrange your shared coverlet—the one big cover with two people squirming inside trying to get comfortable.

According to some medical specialists, male and female of the human species are biologically too dissimilar to sleep cozily under a common cover. The temperature requirements of the two are quite different. Women have protective layers of fat against cold and a built-in thermostat that produces less body heat in summer. Men are prone to suffer more, both from cold and heat.

Even the sleep requirements of the two are different. The average man, often doing heavier work, needs more sleep than his mate.

Snoring presents its own problems. Men snore louder than women, and alcohol intake steps up that roar. Wives too troubled by a mate's snoring are known to shift their pillow to the foot of the double bed—a move viewed by the other party as "unfriendly". This puts some five feet of distance—instead of the usual foot—between her ears and the source of the noise.

How you handle the coverlet is crucial.

You wake up in the middle of night to find, there is nothing to handle. Your mate has somehow accumulated the bulk of what's at least half yours.

You tug at it gingerly. The partner stirs, and seemingly unaware, tightens the grasp and rolls further away, taking another good foot and a half of it. You are left in cold or exposed to a blast from the air conditioner. But then the party responsible for the same is someone committed to lying alongside you for the rest of life. So you pull up the pathetically small segment of coverlet left available to you and scoot up next to your mate. Anyway the partner would be warmer than you.

The double bed is a complex, multipurpose arena, and it's important that the two parties specify which activity they're undertaking after the Conversation Curfew.

"Are we seeing TV, or are we reading?"

"Are we not talking because of some sulk, or because we both just don't feel like talking?"

"Are we sleeping, or we fooling around?"

The good thing about marriage is, there is less pressure to make any given night magical. You always know you have another shot tomorrow. And the next night. That's the whole beauty of Forever.

Possibly the greatest virtue of the double bed is its role as a breach healer. Most marriage rows spring from little things; a small complaint here, a slight refusal there, one partner's feelings are hurt, the other goes into a sulk. The man hurries up his tooth-brushing, gets into his night clothes, and plunks down on the farthest edge of his bed. Draws up the cover over his head and almost peevishly turns his back on his soul mate. She, with a longer nightly toilet routine, later slides into hers.

It's long time before they actually fall asleep, the man usually the first. Till then each keeps on thinking ruefully, "Why not end this silly quarrel? Why not snuggle in besides the partner; no doubt erring but still loved?" But who's to make the first crucial move, to "eat crow"? They often end up having a restive night. And so quite in a mood next day to nurse more grievances, real or imagined.

In beds separated by night tables, it means crossing that horrid chasm of three feet. Even in joined beds, any conciliatory move has to be telegraphed; the "magnanimous" partner shuffling out of covers and tugging at those of the partner. This deliberate gesture takes some doing.

In a double bed, things are apt to turn out easier. A tentative toe stretched towards the centre. Quite by accident it touches a leg. There's no real obligation to withdraw the toe. So it stays. Maybe, it's rewarded by a gentle return pressure. The underlying yearning for amity begins to flow. A hand by chance may brush a side. Heads draw near, arms may reach out. . . . The physical contact has broken the ice, even if no formal reconciliation results before falling asleep.

6

The Family

Family Eating Together

Eating together offers an ideal opportunity for a family to communicate, to interact. Indeed, without a family meal to bring everyone together, there is no other forum of communication, no other focus to family life, no domestic debating chamber, no medium for the exchange of wisdom between the different generations.

Yet the custom of a family eating together has been on the decline in several societies. For example, a majority of the British and Americans have given up eating together. In many homes, nobody even cooks on a regular basis. Anybody feeling hungry approaches the fridge and fashions a meal for himself, or brings along some carry-home stuff. No fixed timings of meals, no fixed place to eat. Each member of the household develops a separate life, fitting eating into his or her own work-cum-recreation schedule. In quite a few families, the only mode of communication between teenagers and their parents is now through slips pasted on the fridge door.

Others, such as the Italians, are still mostly keeping to the custom of a family sitting down to a meal, once a day or at least several times a week, while the housewife cooks. Children learn how to manage a knife and fork, how to behave, how to talk.

In this respect we are more like the Italians. Yet in many an urban, upwardly-mobile home, the Anglo-American pattern seems to be setting in. Children tend to eat in their rooms in the midst of their activities and at their own time. In fact one gets an impression that many a teenager is at pains to avoid any pally talk with parents—keeping such conversation limited to grunts and shrugs.

The family meal, primarily the evening meal, is not only the core curriculum in the school of civilized discourse; it is also a set of protocols that curb our natural savagery and animal greed. It cultivates in us a capacity for sharing and considerateness for others. Indeed table manners are one of the subtlest lines separating civility from barbarity.

Dinner rituals have little to do with the income or the social class of a family. It's not important whether you sit at a big dining table or squat on the kitchen floor. And you could have the simplest food imaginable; plain dal and roti would do.

What really counts is the grace with which food is served and accepted. It's through this practice of family sitting at meals and observing the attendant conventions that youngsters learn the art of human companionship, the culture of give and take.

And the ideal family meal calls for undistracted dining, not sitting in front of the TV. Even otherwise, new research shows that families who watch TV during dinnertime tend to develop poor eating habits, putting kids at risk from obesity or malnutrition. A Tufts University study, recently released by the American Academy of Pediatrics found that when families didn't separate eating from other activities, particularly watching TV, kids consumed fewer fruits and vegetables and more junk food. Left to their own devices, youngsters almost inevitably gravitate to fast food, rarely brimming with nutrients.

In one recent study of 5,000 families published in the Journal of the American Dietic Association, frequent family meals signified an increasing intake of healthy foods.

Another study published in the Journal of Adolescent Health also found that eating evening meals at home was associated with an increased consumption of fruits and vegetables, and healthier eating habits overall.

The more frequent family dinners are, the more likely the youngsters are to discuss and learn about nutritional matters.

Eating is one of the most fundamental health-related behaviors we have. Cutting out distractions at mealtimes, such as TV, is the best way to ensure that healthier foods make it to the table. Once parents manage to separate and structure eating times, incorporating healthy foods becomes much simpler.

A factor undermining the institution of the family meal is the spreading habit of "grazing". People, particularly teenagers, keep on taking snacks at all hours or snatching food whenever convenient. This does erode the imperative of a regular, fixed-time sit-down meal.

Teenagers gulping junk food slouched in front of TV or snacking at odd hours cooped up in their rooms, could not only be nutritionally deprived, they are deprived of the best element of the family life; the family meal. It would be an error to underestimate its importance in the character formation of the young.

Their parents can also be faulted for this development. These parents—often working parents—may be too busy in their business deals or social whirl. Or, they may simply be preferring nice, quiet meals. Eating with youngsters entails enforcing a modicum of discipline and smoothening individual behaviour. That way all rituals involve some degree of sacrifice in time and attention. And the same is true of the sit-together family meal.

"The family that prays together stays together," they say. It could well be said that the family that eats together stays together.

The Onlies

"I can spot an only child at twenty paces. It is something about the space they always need," says David Emerson, the co-author of *Only Child* (Souvenir Press). He and Jill Pitkeathley had interviewed in depth hundreds of adults who were onlies.

"Having all those goodies, all that undiluted parental attention, not having to share with other siblings, missing out on rough and tumble of a sibling childhood—and many more distinct experiences—does create in the only child someone special, someone with behaviour that can seem strange to those who have grown up amongst brothers and sisters," say the authors.

Being surrounded by adult company and being the centre of attraction, the child quickly develops a larger vocabulary and models his behaviour on adults around him. Parents increasingly give him responsible tasks and involve him in decision-making about the house and family. Indeed being the focus of attention can be a very good childhood experience, generating self-confidence.

The undivided attention of both parents means that whatever you say is likely to be heard. The moment his foot crosses the door there's a parent saying, "Hello, how are you? Has it been a good day?" The situation is clearly different where three or more sibling are clamouring for parental attention.

Only children get more parental support in education than what is available to children with siblings. Parents indulge them more in their hobbies; concerned that the only child wouldn't get bored.

Yet there are negative aspects, too. When onlies play with other children, their lack of experience in joining in can hold them back and make them appear stand-offish. Onlies just haven't been used to the jostling and bumping up against each other that is common among other children. And onlies find it difficult to cope with teasing that goes on in schools—they have no such experience at home.

They are often unable to deal with anger in a light-hearted or non-threatening manner because they never had the "squabbling, bickering" and then forgetting it as most children have.

Relating to brother and sister and having to accommodate them, howsoever reluctantly, is an invaluable training for later life. Surely you can get by without it; you can even learn some of it. But what siblings do provide is an emotional training for life that is difficult, if not impossible, to replicate.

No brothers and sisters to borrow or move things. Only children can retain a burning resentment at other people's thoughtless rearrangement of their territory. Borrowing without asking and putting them in the wrong places make the only children (even when grown up) really angry.

The greater time and attention available from a parent means that the only child's needs tend to met fully and quickly. As a consequence, onlies often develop a sense of immediacy. They want things to happen quickly and are usually more restive in queues.

Being in the limelight for a few years is something first-born children may share with onlies, and may explain some of their shared characteristics. But for the only child, of course, this focus is never shattered.

Any talk of onlies brings in China. The country's one-child policy is the most ambitious piece of social engineering in history. Never has any nation attempted something as drastic and of such magnitude as this policy. What will be all its ramifications for the Chinese society? And what about the coming crop of only children; only children born to parents who themselves were single children?

With son-preference strong in the Han Chinese (akin to ours), one-child regime operated harshly on girls.

Yet, unintended as it may be, the one-child policy has done wonders to the status and image of Chinese girls. Millions of middle-class urban families now have one girl child. Parents dote on them, prize them. These girls are receiving almost as much parental attention and investment in their education as single sons. The one-child policy seems to have triggered a silent revolution, leading to greater girl-acceptance and a boost to women's self-esteem in a traditionally male-oriented society.

In the early 1980s, various Chinese research psychologists found that the only children—"the little emperors"—were more likely to have personality and social behavioural problems. They grow more stubborn, moody, irritable, less sharing than non-only children.

Another consequence: these onlies are usually overfed, many to the point of obesity. Whatever they—and they mostly demand foods rich in fats and proteins, such as meats, sweets and fast-foods—they are given. Grandparents are even more indulgent; they tend to cater to every whim of the grandchild. No wonder, single children are known in Chinese as "four-two-ones": four grandparents, two parents, and one spoiled brat.

Besides spending relatively large sums on over-feeding their onlies, parents are seen to spare no expense on their toys and clothes. In many families nearly half the family budget is snapped up by the only.

And parents often go to extraordinary lengths to give the only child the best possible education. That's the top priority, no matter what it costs. Special tutors are hired outside schools. Parents skimp on their own consumption, take loans, to buy the only child expensive educational inputs, such as a computer, even a piano.

No wonder quite a few Chinese surveys concluded that only children were more egocentric, with lower ratings in cooperation than non-only children.

Elsewhere in the world the only-child situation doesn't go beyond the concerns of individual family happiness and the child's psychological adjustment. But in China the problematic character of such children in huge numbers has become an important social issue. It even worries state authorities. Parents are frequently exhorted not to overindulge their only children. And, of late, the Chinese authorities have been relaxing the rigour of one-child norm.

Some prejudice against the only child is age-old in every culture. Popular sentiment still persists that a second child is needed to provide companionship to the first, so that the first won't be spoiled or be selfish or feel lonesome. Parents experience pressure from relatives and friends to have a second child—sometimes even more pressure than to have the first. Many single-child parents feel stigmatized as being selfish.

The only child, however, is faring well in western research. These studies concentrate on IQ and school results, items lending themselves to more accurate quantification than the vague "personality". When it comes to educational achievements, the results are clear-cut: only children have been found to have higher achievements in both length of education and quality of academic work.

As to personality traits such as emotional adjustment and sociability, western research generally finds no significant difference between only and non-only children—the only-children "more maligned than maladjusted". It is not the nature of only children that creates problems, but what is expected of them by their families and society. If they are any different, it is because of the heightened expectations and anxieties that others have about them.

In Europe where single-child families are nearly as common as two-child families, no adverse effects have been observed. Similarly elsewhere, including India, there has been a steady rise in single-child couples. A growing number of our matrimonial ads highlight that the boy or girl in question has the advantage of being an only child.

In recent years a new perspective on only children is emerging. The most noted researcher in this field is Tony Falbo, a professor of educational psychology at the University of Texas. She (herself an only) has conducted numerous surveys and examined more than a hundred studies done since the 1920s.

Falbo concludes that "only children scored significantly better than other groups in achievement, motivation and personal adjustment," and were in all other respects indistinguishable from children with siblings.

The debate, however, still goes on about the advantages and disadvantages of being the only child.

Latecomers: Children Born to Older Parents

Children begin by loving their parents; as they grow older, they judge them; sometimes, they forgive them. (Oscar Wilde, *The Picture of Dorian Gray*)

Ravi, a 40-year old business executive, was born when his father was forty-eight and his mother thirty-nine. His two sisters were fifteen and thirteen when he was born. Ravi says, his parents just wouldn't give up the idea of having a son.

"By the time I was twelve, my father had grown bald and my mother was greyish. I felt a little embarrassed when I saw my parents next to other kids' at school functions. They always seemed less active; I don't remember my father playing any ball games with me.

I was uncle to half a dozen nephews by the time I was in first grade. There were no grandparents to go to, and my sisters were motherly.

By the time I was thirty-five, I was deep into caring for my sick mother, father dying already after a protracted illness. I already feel tired, almost old."

Reenu, a young physician, was born when her father was thirty-nine and her mother thirty-eight. She's the only child of parents who are both doctors.

"By the time I arrived in this world, my parents were successful professionals and moneyed. I had a marvellous childhood. They took me on many trips and gave me lots of toys and books. And my mother, I believe, taught me early to be self-reliant and career-oriented, with her talk and example. I rate myself lucky for being born to parents who were then mature."

Social scientists have rarely given thought to the influences that shape latecomers—children born to mothers over 35 and fathers often much older, whereas children of divorced parents, working mothers, alcoholic parents, adoptive parents have been extensively investigated.

Evidently having older parents does make a difference. But this difference has yet to be studied in scientific terms. Is it a hazard or an advantage? Is the latecomers' childhood different from those of children born to parents in their twenties? And does this feeling of being different continue from childhood into adulthood?

Andrew L.Yarrow, a *New York Times* reporter has made an attempt to answer some of these questions. He queried hundreds of Americans who had been born to older parents. And summed their reactions, along with his comments, in a book "Latecomers: Children of Parents Over 35" (Free Press). The book makes an interesting reading.

Children are born to older parents either by chance or choice. There are those who are the result of an "accident" or "mistake"; the last in the line of children, born with a gap of years separating them from their next older sibling. And when they learn they had been unwanted, this knowledge usually hurts. While some receive lots of attention as the "baby" of the family, others prove weary to their older parents who had settled to a well-defined life after the close of the child-rearing phase. This sort of perceived parental resentment of their children's intrusion into their lives could continue, in some cases, long after childhood. Anyway these cases are set to decline with the prevalence of more reliable contraceptives.

Another category is the long-awaited ones, with couples trying for years to get a child. When such babies arrive, they are the subject of much parental doting. Whether the same does them any great good, is another matter.

Then there are those children whose coming had been delayed because of conscious family planning or of a late marriage itself. The latter can be a significant feature in marriages of the divorced or widowed. Even otherwise many professionals are now marrying quite late.

Childhood of Latecomers: Of course a good deal will depend on a latecomer's particular circumstances and the family situation. Yet latecomers seem to encounter some typical problems and privileges.

The generation gap between the older parents and their offspring is wider. Children often feel that their parents are too conservative, outdated and set in their ways. The generation gap typically worsens during adolescence. Teenagers may feel that the ideas of their older parents on clothes, entertainment and dating are too old-fashioned or rigid.

On the other hand, older parents being more mature and experienced, can be calmer, more tolerant, more understanding. Again older parents are more likely to be economically secure and emotionally stable.

This can yield high quality parenting.

There's an old saying: "Old people have old babies". Many children of older parents tend to feel, they "grew up fast". They imagine they were treated more like adults and given more responsibility than their friends with younger parents. The older parents are apt to communicate with their children in more "adult" ways. Again older parents, it seems, are involved in mature pastimes like reading and music, instead of games and other robust physical activities. Their interests frequently pass on to their children.

As older parents are often too intense at child rearing, the children are under greater pressure to perform than those born to younger parents. These kids are likely to have fewer siblings. And they'll be more individualistic, type-A achievers.

Till recently the normative ideal that it is best to become a parent in one's twenties. Indeed older parents begetting children were the subject of snide remarks. Medically again, mothers were advised that childbirth in late thirties carried more risks to the mother and child.

Social attitudes seem to be changing. People are marrying late; others are delaying children for career considerations or other personal reasons. It is also made out in defence that people today are "young" longer; the dividing line between youth and middle age pushed back from thirty to forty.

Women in their late thirties and forties are still considered high-risk mothers by some obstetricians, but new medical knowledge and procedures has led to changes in perspectives on these "elderly" thirty-five plus. Advances in obstetrics certainly play a role in reducing the perception that later childbearing is "wrong". Actually many older parents get the feel of being young again when a child is born to them.

In some professional circles, late childbirth is being deemed as something chic than deviant. And this trend could well accelerate in coming years. Increasingly career women are delaying children till they have established themselves in their calling. But this could also trigger a certain anxiety, even panic, when they reach the now-or-never stage; the biological clock ticking remorselessly against them.

While older parents commonly derive much satisfaction and pleasure from latecomers, whether latecomers are themselves better off having older parents is not that clear. The emerging picture is rather mixed, with some children coming out as gainers and others as losers. And there are those for whom the gains and losses balance out.

How Significant is Your Birth Order?

The birth-order gurus claim they can predict your personality from your birth order.

The birth-order theory is built around the appealingly simple idea that your place in the family determines your strengths and failings, your very mental make-up.

According to it, if you were the first born or the only born, you received the full charge of your parents' attention and expectations. That made you demanding and self-centred, somewhat overcontrolling and ambitious. The oldest or the single child tends to spend more time with adults. That's one reason why such children are likely to develop faster, and show greater eagerness to assume leadership or responsible roles.

Jawaharlal Nehru, that way, had to be the first born. And Indira Gandhi, the only born. The intensive early education of John Stuart Mill at the behest of his great father was largely a product of the same situation.

The personalities of middle children are harder to define or classify. But they do suffer from some benign neglect; they have fewer pictures in the family album. To cope with the lack of parental attention, they tend to become rebellious and secretive. And because they never got their parents all to themselves, they learn to compromise, act more accommodating.

At its best, the process can make them more sensitive, more human. Tennyson and Tagore were middle children.

What about the last born? By the time they are born—frequently born unplanned—their parents have mostly exhausted their expectations of children; this could make the last born smoulder with thwarted ambition. Parents are content to pamper the youngest one almost unreservedly. Last-borns are described variously as clowns and cutups. And often act more spoiled than the onlies.

Some birth-order experts, to prove their point, make out that many of the world's comedians and clowns were the last born. Others have tried to prove that women who are not fond of children tend to be youngest siblings.

Leman, the author of *The Birth Order Book*, is the reigning guru. His main argument is that the dynamics between the parents and the children plays a crucial part in the formation of personality, and here the order of one's birth matters a lot. "You can use birth order to get a quick handle on people," says he.

Freud is quoted as saying that "a child's position in the sequence of brothers and sisters is of very great significance for the course of his later life".

And the most authoritative work on birth-order comes from the Austrian family therapist, Walter Toman, author of *Family Constellation: Its Effects on Personality and Social Behaviour.* Toman's basic assertion is that the order of one's birth determines certain personality characteristics that shape the choices we make and the likelihood of our success and even how we think about ourselves.

All in all, the birth-order theory is now drawing more flak than appreciation, particularly from the scientific community. It is likened more to palm-reading or astrology.

"Most serious researchers have stopped talking about birth order," says Falbo. A family is a densely woven fabric made up of innumerable threads; the birth order is just a thread in that carpet.

Suppose there is a wide gap between the second and the third child. Wouldn't the third child likely to develop the characteristics of a first born? And what about the second child sharing the traits of the last-born? What if the firstborn was a boy, and all the rest girls? Wouldn't the oldest girl develop a first-born personality in relation to her sisters? And what about the eldest son, with an elder brother who died young? The variations are far too many to draw any hard and fast rules. And family life and child development is too complex a field to lend itself to standard formulae.

Yet the popular appeal of birth-order theory persists. People continue to feel there's something in it.

Sibling Rivalry

In his book *Born to Rebel* (Pantheon) Frank Sulloway argues that the single best predictor of revolutionary creativity is birth order. Firstborns tend to be conservative while laterborns are more likely to become freethinking.

And this he illustrates with a mass of impressive statistical evidence. All in all, more than a million biographical data points were culled from 500 years of history. Special software was created to feed the enormous data into a computer.

Sulloway makes out that siblings employ adaptive tactics to compete with one another in currying parental favour. "Depending on differences in birth order, gender, physical traits, and aspects of temperament, siblings create differing roles for themselves within the family system." he writes.

Firstborns identify more strongly with power and authority than their siblings do. More self-confident, they employ their superior size and strength to defend their special status. In their relations with siblings, they are more assertive and jealous. No wonder they are heavily represented among political leaders, presidents and prime ministers.

Laterborns, as underdogs, are more inclined to identify themselves with the downtrodden and question the status quo. That makes them more creative, altruistic, and independent-thinking. From their ranks have come out revolutionaries, explorers, iconoclasts and heretics of history.

"Like other predictors of radicalism, birth order is fallible." he concedes. "Its principal virtue lies in being less fallible than any other predictor I have been able to identify." According to him, birth order has played a consistent role across twenty countries and five centuries he has examined, in respect of political, religious and scientific revolutions.

Sulloway also raises the basic question: why are siblings from the same family so different from each other? Siblings of a middle-class family often attend the same school, play the same games, participate in the same religious and cultural events, yet they are "little more similar in personality measures than they are to working class or farm boys". What people once thought was a shared family environment turns out not to be shared at all. Though a family seems to be homogenous, from a child's perspective it is a panoply of environments—"a collection of niches, consisting of distinct vantage points from which siblings experience the same events in very different ways".

Siblings are so different from one another because they act in accordance with Darwin's "principle of divergence", he explains. In a family, as in nature, diversification is a strategy that helps individuals minimize direct competition for scarce resources. Childhood, that way, is essentially a search for a family niche.

When a sibling strives for parental attention it is primarily his other siblings that he is competing against. Children become painfully aware when they are loved less than a sibling. They are extremely sensitive to inequality, whether real or perceived.

"No one is genetically destined to be a first-or lastborn; we merely find ourselves in that position and have to make the best of it," says he. The birth order thus is a functional order.

"Even an only child is locked in sibling conflict because he is trying to maximize parental investment in anticipation of a sibling." explains Sulloway when asked what the rivalry would be in a family with just one child. "Children are hardwired to use sibling strategies to maximize parental investment. They don't even need a sibling to do it; they have hundreds of millions of years of biology telling them to do it anyway."

The study of birth order isn't particularly in good standing among social scientists these days. A general impression has gone round that the birth-order influences on personality and I.Q. are widely overrated. Most serious researchers have actually stopped talking about birth order. The family is deemed a densely woven fabric in which birth order is just a thread.

Choosing the Sex of Children

Almost no subject is more steeped in myth and lore than the business of choosing the sex of children. Aristotle recommended placing the bed on a north-south axis for those wanting boys. Some others believed that lying on the right side (considered the superior side) during sex would produce a boy. Various diets or drugs have been advocated through centuries for producing boys.

Yet the only sure way to be certain of having a boy has been, sadly, female infanticide; newborn girls killed through poisoning, throttling, plain starvation or neglect. This gruesome practice should be on decline as science has come up with new ways of knowing the sex of the unborn child, coupled with easier and safer forms of abortion.

Prenatal diagnosis for sex selection misuses a procedure designed to detect serious and fatal genetic diseases. And this scientific tool is being increasingly misused in some regions of our country to abort female foetuses, despite laws forbidding the practice.

Ultrasound technology makes it possible to image foetal genitals as early as 14 weeks. It is a reliable method and easy to operate.

In blood sampling, a new British method, the mother's blood is examined for foetal cells to determine the sex of the foetus. The test is still expensive.

Could females in some way influence the outcome of the competition between X and Y sperm? Till now we are accustomed to the notion that our gender is determined at conception by sheer luck. If the first sperm to penetrate one's mother's egg carried a Y chromosome, one is a male; if it carried an X chromosome, one is a female. Because men produce X- and Y-carrying sperms in equal number, it seems a matter of pure chance.

Some researchers are now of the view that even in mammals a female has an element of choice. A hormonal explanation is offered, especially when hormonal levels are clearly influenced by social status in many species. The hormone gonadotrophin which is released with ovulation somehow favours X-bearing sperm. Thus frequent sex which often leads to fertilization in an early phase of the fertile period during low gonadotrophin levels, tends to produce more males. The phenomenon of soldiers returning from war and producing more boys than girls is explained on this; frequent sex is characteristic of soldiers returning from war.

Human beings have the history of retaining an acceptable numerical balance between the two sexes, despite many cultures biasing their legacies, parent care, and sustenance and favouritism to sons at the expense of daughters. On top, certain societies have actively practiced female infanticide. The cruel fact is that sons often have more economic value than daughters, besides deemed better at fulfilling some other emotional and religious needs of their parents.

But with the new scientific methods of prenatal sex identification, backed up by easier abortions, the situation becomes potentially different. A rare and complex ability to select the sex of an offspring does society no harm, but a cheap and widely available ability could. If large sections of population take to it as in parts of India has ominous portents. Clinics conducting sex determination tests are said to be mushrooming in cities, even in rural areas: And it is very doubtful whether legal and enforcement barriers imposed by authorities will really succeed in curbing the barbaric practice.

If human beings do acquire the capacity to choose the sex of their offspring, a host of ethical questions will arise. And these will have no easy answers till women attain equal status with men.

There is nothing inherently wrong in human beings acquiring an ability to choose the sex of their children—in fact, the choice will be another gift of science to enrich human life. But then the widespread operation of such a choice calls for a climate of essential equality between the two sexes.

Childless by Choice

Families with babies and families without babies are sorry for each other.

These days you occasionally hear the phrase "child free" instead of "childless". To some it almost smacks of eradication like "smoke free" or "pest free". Those who use it make out that "childless" has connotations of loss or regret; "child free" implies satisfaction and deliberate choice. To be child free, they argue, means giving far more thought to not having children than most parents give to having them.

Until recent times, childlessness was simply assumed as an involuntary condition, caused by infertility—the same now increasingly amenable to scientific advances in the fertility field. Voluntary childlessness goes so much against the grain of normative behaviour; the traditional transitions of a woman's life as she shifts from single woman to wife to mother to grandmother.

For centuries, women didn't really have a choice—if they were sexually active, and most of them were—then they would become mothers. Yet there has always been a tiny segment of population whose absence of offspring was intentional. And with women growing more career-oriented, childlessness by choice seems set to rise. To many of its votaries, it's an honourable choice. They seem to have no real heart-searching about not having children, no regrets.

Jean E.Veevers's book *Childless by Choice* (Butterworth), discusses the making of a non-parent. In many cases, childlessness is seen more as an evolving state than a sudden decision. Only one-third of her sample had made the decision before marriage. The other two-thirds arrived at their choice by a series of stages, beginning with several successive postponements of intended parenthood.

Yet they were more effective contraceptors from the start. After successive postponements there came a period when the pros and cons of having or not having a child were given explicit consideration. In half the cases one partner convinced the reluctant other, and in the remainder the decision was mutual.

Asked about reasons for their decision, freedom was uniformly cited as the overriding advantage: more freedom in the use of time and the use of money.

The popular perception that childless women had a morbid fear of childbirth was not generally borne out. Do childless women dislike children? Some of those interviewed felt that they would not be good mothers because of failings of patience or their temper. But overall, only half reported they actually did not like children. Some indeed had special relationships with little nieces or nephews. Others in their professional capacity as teachers or nurses did extensive work with children.

Laurie Lisle in her book *Without Child* (Ballantine Books) concedes that child-tending builds self-confidence and develops capacity for patience and responsibility. However she finds that middle-aged women, mothers or not, base their feelings of well-being on success in their work and pleasure in marriage; other aspects such as the presence of children are less crucial. Again she finds that elderly non-mothers tended to be more resourceful, self-reliant and gifted at friendship that their counterparts.

Childfree couples (excluding the biologically barren) tend to evoke disapproval if not hostility, from relatives and friends, even from strangers. They are deemed selfish or emotionally immature. Some critics even question whether adults who intended no children should marry at all.

The whole debate can be distilled down to the word "selfish". Though "selfishness" is rarely spelled out, it may imply things such as the childless spending money on vain pleasures, even enhanced sexual activity the childfree are presumed to enjoy. The childless are told that if no one had children, there would be no more society. Paradoxically, those who make this accusation simultaneously believe that the childless miss on the deepest, if not the greatest joy known to human beings.

Non-parents counter the "selfish" charge saying that overpopulation is a bigger problem than under-population, and that parents rarely decide to be parents out of a perceived obligation to mankind. Parents have children, non-parents say, because they are selfish—because they want a baby to coo over, or a genetic link to the future, or a prop for their old age.

Wives invite greater pressure as well as censure for the childfree condition; they are assumed either career-crazed or spinster types if not deviant. Only great women aren't expected to have children—writers, poets, painters—if their abilities get revealed early enough.

As having or not having children affects the lives of wives more, childlessness is viewed as essentially dependent upon the woman's decision and determination. Little wonder, there is the general tendency to neglect the study of childless husbands.

How do the childfree handle the situation when quizzed about their intentional childlessness? Most of the respondents report considerable practice in suiting their reasons to the audience; giving one justification out of a complex of reasons to parents or grandparents, another to colleagues or friends, another to strangers. Some couples deflect criticism by announcing an intention to adopt.

And the childfree respond to criticism in various ways, ranging from cheerful acceptance to guilty defensiveness, from thoughtful discussion to a brusque reply. The women's responses are usually more diffident. Some readily admit to "indulging themselves disgracefully". Others may well retort, "What's wrong in being selfish?" Money is seldom given as a reason for refusing the responsibilities of parenthood.

What about childfree couples in their old age? Won't they be impoverished without the support and companionship of children? And who will carry the family name after their demise?

In this context, it has to be noted that couples childless by choice are on the average better educated and more career-oriented. And they are usually well-off to be financially independent in their old age. Even otherwise some studies have shown that these days older people in their 60s and 70s are more likely to help their children financially than the other way around.

Again many of the elderly these days prefer to live on their own than move with their children. They may well engage professionals to provide healthcare than be a burden to their busy children. The non-parent's sense of loneliness, however, could become acute when one of the partner dies. The childless elderly try to make up with more active social life and hobbies. A few studies have thrown up an astonishing finding: non-parent elderly tend to be feel happier and healthier than their counterparts.

Perhaps the greatest drawback that the voluntarily childless experience is the lack of social approval by the wider society. Even the feminist movement favouring women's interests assumes universal motherhood as the marital norm. And there's pressure of the popular culture, let alone family and friends, on women to "fulfill" themselves by having a child, if not children. We, as a people, are possibly more psychologically tuned to parenthood.

Some attempts have been made by the childless themselves to organize support groups. NON (National Organization of Non-Parents), later changed to NAOP (National Association of Optional Parenthood), operates in United States. Leslie Lafayette started "Childfree Network" in 1993. "I want to make this kind of life more acceptable," says she. "Not everybody needs children to have a full life." A corresponding group in Britain, called BON, highlights the positive aspects of being without children. No similar organization is known to be yet operative in India.

Jerry Steinberg, a Canadian schoolteacher, became founding "nonfather" of the group No Kidding! "Conversations with child-burdened friends became monlogues," he says. "I'd say, How's it going?" and they'd bombard one with information about the kids." The childless by choice have their point of view. Yet such choice would mostly remain an exception than the rule.

A Baby's Smile

The heart which is not struck by the sweet smiles of an infant is still asleep.

Hazrat Inayat Khan

Is there anything quite so heart-warming as the smile of an infant?

What makes a baby smile? Where do smiles come from? How are they born? How do they grow?

All sorts of theories have been advanced on the subject. Indeed, experts agree to disagree.

Some parents believe their babies learn to smile from the smiles they offer them. Parents spend a great deal of time in intimate face-to-face encounters involving mutual smiling and baby talk.

Yet smiling is not a learned response. Rather, it is deeply ingrained, inborn facial expression of our species. Blind babies smile. Deaf babies smile. All babies of all cultures smile.

Smiling, as well as crying, are deemed a child's first language; a way of communicating and interacting.

Behavioural psychologists tend to believe that a baby's smile begins as one of the many insignificant random muscular facial movements. The very first smile is, therefore, almost an accident. But because it gets such a positive response from mother, or whoever is around at that time, the child performs it again, and again. The bigger and better the performance, the bigger and better the adult response, and so on. Smiling is therefore a product of positive reinforcement. As a corollary, smiling declines if supportive responses are weak.

Some psychologists describe smiling as a physical reflex that responds in particular to tickling. A child smiles when touched in the most ticklish areas of its body, such as the armpits, the ribs, the soles of the feet, and around the neck—a "pleasure response" to stroking.

Then there is the "wind theory", which suggests that smiling first evolves from the effort, pleasure and process of "bottom snorting". Passing wind is the process that triggers the first smile.

Most smile theories acknowledge that smiling is initially a physical behaviour that develops in time into an emotional and mental one.

Desmond Morris, the noted zoologist, puts forward his explanation of what makes a baby smile. Human babies smile while apes and monkeys don't, because they have fur and we do not. We share crying and screaming with them. Such signals alert the parents, both human and simian, to the distress of their offspring. They rush to their aid. Once there, the ape or the monkey baby flings its arms around the hairy body of its mother and clings as tightly as possible, thus ensuring closeness to the protective parent.

The human infant, having attracted its parent with its crying, has no such ability to stay close to the parent. It needs something extra—something that would be so appealing to the parents that it will not let themselves be dragged away—and that something is the smiling face. An enchanting smile from a human baby can keep a loving parent as close as any tight fur-clinging; at least make the parent stay with it a bit longer.

Desmond Morris also details the process how smiling develops.

Babies start with a *reflex smile*, as early as three days after birth. And this way it continues for a month or so. Fleeting and poorly formed, it is barely recognizable as a true smile, but it certainly seems to be the precursor of big grin that comes later.

The reflex smile is often triggered by tickling. That fits well with the origin of the smile. Like all facial expressions involving the pulling back of the mouth corners, it has an element of fear it, albeit a very mild fear. Tickling, for example, is fun, but there is always a lurking worry that it might go too far.

The *general smile* arrives at about four weeks of age. Now it's a proper greeting smile; each smile longer, broader, and accompanied by expressive twinkling eyes. The voice of the parent is still the trigger for this fully formed type of smiling, but now the more common stimulus is the appearance of an adult face close to the baby's face. This is mostly a non-specific smile, not only confined to a parent's face but to any friendly face.

Specific smiling comes much later, any time between five and six months. Anyone can receive a general smile but only close contacts—individuals whom the child has come to recognize—are honoured by the specific smile. Strangers, who a few weeks earlier, were able to peer closely at the baby and were rewarded with a grin, are now upset to discover that a similar tactic causes crying.

The baby has at last learnt its parents' faces and differentiated them from those of all other people. Smiling is now a highly personal greeting, and this makes it even more special for the mother and father. They belong to an exclusive club where strangers are no longer welcome.

And somewhere in the fourth or fifth months of life, the baby starts to laugh. Some theories state that laughter evolves from smiling. But then others claim that laughing and smiling are two separate behaviours.

The mother does something and the baby chortles—the first laugh of life. The mother is delighted and repeats the stimulus. The baby laughs again, its face lighting up as it beams at its mother's face.

What action of the mother produced the first laugh, and so the subsequent ones? It could be the mother bouncing the baby up and down on her knee; making a funny face; burying her face in the baby's chest, puffing her cheeks and making blowing sounds; clasping her hands together loudly in front of the baby; hiding and then suddenly jumping out in front of the baby; or when lifting the baby high in the air and bringing it back safely in her arms.

All these actions have one element in common: performed too vigorously the baby can become scared. But hugged and cuddled immediately thereafter, the infant quickly recovers its composure and may soon start laughing. That way all laughing and crying are closely related.

7

Teenagers

Teen Troubles

Pawan, a lanky lad of 17, seems to be slipping. That's what his parents, both doctors, have been noticing for the last few months.

Pawan, known never to miss a school assignment, is often skipping homework. And there has been a perceptible dip in his school grades. Once a voracious eater, he dines with lesser enthusiasm. A neat kid, he's grown somewhat sloppy about the upkeep of his room. He even doesn't bathe as often as before or care that much about his daily grooming. There has also been a subtle change in the composition of his core group of friends. The new ones are not in the top rungs of the class, though not necessarily bad kids.

Ranjit and Ritu are feeling uneasy. There is nothing alarming about the situation, but small signs of slippage keep on showing up. That he's doing poorly in school seems to concern him less than his popularity with peers. Has Pawan taken to alcohol, or worse still, to drugs? Or, is it just the company he has started keeping? (unknown to parents, Pawan is sliding into all these.)

Direct queries from him draw a blank: he simply repeats, "There's nothing". At one time the parents had assumed," Our son tells us everything". "My boy would never lie to me," insists Ritu.

Actually, teenagers can tell prodigious, bold-faced lies to their parents. Most modern adolescents—and adolescence arrives earlier these days—don't feel the slightest guilt about lying because to them it's simply a matter of getting what they want. Everybody does it anyway, they say in justification. So lying becomes an everyday tactic of self-preservation. Freed from the old-fashioned baggage of guilt or remorse, teenagers are able to spin the most intricate tales without as much as batting an eyelid.

Evidently you can't stop a teen from lying. But you can be smarter than a teenager thinks you are, to figure out the deception. Teenagers, it seems, develop a particular lying "style": fast talkers, slow talkers, confessors, pledgers, plotters. A good strategy is to pay close attention to a teenager's explanations and rationalisations. You'll probably begin to notice certain ways of talking, types of excuses, perhaps some mannerisms that alert you to a simmering deception. Some kids look down; others get wide-eyed. Some shuffle around a bit; others try to stare you down. Don't let a teen steamroll you with fast talk or dazzle you with details. If the facts don't make sense, you demand more information.

Pawan's parents would love to know more about his current involvement and activities. Even his friends when asked, stay clammed up. It seems, on Planet Youth there's a conspiracy of silence, whereby kids manage to keep from parents or teachers just about everything they or their friends do. Teens zealously guard their privacy and their independence. They close ranks when it comes to adults, protecting each other against prying adults. Even older siblings will rarely share their information with their parents. In fact, researchers find that increasingly it's the older brothers and sisters who are the first to introduce their siblings to some of the pleasures and damages, such as drug use or sexual experimentation.

With parents, particularly dual-career couples, spending increasing amounts of time away from home, children are spending more and more time away from home as well. As adults become increasingly individualistic, children become more egocentric, too. At worst, the latter care little about others' feelings and believe that the world revolves around their needs.

Take the modern teenager's fascination for rock music; they seem to spend every vacant moment listening to it. They install loudspeakers in their bedrooms so that nothing else could be heard in the house. In fact the sounds around them are so loud, they often have no idea what a parent is saying.

Sure, teenagers have always set themselves apart, broken the rules, irritated grown-ups. But the modern day teenagers are a mystery to most parents—and parents' demands are equally mysterious to them. A certain disconnection from their families can be sensed. It's the incomprehensible disregard for anyone who isn't in their world.

Thus, the quality of family life has changed dramatically. Even when parents are available at home with the kids, they may remain less connected and, as a result, exert less gravitational pull on children than the outside world of peers. It's not that parents aren't trying to exert influence on their adolescent children, or to rein them in. It's that they have few ideas about how to go about it.

Buried by an avalanche of child-rearing how-to's over the last decade, parents today have become so anxious about doing the wrong thing that they are often paralyzed. Parents are often not sure what exact values they should espouse. For example, should they stay strict with teenagers about sexual escapades or adapt a somewhat liberal approach?

Experts have finally come to admit that the only way we can help teenagers stay on course is to lay down clear expectations, or what could be crudely termed bribes and punishments. Label it as you will, an incentive, a reward is what gets kids to pay attention to parents.

So, if Pawan wants a Hero Honda motorbike when he goes to college, he must clear his finals in first division. And, on top, a month's trip to Europe if he stands first in his class. He gets double daily allowance, the day he's home by dinnertime, but then he forfeits it all in case he defaults.

Some parents may find such bargaining distasteful. Others make out that we should expect certain behaviours from our kids without having to reward them for it.

Yet, one has to remember that teenagers always have some next big thing that they want—permission to go somewhere or to buy something. Threatening to take away a favourite TV programme or denying access to the Internet may get their attention a lot faster than yelling. What's more, bribery or/enforceable punishments also create that pause—time to really talk—which, in turn, motivates teens to step back from their peers and take more seriously their own family.

All in all, setting clear rules of conduct and behaviour, and staying steadfast in enforcing them through a well-drawn system of rewards and punishments, could be a workable parental strategy for dealing with modern teenagers, more so with the ones giving some cause for concern. Surely the strategy is no secret; most parents know of it. Yet few succeed in exploiting its maximum potential.

Teenagers Driving

Recent American studies of fatal road crashes by teenage drivers have thrown up a few revealing findings.

According to these, a teenager driving solo is safer. A teenager driving with one teen passenger doubles the fatal crash risk. With more than two teenage passengers, the fatal crash risk is almost five times as high as driving alone. And gender matters; the highest-risk situation is with male teenagers. (Having passengers or not has no effect on safety with older drivers.)

And the biggest reason for fatal teen accidents has been shown to be inexperience and immaturity. Teenager drivers tend to get themselves into situations they can't recover from. New drivers make mistakes such as overcorrecting at a corner or slamming too hard on brakes and skidding.

As a consequence, several American states are putting restrictions on teenager driving. One favoured approach is to issue a provisional driving permit at the age of 16. The provisional licence—commonly valid for six months in the first instance—restricts teenage passengers and late-night driving. And the permit is suspended if the teen has an accident, commits a driving violation (as minor as not wearing a seatbelt), or is caught driving after drinking even a trace of alcohol.

Of course, it isn't as much fun driving with parents as with one's friends, yet teenagers are being advised to undergo a certain amount of supervised driving, just to get a feel for judging distances and speeds.

We here are also witnessing an alarming rise in teenage fatal crashes, more so in Delhi. In one case, a 19-year-old driving a Maruti Esteem at midnight suffered a crash. He died on the spot and so also a young girl with him; the third youngster surviving miraculously amidst the wreckage. Riding the pavement, the speeding car also killed two pedestrians.

The accident throws back memories of the infamous BMW case. The speeding car, driven at night by a youngster in the company of other buddies, rammed into a group of bystanders, killing six of them.

The usual scenario: youngsters driving in the company of friends, often after a drinking session. And speeding on the city's wide roads that are invitingly empty in the wee hours of the night. These are single-vehicle accidents and severe.

The youngsters' company encourages speeding, even an element of daredevilry, combined with a young driver's lack of driving experience. And on top, the young driver's inability to handle alcohol compared to older adults who are habituated to it over years of drinking.

Moderating teenage driving through licence control may not be very effective in our conditions. A lot of teenagers are known to be driving without licence, often within the knowledge of their parents. And our system of issuing driving licences itself stays far too lax to assure driving competency.

Consequently we have to rely more on education. That's educating parents about the risks of unsupervised driving at the stage when the teens are immature and inexperienced. And educating teenagers about the added risks they run in driving with buddies as passengers, and worse still, driving under the influence of alcohol.

Teen Drinking

Arvind, a lively lad of 18, is in his first term at a Delhi college. He has been taking an occasional beer since he was 15. But now he's given to bingeing, mostly in the company of his hostel mates.

Does he drink excessively?

"I don't think," says he. "My drinking averages no more than once a week and I deem it stupid to get really drunk."

Asked what constituted for him a reasonable limit for a drinking session, he puts it at three large bottles of beer.

Three big beers (at 4 to 5% alcohol) equal six standard drinks. That would be bingeing; defined as consuming at least five drinks (4 for women) during one sitting, no less than once in a fortnight.

Recent studies reveal that an increasing number of undergraduates are becoming binge drinkers. Even the percentage of college girls indulging in it has arisen significantly. "If a party is going good, I may well down 3 to 4 gins," admits Ruby, a fresher at Miranda.

Many people tend to view college students as essentially children, and so must be shielded from the pernicious effects of alcohol. They quote laws under which persons below 21 are not allowed to drink in bars or buy alcoholic drinks. But this argument seems to cut little ice with young folks. "I'm not hurting anyone," says Sawrup, 19-year-old IIT student, sipping his third tot of rum-cola. "I'm just having a great time."

Indeed the age limit makes it all the more exciting for the below-21 to drink, with that extra high from breaking a rule. And they have little difficulty in obtaining alcohol.

Quite a few freshers come to college thinking that binge drinking was expected of everyone who wanted to be popular. Some may drink to seek the fellowship of their seniors or just to impress them with their capacity and maturity to stand heavy drinking without puking.

College drinking has this distinctive feature; it's primarily social drinking. Drinking isn't something to do—it's something people do together. Freshmen often make friends over drinks.

Drinking too much or far too quick at a session can pose serious health hazards, especially to a novice. People are known to choke on their vomit or fall into a coma, even die if medical aid gets delayed.

The other trouble with bingeing is the risk of generating irresponsible behaviour. Some lose control, get into fights, even use alcohol as an excuse for sexual aggression. Binge drinkers are known to indulge more in unplanned sexual activity than non-binge drinkers. Even women can blame their lack of sexual control on alcohol.

In many cultures, including ours, drinking still carries negative connotations. One reason, why people drinking tend to match that image; indulging in irresponsible behaviour as if it was something expected of them.

Possibly the most disturbing aspect of teen drinking: more and more teenagers taking to it in younger years, sometimes from the age of 14-15 onward. According to the National Centre of Addiction and Sustance Abuse (CASA), USA, the proportion of American children who start drinking alcohol has increased by nearly one-third since 1975. Boys no longer do the bulk of drinking. 14-year-old girl students are just as likely to drink as their male counterparts. Situation in our cities may not be as alarming, yet we do seem to be moving in the same direction.

New research suggests that young drinkers are courting danger of another sort. Because their brains are still developing well into their twenties, teens who drink excessively may be destroying significant amounts of mental capacity in ways that are more dramatic than in older drinkers.

It has been long known that excessive alcohol consumption among adults over long periods can create brain damage, at least a mild loss of memory. But less has been known about the impact alcohol has on younger brains. Till recently it was assumed that a youthful brain is more resilient than an adult brain, and could escape many of the worst ills of alcohol. But several recent American studies indicate that the younger the brain, the more it may be at risk. "Binge alcohol exposure in adolescence appears to produce long-lasting changes in brain function," says Dr Arron White, a noted biological psychologist at the Duke University. "The younger brain tissues, being more sensitive, are more vulnerable."

Teen drinkers appear to be particularly susceptible to damage in the hippocampus—the deeper part of brain responsible for many types of learning and memory, and in the prefrontal cortex—the brain's chief decision maker and voice of reason. Both areas, otherwise, undergo dramatic development in the second decade of life. Excessive teenage drinking could interfere with their development.

This is suspected to have a significant impact on the ability of affected adolescents to learn. Not that he or she can't function normally, but it could mean a difference in grades at school or college. In some studies researchers found a 10 percent difference in performance.

The rising incidence of teen drinking is mainly blamed on alcohol and entertainment industries. You see TV ads glorifying beer. And drinks glamorized and sexualized in movies—many a film equating alcohol with wealth and with sexual activity. Anyway today's children are growing faster, and so also adopting adult habits at an earlier age

Some of the recommendations made by CASA (USA) to curb teen drinking are as follows: .

For Authorities

Hold parents legally responsible for their children's alcohol use.

End all alcohol ads (in our case, it should mean ending all surrogate ads that circumvent the ban on alcohol ads)

Step up enforcement of underage drinking laws, especially on establishments that provide alcohol to them.

Restrict home delivery of alcohol (Delhi Administration has lately been mooting home delivery of beer).

For Parents

Eat dinner together (the magic of the family meal).

Don't accept teen drinking as a rite of passage.

Know your children's friends and where they go.

Discuss negative consequences of drinking.

Set rules and enforce consequences.

Possibly the answer lies in changing the environment which supports drinking. And this is a challenging task not only for the parents and school/college authorities, but also for the young students themselves.

Adolescent Impact on Marital Life

Every family experiences a wave of anxiety when a girl turns thirteen or a boy reaches fifteen. As a child enters adolescence, this puts pressure on all aspects of family life, on marriage itself.

The anxiety is not necessarily in response to the teenager's overt behavior; just as often it comes from the parents' fear of the imagined behaviour. What's she actually doing, gone for hours to a friend's house or staying late at a party? How safe is the neighbourhood for her to move about after daylight? What's the boy doing spending long evenings with his chums? Are they experimenting with drugs? Will he drive his motorbike rashly? Fears extend to accident, death, rape, pregnancy. And these are no small fears.

I know of a well-placed Indian couple in Washington who fear leaving their 17-year-old son by himself overnight. They apprehend he may have a "party" in the house; his buddies guzzling too much beer, doing drugs, making trouble with girls, even causing a house fire. And mind, their son is a fairly straight chap; only he has picked up a few cronies with a weakness for "partying".

Of course, most parents grow more anxious when their daughters reach adolescence than when their boys hit that stage. Not only girls are sexually more vulnerable, their bodies change more obviously than those of boys.

Renu at 15 hogs the family bathroom and walks about in the house in a flimsy nightgown. She's proving more provocative than her brother of 17; Rajan isn't seen flaunting his sexuality, at least not at home.

Even when teenage girls stay demure and well-behaved, anxiety about their potential behaviour is rarely absent.

Parents harbour a brooding awareness of the dangers lurking for the young lives: auto accidents, sexual complications, alcoholic binges, introduction to drugs. They feel panicked by things that adolescents themselves approach in obvious confidence. Indeed, nothing that parents say will dissuade the young from their youthful flings—we all remember how we ignored our parents' admonitions. The parental anxiety is often compounded by the fact that the sight of the teenager revives memories of their own adolescence. And these vivid memories of the thrills experienced and risks encountered add another emotional charge.

Bit by bit the teenage pressure mounts up. In staking his manhood, the boy pushes at the father, who may see the behaviour as insolence or defiance. Surely the boy needs his father but he also needs to assert his independence.

Father-daughter relationship is no less complex. She wants her father to find her charming, irresistible but totally off-limits. The situation gets more complicated where he isn't her biological father.

To the mother, the daughter's growing sexuality often serves as a reminder that her own youth and beauty may well be on the wane.

And there's the impact of adolescence on marriage itself. It may impel parents to turn to each other with new needs, especially sexual needs, stimulated by the teenager's presence.

Many a couple at this stage is forced to look afresh at their marriage. Is it good or bad? What lies ahead?

Oh, to be young again, to begin life afresh! Not surprisingly, the narcissism of the adolescent is contagious. Some parents get preoccupied with their appearance. Am I too fat? Am I looking old? Am I still attractive?

Yes, all adults do have the wish, consciously or unconsciously, to be the adolescent they are bringing up. We love our children, but at the same time we envy them. We want them to grow, but we know that it's us they are replacing. Our pride in their achievements mutes our envy, but it does not banish our wish to be young again.

Renu's mother often experiences a tinge of envy when she sees her daughter developing. The girl is growing in a far more open, exciting world compared to the traditional one of hers. Kamala had gone from being a protected daughter to a protected wife, and then on to the relatively limited life of a homemaker, including a somewhat inhibited marital sex. In comparison, Kamala sees for Renu all the possibilities of a fuller life.

In a way a child's adolescence is also a time of parental sadness. We recognize that the teenager is getting emotionally detached, the first step towards his or her eventual separation from us. We lose our special relationship with the child and the feeling of being essential to his or her life.

Disciplining Children

Some parents begin with giving in and end with giving up.

Romi, an 8-year old, repeatedly grabs toys from his younger brother aged 5, even hits his sister of 6.

And there's Rana, a 5-year-old, who merrily flings things down including items of his food. And refuses to go to bed in time.

But my most disconcerting encounter was with a 4-year-old who went by the name Tony, when I happened to be visiting his parents. As soon as Tony entered the room, he set up a howl looking at me: "He's sitting in my chair". My mistake; I had unwittingly sat on a chair that was Tony's favourite. On a sign from Tony's mother that he won't stop crying I changed to another (could never imagine in my childhood an adult giving up his chair to me).

Now, instead of sitting on the vacated chair, Tony ran out in rain, ignoring his mother's plea not to do so. And he soon returned with muddied shoes making marks on the carpet. On being ordered to get off the rug, he flung himself on the floor and commenced a tantrum.

In truth, the three kids are turning out fairly unpleasant. And they are no solitary exceptions. Quite a few children these days grow whiny, rude, defiant—in short, thoroughly spoiled.

Is there anything wrong in their upbringing? Are present-day parents getting too indulgent? Or simply keep on humoring small children? Some parents argue, they don't want to pick battles with kids all the time. Others blame it all on television or even on environmental toxins?

The age-old recipe of spanking is no longer in favour, though an overwhelming majority of parents still continue to spank younger children between the ages of 2 and eight.

Defenders of corporal punishment say or imply that no-spanking is the same as no-discipline. When alternative disciplinary strategies such as explaining or deprivation of privileges don't work, a slap does. And there's the popular perception that "mild" corporal punishment is harmless.

Of course, corporal punishment has to operate under certain limitations. Kids below two are not to be spanked, because the risk of causing physical injury is too great. No hard object such as an umbrella or stick to be employed: only an open hand to be used, and that also to hit extremities like a child's buttocks. The intention should be to modify behaviour, not to cause pain; in effect, to secure a child's attention and send a clear message of disapproval and direction. The frequency of spanking shouldn't exceed once or twice a week; overspanking tends to lose its effectiveness. And to avoid verbal abuse, no less harmful than physical abuse. Finally, spanking is to be done in private to spare humiliation, and without anger.

These days, however, the very concept of spanking children is being challenged by quite a few social scientists. One in the lead is Murray A. Strauss, author of the book *Beating the Devil Out of Them*. Strauss builds a cogent case for the benefits of never-spanking. The main approach is to set clear rules of conduct, and staying steadfast in enforcing them through a well-thought regime of rewards and deprivations. This is deemed a workable alternative to corporal punishment. Admittedly, corporal punishment may secure a child's immediate compliance, but it increases the likelihood of negative outcomes, such as increased physical aggression by the child, not only against other children but even assaulting the parent subsequently, and the greater probability of hitting a spouse later in life.

Of the non-corporal punishments, the one commonly advocated, especially in USA, is what's called Time Out. It means removing the errant child from all rewarding activities for a short period. And exposing it to a very boring, unrewarding environment, such as made to sit or stand facing a blank wall. You have to stand close enough so that if he or she attempts to leave you can immediately return it to the same position. Never let the child leave until it has been well-behaved at least for a minute or two.

Once the child realizes you mean business, the Time Out will proceed more smoothly.

However, the most recommended measure for curbing bad behaviour in small children is to ignore their tantrums, to give little attention to their whimpering. On the other hand, all good behaviour must be noticed and applauded. This approach is based on the well-established fact that children do what gets noticed, that adult attention usually makes behaviour more likely to occur, not less.

There is nothing more important to a child than the undivided attention of a parent. If a child is able to secure such adult attention through tantrums or make its parents run to it for comfort at the first sign of crying, it will be encouraged to do the same more and more. Parents giving too much attention to whimpering or rude behaviour are actually playing into the hands of the child.

Parenting is a complex undertaking these days. Everyone wants the best for their children. But there are no hard and fast rules for providing perfect upbringing. Parenting magazines and self-help books aren't really much of a help. That often leaves parents with difficult questions: How much to indulge a child? When a 'No' should mean 'No'? Do adults have the right to expect children to defer to them?

Possibly the only sound advice on offer: if you want your children to be well-behaved, don't shower attention on them when they are behaving badly. On the other hand, extend every encouragement whenever you encounter good behaviour on their part.

Sexually Abused in Childhood

The popular notion that it's mainly pubertal girls who are sexually molested has been found to be an oversimplification of the actual situation. Much smaller children are being sexually abused, girls as well as boys.

A most shocking aspect of child sex abuse was brought out a few years back by two UK doctors, Marieta Higgs and Robert Wyatt. Through the "reflex and dilation" symptoms they found that many small children, even toddlers, had been assaulted anally. Of 900 cases referred to them in one year, 274 were confirmed as sexual abuse.

The passage of faeces through the anal canal is controlled by two rings of muscles called sphincters. The internal sphincter operates automatically whereas the external one can be relaxed or tensed voluntarily. "Reflex and dilation" is the condition where both sphincters open up when the buttocks are parted. The inference is that the sphincters perform in this way because they have been conditioned to allow penetration by the abuser. Some doctors maintain that the same condition can be the result of serious constipation. Yet the consensus is that anal dilation is a significant indicator of sexual abuse.

The Cleveland study further brought out that buggery was more practised by child molesters than vaginal penetration when it came to very young children. Evidently the abusers were aware of the physical damage they could cause with vaginal penetration of small children and the greater risk of the abuse getting identified.

World over, surveys and studies show that most child sexual abuse takes place within the family itself. The offenders are not only uncles, older cousins, stepfathers and stepbrothers, but even biological brothers, fathers and grandfathers. These perpetrators operate most secretively while the victims are often helpless or stay silent. The abuse proves particularly secretive among middle classes as the people involved are better equipped to deflect suspicion of abuse away from them. Even when sexual abuse is recognized within a family, there is often strong pressure to keep it secret from the outside world.

With increasing public and professional awareness of child sexual abuse, new approaches are being sought to unearth and tackle the problem. Doctors are trained in identifying an abused child from suggestive signs. The child's response to medical examination itself, particularly of the genitalia, may provide a few clues. Some children will strenuously resist examination, indicating the degree of traumatisation. Others will accede too readily, assuming sexualized postures, and indicating the degree of habituation which regular use has caused them.

Teachers are trained to identify abused children. Sometimes young children who are victims of sexual abuse, especially if it has been going on for some time, will begin to behave in a sexual way beyond the bounds of what would normally be expected. Oversexualized behaviour of a child should alert its well-wishers to a likely abuse going on.

Social and medical workers in this field have been devising ways that could encourage young children to speak out of their abuse. Children rarely make false spontaneous allegations, unless induced by someone to claim non-existent sexual abuse. Debbie Glassbrook in England, for instance, runs a special room where a child and a counselor work undisturbed. The room contains several sexually explicit dolls through which the child is helped to explain what happened to her or him.

Yet the most common time for the sexual abuse of children to begin is when the victims are aged between 8 and 12 years. Girls are more likely to be abused by family members—stepfathers five times more likely to abuse their daughters sexually than natural fathers. Boys are more at risk from people outside the family but known to them.

Most of this sexual abuse remains undetected or unreported. Only, of late, adults are increasingly coming forward to tell of the sexual abuse they underwent when children.

One recent sample survey in UK revealed that out of 2000 interviewed, 206 admitted to sexual abuse in childhood. A similar study by the Tata Institute of Social Sciences, with the majority of respondents being between 20 and 24 belonging to the middle economic strata in Bombay, found that one out of every three girls and one out of every ten boys had been sexually assaulted in childhood.

More and more cases of "recovered memory" are coming up. Adults, particularly women, recollect how they were sexually abused as small children. Some of these revelations are so astounding as to put their veracity to doubt. At times it makes one wonder whether the recall after a lapse of so many years is all correct or harbours an element of imagination. Persons known as pillars of respectability have been accused by their daughters of molesting them in childhood.

Typically, most of these "recovered memories" speak of sexual molestation or even rape by fathers, natural or the step-ones. If all these accounts are to be believed, incest seems more widespread that is commonly assumed. It's all the more in societies where stepfathers abound due to prevalence of divorce.

The incest theme has also started figuring increasingly in books by women writers. In USA particularly it's become the latest literary vogue. A whole crop of current reminiscences and novels dwells on the subject. Indeed many of the problems experienced in later adult life—sexual dysfunction, depression, guilt, impaired self-esteem, alcoholism, even obesity—are blamed on incestuous assaults in childhood. To name only a few of these books: Marilyn French's *Our Father*, Margaret Atwood's *The Robber Bride*, Amy Bloom's *Come to Me*, Saphire's *Push*, Donna Tart's *Secret History*, and Mary Gaitskill's *Two Girls, Fat and Thin*.

Possibly the trend for giving graphic descriptions of the incest scene started with Toni Morrison's *The Bluest Eye* (1970) and Maya Angelou's *I Know Why the Caged Bird Sings* (1971). Now you get descriptions that are cinematic in detail and rendered with pornographic precision.

Critics are not wanting who deplore this trend as more of a tactic to boost book sales. Sex sells and perverse sex sells more. And so also the bid to shock the virtually unshockable modern reader—with the purest rage, the most lurid crime, the most innocent victim.

Despite their quota of sensationalism, these books are surely giving the reading public a better awareness and understanding of incest.

What about men who sexually abuse children?

Social scientists feel that sexual abusers are far too diverse to be usefully identified into two or three behavioural/ personality groups. Actually, abusive men form an extremely heterogeneous lot. For instance, some seem to be motivated primarily by sexual desires, while others are motivated by the need for closeness or aggression. Some men prefer young children as their targets; others adolescents; others any child who is available. Some men are incestuous, others take children outside their family. Many abusive acts are committed when men have been drinking. In fact, most abusers present a picture of being generally "normal"; no easy way to spot a potential abuser.

What can be done to combat the menace of child sex abuse? The minimum we can do is to train doctors to diagnose physical symptoms of abuse. Selected teachers could be oriented towards reading the signs of sexual abuse in their small wards. The rest is up to the familial and societal forces.

8

Parents and Grandparents

Parents and Peers

Peers matter much more than parents. And so whatever our parents do to us is overshadowed, in the long run, by what our peers do to us.

The above in a nutshell is the argument advanced by grandma Judith Rich Harris in her book *The Nurture Assumption* (1998), a book carrying enthusiastic blurbs from some of the world's top psychologists.

What Harris makes out runs counter to nearly everything that a century of psychology has told us about child development. Freud put parents at the centre of the child's universe, and there they have remained ever since. "That's the way I was raised," is quite a common comment, by which we mean that children instinctively and preferentially learn from their parents—parents proving good or bad role models for children. Child development has been, in many ways, concerned with understanding children *through* their parents.

Since genes account for about half of personality variations among people, parents' contribution in the nature part is obvious. What about the nurture part? The accepted wisdom is that it's the parents who mould the personality of their children by doing all the right things: providing them with every lesson and every experience, buying them the right toys, saying the right words, helping them in work and games, and not spanking them or publicly scolding them.

The nurture assumption places the credit and blame squarely on parents, in the process turning modern parenthood into a high-responsibility, high-anxiety undertaking. Those who fail to measure up to the strictest standards of supposedly optimal parenting often labour under a sense of guilt. "The frightening thing about heredity and environment is that parents provide both," says a wit.

Harris does not see children as delicate vessels and does not believe they are easily damaged by the missteps of their mothers and fathers.

"Kids are not that fragile," she writes. "They are tougher than you think. They have to be, because the world out there does not handle them with kid gloves. At home, they might hear 'What you did made me feel bad,' but out on the playground it's 'You shithead!' " Observing teenagers around, it began to dawn on Harris that adolescents were wanting to model themselves more on their peers than parents. Children were identifying with and learning from other children. And so her realization that in a key sense, what's important is not what children learn inside the home but what they learn outside the home.

Harris argues that we have been in the grip of what she calls "nurture assumption," a parent-centred bias that has blinded us to what really matters in human development.

She cites the story of Cinderella. "Cinderella learned when she was quite small that it was best to be meek when her stepmother was around, and to look unattractive to avoid arousing her sisters' jealousy," Harris writes. But outside the house Cinderella learned that she could win friends (even a prince) by being pretty and charming. Harris concludes: this lesson—-that away from parents children can reconstruct themselves—-is one that all children learn very quickly. It is an important limitation on the power of parents. Even when they do succeed in influencing their children, those influences very often don't travel outside the home. And Harris pulls together an extraordinary range of studies and observations in support of the idea.

Just the fact that a child wasn't getting along with his mother didn't necessarily mean that he wouldn't get along with his peers. (Children, after all, are born with individual temperaments. Some children are easy to rear from the start and others are more difficult. And those innate characteristics can strongly influence how parents treat them.) In one Swedish study of picky eating among primary-school children cited by Harris, some kids were picky eaters at school, some were picky at home, but only a small number picky at both home and school. A child who pushes away carrots at home might gobble them down in school cafeteria.

In the same way, a child might stay reserved at home but be a chatterbox in school. In families, the eldest child does seem more serious, responsible and bossy, while the youngest behaves in a more carefree fashion. But outside the home, the younger brother no longer cowed by his older siblings, is perfectly capable of being a dominant, take-charge figure when he's among his friends.

"Socialization research has demonstrated one thing clearly and irrefutably: a parent's behaviour towards a child affects how the child behaves in the presence of the parent or in contexts that are associated with the parent," Harris concludes. "I have no problem with that—I agree with it." But this doesn't necessarily cross into the life a child leads outside the home.

That brings us to one of the Harris' central observations; namely, kids aren't interested in becoming copies of their parents. Children want to be good at being children. How, for example, do you persuade a preschooler to eat something new? Not by eating it yourself and hoping that your child will follow suit. A preschooler doesn't care what you think. But give the same food to a bunch of preschoolers who like it; it's quite probable that your child will happily follow suit. Children like to wear the kind of clothing other kids are wearing, not the kind their parents are patronizing. From the very moment children meet other children, they take their cues from them. There is a real, strong emotional satisfaction in copying, sharing things. Even for a child of three or four, the group is critical. Advertisement people know it well; ads targetted at children always show children merrily consuming the advertised product.

Here Harris poses the question: "And, from an evolutionary perspective, who should children be paying attention to: their parents—-the members of the previous generation—-or their peers, who will be their future mates and future collaborators? It would be more adaptive to be better tuned to the nuances of their peers' behaviour. That just makes a lot of sense."

That's why neighbourhoods and schools play such a crucial role in the development of a child; a role often as potent as that of home, if not more.

Is Harris right, as she challenges people's cherished ideas about parenthood? She herself admits that what she has provided is only a theory; the same calls for a multi-million dollar, multi-year research to back up. Yet she has helped wrench psychology away from its single-minded obsession with parenting—one that sees the development of children almost entirely a story of their parents.

To Harris, parents matter but peers seem to matter more.

How Good are Grandparents?

Grandparents are people who come to your house, spoil the children, and then go home.

"The entrance requirements for grampahood are comparatively mild,

You only have to live until your child has a child."

_____the poet, Ogden Nash,

We recently had a month's stay with our son's family in USA. We have one son and he again has only one. Our single grandchild came rather late; he's 5, his father 45, and me 75.

We had a jolly good time interacting with the lively lad, playing with him, plying him with presents. Did we spoil him? It set me thinking about our role in the boy's life.

The significance of grandparenthood evokes much interest and speculation. Yet it is backed by scant verification and research.

Grandparents themselves seem unable to speak of their role in anything but laudatory terms. Most speak glowingly of the joys of grandparenthood, particularly of the fun with those adorable, small grandchildren. That way, "nothing makes a boy smarter than being a grandson".

In the process, grandparents may indulge their grandchildren in a way parents cannot; in fact, in ways parents may not approve. Yet this is a relationship from which grandparents derive much satisfaction. Indeed nothing is harder on a grandparent than having to watch a grandchild being disciplined.

It is sometimes made out that such indulgence from grandparents served a salutary purpose for the grandchildren, as it functioned as a relief from the tensions caused between the parents and children by parental authority. But then, modern parents themselves are becoming permissive these days, and usually adopt an egalitarian and friendly relationship with their children. Hence children don't need grandparents as mediators or allies against parental authority.

Many a sociologist has come to believe that in modern times, grandparenthood is "a largely inactive role" that does not bring continuing interaction into the lives of grandparents. They are just permitted to dispense certain services and material support, and to engage in certain expressive activities, yet mostly prohibited from encroaching upon the parental responsibilities of their adult children or interfere with their authority.

These sociologists attribute this downsizing of the grandparental role to the high value being placed upon the independence of the nuclear family in child rearing. Their writings create an image of grandparents as "meddlesome intruders" in family processes. The once favoured position of the grandfather and grandmother is getting undermined.

Others make out that grandparents live on the fringe of a nuclear family, so long as the family remains intact. However, in the event of a breakup or the death of a spouse, grandparents assume a vital function, providing a source of rescue or refuge for grandchildren. And grandmothers often take on major household responsibilities when the mother is working or giving birth, and lend assistance in times of illness or crisis. Even economic help is sometimes given in the form of shared living arrangements. The flow of aid, particularly financial aid, is chiefly from the parents to the children, especially in the early years of the latter's marriage.

That way, despite a decrease in joint family living, middle-class parents and their married children usually do develop a regular pattern of mutual aid in nursing care, festivities and other activities.

Where young married middle-class couples deem it important to avoid obligations and keep their independence, their parents find indirect ways of helping their married children: the most common method is to give substantial gifts to their grandchildren. Parents help their children to establish their homes and families; in return they expect their children to give them continued affection and personal attention, and to include them in some of their activities.

What's the significance of grandparenthood to grandchildren? Very few investigators have examined the grandparent-grandchild relationship, often called a magical relationship.

One interesting thing revealed in studies is that young people with grandparents and great-grandparents harbour fewer age-prejudices than those with no grandparents. When the grandchild sees his grandfather organizing his life with meaning and purpose, the former entertains not only a certain pride in owning up the latter, but also actively indulges in even exaggerating grandpa's busy schedule.

Studies also show that grandparents have different meanings for children at different development ages (4-5, 8-9, 11-12). The youngest group valued grandparents mainly for their indulgent qualities; the middle group preferred active, fun-sharing grandparents; and the oldest group appeared to have become distant from their grandparents. It seems, as children grow up, they grow away from their doting grandparents. In a survey where American college students were asked as to whom they deemed their most important transmitters of information, almost all named their parents during childhood and peers in adolescence. Hardly anyone made a mention of grandparents.

The changing status of grandparents, and the influence this will have on the grandparent-grandchild relationship, should be an area of emerging interest in family research.

Most grandparents appear to find the grandparental role comfortable and pleasant—-you have all the fun and none of the responsibility. They don't hold themselves accountable for the mistakes or shortcomings of their grandchildren, but like to bask in the reflected glory when grandchildren achieve success.

Seemingly, grandparenthood is a relatively undemanding role; few, if any, clear-cut demands are made on grandparents as a category. Yet the older person has an opportunity here to create a role that is valued by the family. Such a valued role, presumably, has to be learned; it's not something automatic and traditional.

A person wishing to become a valued grandparent should learn to accept change, and should be able to relinquish the parental role with his children and enter into a new role with his grandchildren, a role that supplements the parental role and in no way conflicts or competes with it. The general advice is that you have to be careful not to get too tied up in your grandchildren, as it isn't good for you or for them.

It is still to be established whether grandparents influence their grandchildren directly, or whether their influence is largely indirect (through their children in the middle generation). And here again, tension in relations with one's adult children may often prevent a satisfactory relationship from developing between grandparents and grandchildren.

Grandparenthood is one of the few "ready-made" roles available to the ageing person at a point in his life when his former roles are lost or decrease in significance: "A man begins to show his age about the same time he begins to show pictures of his grandchildren".

When an individual retires or is widowed or exits from other roles, grandparenthood begins to assume greater importance for him. Surely grandparents look for every opportunity to play host to their grandchildren. But then small children with their pranks and noise can prove quite tiring to elderly grandparents.

Nowadays, however, many people become grandparents when they are relatively young (men in fifties, women in forties) and active in their jobs. With the longevity trend, grandparenthood has become a middle-age rather than an old-age phenomenon.

At the middle-age stage, grandparents are often not in a position to give the desired time and attention to the little grandchildren. In later years, when major roles are gone and they have plenty of time for grandchildren, this role may have lost its salience. With grandchildren grown up into adolescence or adulthood, the opportunity to develop a meaningful relationship or even enjoying their company may have elapsed.

Parents of NRIs

Dr Mehta and Sandhu, both in their mid-seventies, are buddies; they play in a fixed foursome every morning at the Delhi Golf Course. And both have an only son living in America.

Their conversation, outside of golf, commonly veers around to a discussion whether to move with their son or stay put here. Both couples are green-card holders and make the obligatory annual visit to USA.

Sandhu: Manjit keeps on asking us to sell our house and move permanently to USA. He even offered to buy a flat nearby if we preferred to live separate. Rani has almost agreed. Her diabetes is throwing up all sorts of health complications. She feels she'll get more advanced medical attention there, especially when Manjit's wife is a doctor. But most of all she wants to be with her two grandchildren—kids at whose births she was present and stayed on every time for nearly a year.

Dr Mehta: Not a bad idea. You'll escape the heat and air pollution of Delhi. And so the daily hassle of bijli/pani. Only we'll have to find another player in your place.

Sandhu: But why should you stick on here? You can chuck your practice; it's a trickle of what it used to be. Your son and his wife are dental surgeons, and these professionals earn a lot there. You can have a good time.

Dr Mehta: Three years back I and Prabha experimented with living there for four months at a stretch. Frankly we got bored within a few weeks. My son and daughter have just no free time. Even the ten-year-old grandson is too involved in his studies, hobbies, and friends to be available for us. Maybe, our son and daughter-in-law are by now too westernized; one senses a feeling of strain when we stay beyond a month or so.

I did play a few times at my son's golf club. But it wasn't the same thing as the game here; we are so accustomed to caddies. Anyway the conviviality of playing golf with cronies was missing.

I and Prabha propose to stay on here, as long as both of us are alive. Well, the situation changes when one of us pops off—I'll probably go first, being ten years older. Our son may then persuade Prabha to join there. Mothers are easier to put up than fathers; they are more of a help in the house, and are less demanding.

I, for one, won't migrate if left alone. It will be frightfully lonely but I'm not cut out to be a permanent fixture at someone else's place, even at my son's place—mind, a good son. Anyway I won't last much longer after Prabha is gone.

Sandhu: We are planning to migrate next year. The builder buying our house will give us a small flat therein; we can always return if the move misfires.

Luckily in the area where our son lives, there are nearly a hundred Indian families, even a gurudwara. And several families have their old parents with them. We would have some company.

With our son taking care of health insurance and gifting us a car and basic furniture, we can manage to live modestly on our savings, needing no regular financial help from him. I propose to spend some time every day in the local library—a very good library. And possibly play golf once or twice a week on a public golf course; our son's hobby is boating and fishing, not golf.

Yet, howsoever I organize myself and enjoy being near our dearest ones, I shall miss the life here: the gupshup, the air of informality, the multitude of relatives and friends—and good household help.

Dr Mehta: Our son was at one time reconciled to working in India. I pushed him, spending a lot of money on his foreign exams and travels. I wanted him to have the best of education and the best of openings. We knew he could be going for good, but selflessly we denied ourselves the pleasure of his proximity.

When Raj left, I was in my fifties. I never gave a thought to my old age. Now I sometimes wonder whether it was the best thing to send him so far away. At times we wish we had another child in India, preferably a girl; the latter are more caring, more so when one is in need of care.

In fact as we are getting older, we are finding it quite a strain to make the annual USA trip. Our son and his family will have to come more often if they want to see us, to come at least once a year. Only I'm doubtful whether they will ever stay longer than a fortnight each time. Such visits are over so quickly.

The parents of Non-Resident Indians are a segment that is fast swelling. And many of these parents are elderly. This can mean much loneliness. There's the pride in children's achievements but also the yearning for their company.

The average Indian life is mostly centred round the family; till a generation ago, joint families were the norm. No wonder, we are unprepared for being left alone or in pairs. Couples who have not developed any special interests feel lost once they retire. They have all the leisure but no grandchildren to while it away with.

Where some siblings are still in India, the nearby presence can be comforting to parents. But then these sibling sometimes resent the fact that they have to bear the actual burden of looking after their elderly; NRIs limit themselves to lending electronic support—telephone calls and e-mail.

Joining one's children abroad is no easy option. And for North Indians it has to be a son; only the South has some tradition of parents, particularly mothers, moving with their married daughters.

Human nature as it is, you better be useful or free with rich gifts to be really welcome to your progeny. And if one can't drive abroad, the house takes the shape of a "gilded cage". New friends are difficult to make at that age. Neighbours have no time for you except saying a friendly "hello".

Roles Reversed

"Careful. Keep a hand on the railing, negotiating stairs," I say to my father. And insist, he has an escort when taking a walk in the adjoining park. At the table we heap food on his plate, instead of letting him help himself. I even dish out advice how he should conduct himself in the bathroom without risking a slippage.

The lively eighty-five-year old, a widower since six months, is visiting us for the winter. In fact he wasn't keen on stirring out of his home but for our going out there to fetch him.

Here's a man who was once the most commanding figure in my boyhood, an overpowering presence. I used to hang on every word of his. He taught me how to handle a shotgun and knot a necktie. Tall and muscular, he was strong enough to fight off a robber or beat the hell out of a street bully, so I imagined. When he was annoyed, the whole household shivered. Indeed, all quarrels and loud voices stood suspended when he was sighted coming. As the headmaster of a prestigious high school for twenty years, his standing with students was something special. He was both feared and respected. Whenever seen approaching, boys would sound an alert, "Hark, the headmaster". This put everybody on his best behaviour.

Parenting is said to be an invigorating experience. And a good deal of fun too, despite its quota of conflicts and problems. But 'parenting' one's parent is rarely a smooth affair. The role reversal, a truly complex phenomenon, is never free from an element of frustration and embarrassment.

Is it so because it goes against nature's very scheme of things? In the animal world, the old aren't ever parented by their offspring.

The elderly parent, more so a widower, is often anxious to retain a measure of independence, at least a semblance of it. Physical assistance is accepted but with a marked preference for the unobtrusive variety, not the showy sort. Old men tend to be touchy about it; they don't want their physical infirmities to be advertised.

The elderly parent again wants to preserve his or her lifestyle to the extent feasible. No wonder my father feels far more comfortable in his own modest home than as a guest at a more affluent one.

And the elderly mostly wish to be no burden to their progeny, as long as one isn't disabled. Of course, one has to be in possession of ready cash. The lot of a penniless parent is rarely free of humiliations.

The dilemmas of those parenting a parent perhaps lie even deeper. Whatever he or she does, it never seems to be enough. One always ends up feeling a bit guilty. A dutiful daughter with an old, infirm mother on her hands, can harbour an uncomfortable feeling, she isn't discharging her obligations well—no matter howsoever irritatingly the mother might have treated her as a girl. Many a mother in senility is known reverting to a petulant, demanding toddlerhood.

The task of parenting the parent becomes more daunting for the only child. And it can give rise to a sense of frustration, as the parent is often emotionally more demanding. At times, previously unresolved conflicts have a way of surfacing up.

An elderly single parent, independent, well-off, and enjoying 'good life' is now an increasing possibility. Yet numerous ones can't escape a state of dependence on their middle-aged children—a state that could turn out an embarrassment to the elderly and irksome to the parenting children.

Taking care of the elderly is quite different from childcare. Anyway the elderly consider it demeaning to be treated like children. Again moving the parents permanently into your home may not be always the best solution; in many cases the old may be happier in their own place if otherwise managing appropriate domestic and nursing help.

Chances are, your parents won't need much outside help before they are in their late 70s. But with the increasing longevity, it is quite likely that you would be called upon to take care of them at some stage, at least of a surviving parent. And it almost changes your life if you have to take care of an incapacitated parent.

Raising the subject of old age with one's parents is always an awkward affair but the consequences of not planning for the old age can be severe. When a crisis hits, one may not have the needed information or the requisite authority to act on behalf of a parent. It is even helpful if someone has the authority to act on their behalf during their life if they get incapacitated. Usually a good strategy is to have the whole family involved in the discussions; not only brothers and sisters but also their spouses. Again it isn't fair to load all the responsibility of old-parent care on to a daughter, divesting yourself of it in the process. Remember, your own children will be watching. And someday you may be on the receiving end of elderly care.

While they are healthy and can afford it, staying in their own homes is generally the option for old parents. At this stage, it may even be a better bet to aid them financially if needed, than to move them into your home. They get cut off from their friends, lose autonomy, and often bicker with their children. "There is no kitchen big enough for two women," they say.

Yet there is no escape from bringing them to your home when they require 24-hour care. The option of good nursing homes for the old is as yet rather limited in the country. And the cultural factors also favour home care by children.

Parenting the parent presents its own problems. The role reversal, a truly complex phenomenon, is never free from an element of frustration and embarrassment.

How Are you Today?

In inventiveness, it would be hard to beat the Americans. Here's another instance.

Someone there has come up with a service which alerts you the same day your elderly parent or relative living alone needs attention. It was found that many people were wanting to inquire every day about the welfare of an elderly relative or friend in questionable health. But somehow they weren't managing to ring up with the requisite regularity and timing.

Now for a monthly fee of $15, a Minnesota company offers a computerized telephone service that calls every on the home-bound elderly and disabled to find out if they are okay.

The system works like this.

Once or twice a day, the company's computer calls the telephone number of the cared-for. When the phone is picked up, a recorded voice says, "Hello, this is the How Are You Today service. We are calling to check on *Mr or Mrs X*. If you are okay, press 1 on your touch-tone phone. If you are in need of any assistance, please press 0 on your phone,and we will immediately alert the proper people of the same. Thank you and have a good day."

If even after ten rings the individual does not answer, the computer calls the help number or numbers provided by the subscriber. And says, "Hello, this is the How Are You Today service calling to alert you that *Mr or Mrs X* has failed to respond to all our calls during this day. Please check on the person."

The subscriber can then rush to the cared-for person or arrange assistance in any other way. The new service is said to be playing a significant role in reaching timely attention to many a person in trouble. And it's also saving its subscribers of considerable unease and tension.

Critics are not wanting to whom this device is another heartless way of dumping the elderly, instead of keeping them under the same roof and caring for them. But then there are some elderly who prefer to stay in their own homes, retaining a measure of their independence.

How relevant would be this service to our conditions? Most of our elderly and disabled have someone around to help or at least someone to summon help.

But we again are moving towards living in nuclear families, while the number of elderly is rising with the rise in longevity.

Innovations such as the How Are You Today service may well start here.

Back into the Empty Nest

Teenagers haven't changed. They still grow up, leave home, and get married. The big difference is that today they don't always do in that order.

Sudha, a Delhite, married a software programmer in Bangalore and left for that city. After five years, the husband opened his own consultancy firm in Delhi. She moved back into the empty parental nest—a big four-bedroom house in Vasant Vihar—with her husband and two kids, a boy and a girl.

Originally it was for want of readily available accommodation. But now Sudha's family is well adjusted living there. And she runs the kitchen in lieu of rent. The ageing parents—their son stays in USA—now live like guests in their own home.

Raman is a dentist. He lived with his parents in Panchsheel, Delhi, the father a retired chief engineer. Raman married a dentist. They moved to a flat in Safdarjung Enclave but found it hard to run a comfortable home within the constraints of their newly started practice. So when Usha got pregnant, they moved back to his parents.

With both Raman and Usha busy in their dental clinic, the two small girls, twins, are mostly left in the care of grandparents. Ramans—who have started contributing a fixed sum of Rupees 20,000 per month towards house running—have the use of first-rate accommodation, excellent day-carers for their kids, and nice hot meals on return from work. Usha is quite reconciled to a stray sarcastic remark from her mother-in-law as long as the cozy arrangement continues.

Unmarried sons and daughters, even in their late twenties or early thirties, mostly continue to stay with their parents. To these older children, living at home seems far nicer, much more comfortable.

Parents, particularly parents in Delhi, seem to be subjected to a peculiar phenomenon. Their sons who moved out on marriage are often wanting to return to the "empty nest". This means living rent-free and subsidized, with no scheduled date for departure. Sometimes even a married daughter returns, not necessarily a divorcee, but with her hubby and children in tow. Again grown-up sons and daughters are showing a marked preference to staying on in the parental home than seeking lodgings elsewhere.

Cynics say, it isn't a resurgence of filial affection; it's the city's housing shortage and soaring rents that is forcing the trend.

Another or an added reason is advanced like this. Many young couples are now working couples—it's becoming increasingly difficult to sustain an urban middle-class lifestyle on single income, let alone women's desire to be engaged in satisfying work.

Once young wives used to harbour a horror of joint-family living, and were often instrumental in setting up separate establishments. But now when she has kids and a full-time job, the advantages of joint-family living loom larger than its drawbacks in reduced privacy and occasional unpleasantness (the proverbial nastiness between mothers-in-law and daughters-in-law is clearly on the decline).

You get babysitters gratis. And what babysitters! You can't match grandparents in the quality of their caring, and available on tap. When you come home tired from work, you have things tidied up and a hot meal cooking.

In the West, particularly USA, leaving one's home on reaching adulthood was deemed something normal, almost taken for granted. Let alone the boys and girls, parents themselves were insistent about it.

Of late, there has been a perceptible change there, too. With inflated rents and job insecurity, young adults are returning home in increasing numbers. And parents have grown generally indulgent in receiving them back.

So far so good, as far as the "children", their spouses and kids are concerned.

But what about the parents, turned into permanent parents? Is it a rewarding experience for them to play the extended host? Or, does it usually turn out to be a tiresome affair?

It is hard to generalize in such matters; the range of possibilities is enormous. A great deal depends on personal equation, and on the personalities of the players involved, with the role of the daughter-in-law as crucial. Factors like family finances and the space available are important.

One can, however, venture a few general observations in this minefield of human relationships.

Where the parents, especially the father in his sixties is active and working, he could well see his thirty-year-old live-in "more as a buddy" than father and son. The two may be dressing the same way, going to the same clubs, or playing together, say golf or bridge. Or, a vivacious daughter of twenty-eight who's making the parental house lively with her presence. Today's twenty-somethings and their modern parents communicate better and closer. And people tend to prize the closeness of family relationships.

When the nest is doubly empty (one parent dying), the surviving one often pines for close relationships with children, more so a surviving widow. But then widows in their 50s or 60s can make a mistake getting too involved with their adult children. They have decades ahead and need to find a way to approach their lives as individuals.

Parents like being in a position to help their kids financially or otherwise, and they like the fact that they get along well enough to live together.

Yet perma-parents do suffer potential emotional repercussions. The empty-nest years are a crucial time for them to bone up retirement, rather than feed their adult children. Keeping the kids also prevents couples from reconfiguring their lives in the post-parenting stage.

Having an adult child lurking around the house and feeding off the parental nest egg robs parents of some of this latitude. Experts tend to agree that having an adult kid at home is generally a bad idea. *How to Survive and Thrive in an Empty Nest: Reclaiming Your Life When Your Children Have Grown* by Robert Lauer, Jeanette Lauer (Counterpoint Press) dwells on this theme.

Anyway, everyone must understand his or her role when living together. Some parents, especially mothers, make the mistake of imagining that their adult children are still somewhat helpless. Adult children have to be treated as adults with adult responsibilities and obligations. Whether age 25 or 45, these "children" should shoulder their share of household tasks. They can't expect everything to be just as it was before—with the mother saddled with the bulk of work. Many parents who have re-nesting children get frustrated, because they feel as if they were slaves to their children.

This becomes particularly galling to parents who were looking forward to their "empty nest" years—these years getting longer with the lengthening life spans—for a relaxed life of peace and quiet, with time enough for each other and for pursuing their interests. Instead they find themselves landed up with the same tensions and problems they had encountered at the child-bringing stage. The cooking remains more elaborate and the house is disorderly.

Besides sharing fully in household tasks, the re-nesting children must regularly pay the agreed rent. Pay it regularly and unobtrusively, such as by an automatic bank transfer on the first of every month. Face-to-face payments are not only embarrassing, these often tend to fall in arrears or get "forgotten". And presumably other expenses would be shared in proper proportion.

Parents' privacy has to be respected as zealously as you would want yours. Older people are a little more anxious to keep their love life secret; and their love life may be more active than you imagine.

And you can't always buy peace by shoving your rowdy kids into the old couple's rest periods. One's grand children can be great fun but only if the fare is served in controlled quantities.

All in all, re-nesting children should not make their parents feel as if they were being taken advantage of.

A Peep into Parent-Offspring Conflict

We know the scene too well: a boy of four whining loudly in a shop when he can't wheedle an extra sweet from his exasperated mother, or a girl of six throwing tantrums at her parents' refusal to buy her a particular doll. Children as young as two or three come to learn that making a public spectacle of their unmet demand can put a lot of pressure on their parents. They often also know that they are safe from parental on-the-spot chastisement in front of others.

Curious as it may sound, such parent-offspring conflicts aren't unique to human beings or peculiar to today's children. They are a natural and widely occurring phenomenon in the animal world.

Biologists have found that the animal kingdom abounds with examples of clashes between parents and offspring. And they have developed theories to explain these conflicts. Admittedly, the human scenario is far more complex. Our behaviour is not only dictated by survival strategies that every species adopts, it's also influenced by our social and cultural mores.

According to Robert Travers, a biologist at the University of California, there is inherent conflict of interests between parents and their offspring in species that reproduce sexually. In such species, each of the two parents contributes exactly half of each offspring's genetic material. So an offspring is not an exact copy of any parent. And it shares even less than 50 percent genes with its siblings. Because of this genetic differential, each infant has a separate identity and is fully engaged since birth—or even since conception—in single-mindedly pursuing its own interests. And that makes an infant want its parents to lavish all their care on itself, rather than share it out among its siblings. Conflicts arise as the infant struggles to gain maximum parental attention.

Nesting chicks of many birds have been observed raising a frightening ruckus to get the maximum food from their parents, even hurting themselves in the process to gain attention. By their crying and begging and protesting, they want to convey the message that withholding food supplies would have serious consequences on their survival. And chicks wouldn't hesitate to push away other siblings for optimizing their share.

The parent-offspring conflict in the animal world usually works in some sort of a cycle. In the beginning, an offspring often gains the upper hand by impressing parents with its crying and begging. First-time mothers are less immune to such "deceit" and pressure tactics. In due course, parents get more "sceptical" and tough-minded. They refuse to administer the amount of care that the infant demands, if it amounts to unfair distribution among the offspring, or places inordinate demands on their capacity or well-being.

Parents get manipulated because they never have perfect knowledge of the needs of the offspring. In reverse, the offspring also does not know how much care the parent is capable of providing. So the tussle continues till the infant abandons deceit and becomes more truthful about its needs.

Problems sometimes arise in the intervening period when the mother may think that the infant is still crying wolf while the infant is actually truthful.

Marc Hauser of Harvard University talks of a case he came across while studying vervet monkeys in Kenya's Amboseli Park. A particular infant continually demanded care from its mother until she eventually began to ignore it. One day the infant ran into trouble following its mother and began to scream for help. The mother took no notice and continued on her way up—at which point the infant fell out of the tree, and died of injuries a few days later.

Budgerigar mothers are known to be quite immune to infant manipulation. They feed their chicks in strict rotation, distributing food in proportion to their age and size. No amount of begging will persuade a budgerigar mother to change this course. In contrast, the budgerigar male, on the rare occasions he feeds the offspring (he mostly feeds his mate), gives more food to those chicks who beg the loudest and the longest.

Louise Barrett and Robin Dunbar, two anthropologists at the University College, London who studied the nursing behaviour of gelada baboons in Ethiopia also highlight some areas of the parent-offspring conflict.

During the first two months of life, gelada mothers allow their infants to suckle and cling to their chest much of the time. But with an infant getting bigger, it proves more of an encumbrance when she's feeding herself—extra feeding required during lactation. Gelada baboons feed on grass, squatting on ground and harvesting blades immediately in front. The efficiency of this mode of foraging suffers if a female has to reach around a screaming infant before she can get her hands on some food.

So a gelada mother refuses to entertain her infant during her food gathering, despite all the whines and grizzles the enraged infant indulges in. She just ignores it. The infant in due course learns that it can have the same amount of time at the mother's nipple, but when she's resting or grooming. The infant soon adjusts accordingly, keeping a wary watch when the mother is free from foraging.

The yellow baboons of Amboseli Park in Kenya are observed to behave differently. Here a mother allows an infant to cling on to her chest till it's almost 4 months old. The likely explanation is that the yellow baboons mostly eat fruit and this they do standing. An infant clinging to the chest is not such an obstruction as it is to a grass-eating gelada mother.

Monkey mothers living in captivity show much lower levels of conflict than gelada and yellow baboons, because the mother does not have to spend such a large proportion of her day feeding. She has more time to devote to her infant. Nevertheless they push away infants ruthlessly during the mating season, when a suckling infant can be a great nuisance. Eventually the little one learns to keep out of the way when its mother is preoccupied with matters like mating.

So don't be too upset when your child throws a tantrum. It happens all the time in the animal world; it's a part of the game of life. Of course human children are cleverer. They learn faster and become more skilled at manipulation. How quickly little children learn that most parents will go along than let their children scream in public.

Playing One Parent Against Another

Raising kids is part joy and part guerrilla warfare

Ed Asner

Children can be very good at playing one parent off against the other.

How many times have your kids asked you permission to do something, when unknown to you, your partner had already said they can't? And when you say "Yes", you irritate your partner, who feels that its authority has been set at nought.

And how often trying to avoid this situation, have you asked, "Well, what did Mummy/Daddy say?". This gives the clever child quite an opportunity to bend the truth by blurting out, "Mummy/Daddy didn't actually say no, and that's why I'm asking you."

Instead of asking your child as to what the other partner said, you better ask the partner yourself.

Better still, whenever you can, stay ahead of the game by discussing things with your partner and agreeing to rules well in advance. United you stand, divide you fall.

But then there are numerous occasions when you find yourself taken by surprise. Your child asks for permission to do something that requires an instant on-the-spot judgement, and the spouse is nowhere near.

"Can I have that chocolate bar?" "Can I have a Coke?" "Can I go to the cinema tonight? I need to know quickly as my friend Rajan is on the line and he needs my OK to buy the tickets."

In these cases you'll have to decide one way or the other, and later explain your decision to your partner, especially if the other one has strong views on the subject. You're bound to make the odd slip-up, and you'll have to live with the resulting tension with your partner.

There's the other situation where you shift the burden of disciplining an erring kid on to your partner.

"Wait till your father gets home" was the ultimate threat Mummy would make. Or, in these days of dad devaluation, a father warning, "Wait till your mother returns."

It may all seem like an effective tactic—good cop, bad cop. But dumping the burden of discipline for "serious offences" on to the other parent can prove a poor recipe. It just reinforces stereotyped ideas about the different roles of men and women in the family. It makes the father look like an awful tyrant, and rather than making the mother look good, it presents her as being weak. It's like saying, "I don't have the authority or stomach to discipline you." As a result, it eats away at the respect children have for both their mother and father.

Fair discipline is always best administered by the parent who was there when the “crime” took place. No point dumping your problems on to your partner in a situation the other one knows much less.

Of course, if the offence is serious and you need time to calm down and think before you act, you could say something like, “I and your father will talk about it, and then decide.”

9

Women at Work

Men and Women at Work!

Are men and women the same at work?

To feminists, a perfect gender balance is achievable in all occupations. Many a psychologist thinks otherwise.

Feminists themselves continue divided into minimizers and maximizers of the male-female differences. The issue actually confronts them with an awkward ideological dilemma. If men and women are basically the same, the feminist goal becomes equality—that also restrains them from attacking men or celebrating women. If the two are inherently different, feminists can point with pride to women's special attributes—but then the concept of equality takes a backseat.

Psychologists rely on a wealth of accumulating evidence that shows men and women having different intellectual aptitudes. Men excel in mathematical and scientific pursuits, women have an edge in language skills. School examination results amply bear out the same.

The differences in ability are now known to result from differences in brain structure as influenced by hormones during prenatal development. The most striking difference is that male brains are more specialized in spatial processing in the right hemisphere. Female brains appear better equipped for communication between the two hemispheres. One result: male brains are more susceptible to damage as they have no back-up if something goes wrong in one hemisphere, hence more prone to disorders such as stammering or dyslexia.

Women are surely moving into many fields of work that were once male preserves. Their performance should be no different from men in occupations that were male preserves from arbitrary convention or vested power (office work, administration). But performance differential isn't likely to be eliminated totally in occupations that have a biological foundation (scientific research, engineering).

Another major difference between typical men and women that has relevance to work pertains to personality traits, such as competitiveness and ambitiousness. Men are typically more motivated than women in pursuit of status and economic rewards, whatever occupation they choose. And this tendency of males to be more competitive than women has been observed as common to almost all societies in the world, thus confirming its probable biological origins.

No wonder, most bank managers, company directors, top doctors are men, though women have been coming into medicine, law, business. Some element of male discrimination may be there and men admittedly had a head start, yet men's higher competitiveness may be the crucial factor.

Dominance is a personality characteristic largely determined by male hormones. Here the role of evolutionary psychology would be hard to ignore. During evolution, high male status must have expanded sexual access to females, as it does in many species of animals. Given this distinctly male link between social achievement and genetic proliferation, it is plausible to assume that millions of years of evolution would endow males with a distinctive thirst for power. In almost all societies, the average male is seen pursuing status and power more fiercely and opportunistically than his female counterpart.

Not only does prenatal testosterone cause competitive aggressiveness, but the experience of triumph releases further testosterone. Thus a sharp elevation in status, even a victory in sports, operates as an aphrodisiac, while failure or defeat changes a male's brain chemicals towards those seen in depressed patients.

Female sexual responsiveness, by contrast, is said to be actually enhanced by the sense of being overpowered. Anyway success in life does not boost female sexuality; possibly diminishes it.

None of this is to say that women cannot achieve equality with men in work; only the motivation to do so is greater for the average man. The innate sex difference in ambition is a fact of life. To that extent, the rationale that men and women should be equally represented at the higher level of all jobs falters; an average man works harder at self-advancement and is inclined to make greater sacrifices for it than an average woman. Maybe, things will change but changes in evolutionary psychology have a long lead time.

In the book *Feminism and Freedom*, Michael Levin describes the case of a prominent US Company that was attacked for not promoting enough women to management positions. The company's leadership, which prided itself in being very fair and open on gender equality, hired a famous firm of consultants to find out what was going wrong. The consultants, after an elaborate study, concluded that the difference in promotion was due entirely to motivation. Women clerks were less ready to work longer hours or be relocated and were less inclined to see their jobs as the first rung on the corporate ladder. Work was seen as important but not as all-important as it was with men. Compared with women, men showed a sort of tunnel-vision aimed at power and dominance. They even strove at the expense of friendship, time and physical health.

No doubt, women are more likely to have conflicting family and childcare obligations than men. They have other priorities than just power and prestige at work.

Of course, there are always going to be some women who are just as independent, aggressive, competitive and risk-taking as any man, and they rise to top positions. They often have a childhood background of highly active, near boyish behaviour.

And women enjoy an advantage in work involving social situations. They are far better than men at reading non-verbal signals of emotion, what's called the body-language. And they are more alert at assessing the significance of small details. This superior social perceptiveness is commonly referred to as "female intuition".

The experience of dealing with the needs and wiles of young children may also be equipping women particularly well as better negotiators. Women clearly show greater understanding of other people and this is a valuable asset in many professions, such as teaching, nursing, counselling, even in areas like real estate and insurance.

If women lack aggressiveness in the sales field, they evidently make up for it with other advantages, such as verbal fluency and the management of social situations. Men are more likely to evoke resistance by adopting the hard-sell approach.

In short, men and women are somewhat different at work, and these differences are largely innate. Men are almost certain to predominate in many occupations while women enjoy significant advantage in certain callings. To that extent, the two complement each other than work in opposition.

Men and Women in Management

Do men and women follow different approaches in management? Are men and women profoundly different in their thinking and approach? Does biology influence our business behaviour?

People opposed to sexism resist, with the best of intentions, any such ideas and their implications for the workplace. To them men and women are not only equal but mentally identical as well.

Now this is hard to square up with the evolutionary theory. Indeed, for evolution to have given men and women radically different physical attributes, capabilities and functions, and then equip them with exactly the same mindset, would constitute a crucial "design fault".

Gary Johnson, a marketing specialist with a medical degree, dwells on the general pattern of differences between the sexes, taking the analogy of other mammals, in his book *Monkey Business* (Gower).

According to him, by and large, animals have been adopting two opposing investment strategies. Females generally take the low-risk "bank deposit" approach whereby they produce few offspring and concentrate all nurturing effort to give these a good chance of survival to the next generation.

Male animals, on the other hand, have generally taken the high-risk "venture capital" approach. A male animal, after mating with one female, diverts his efforts to the riskier course of securing more mates to propel a greater number of his genes into the next generation. As all other males are in the same game of securing an "unfair share" of females, it becomes a highly risky venture, calling for strength and aggression.

Johnson typifies this behaviour in elephant seals. The strongest, dominant male elephant seal establishes an exclusive harem of females with whom he mates. This results in many other males failing to mate. The best male strategy therefore is to be big and fight hard to be one of lucky few who pass on their genes to the next generation.

And this is exactly what happens. Right from an early age male elephant seal pups are taking risks to grow to be the biggest, strongest bulls. They engage in "milk thievery"—taking extra milk from nursing seals who are not their mothers. This can be deadly, each seal mother is making a massive investment in producing milk and she intends for her offspring. She could well injure or kill a pilfering pup. But for the male pup, it's worth the risk to steal a lead on the competition to be strong.

Meanwhile, female pups suckle contentedly, solely from their own mothers. Their chances of reproduction are relatively high; there is bound to be a high quality, dominant male only too willing to mate with her. It is not worth her while to take the sort of risks associated with milk thievery.

The same seems true of human beings. Baby boys tend to be more colicky", they cry more than baby girls. Effectively baby boys are demanding more attention and food from their parents. This is not without its own risks such as baby-bashing. But if you want to be one of the bigger, stronger males you need all the nutrition you can get as a baby.

Johnson divides mammals into two broad categories: polygamous and monogamous. And the human male is put as genetically polygamous—*inclined* to be polygamous. Monogamy is a fairly recent invention at that; some 4,000 years back many human societies were polygamous. The genes that determine the polygamous inclination have been selected over millions of years, often in very different circumstances to those that now face us. Of course, this is no excuse for infidelity. Much of our biology is out of date and this is one example.

Johnson cites a few facts to support his point. It is a feature of polygamous animals that males tend to be larger and more aggressive than females. The reason is obvious: you have to be big and aggressive to be more successful in securing females. Maintaining a large body has its own costs; more muscle and less fat in the form of fat. Such males are less likely to survive in periods of starvation. And the added risks of injury or death in fights with competing males over females.

Among the primates, for example, the highly polygamous male gorilla is vastly bigger than the female. The larger the successful male's harem, the larger this difference in size. In monogamous species, males and females tend to be the same size; it's possible for practically all the males to reproduce so there's no pressure for larger males. Among the primates again, the monogamous male gibbon is the same size as female.

Men are significantly larger than women—5 to 12 percent larger.

Another feature of polygamous animals is of reaching sexual maturity much later than females. Sexually mature males invite hostility from competitive males. It therefore pays to delay their maturity until they have the size and experience to stand a chance in the competition for females.

Human males reach sexual maturity significantly later than females.

Johnson concludes that men are genetically predisposed to riskier lifestyle than women; flamboyant, accident-prone behaviour in general tends to be male. That explains men being involved more in auto accidents and drunken driving, suicides, fights, and crime. They change their jobs oftener and are prone to risk a career move in order to gain the status and resources that their genes crave for. That way men have a greater propensity to take rash risks.

Men tend to try and dominate and be aggressive, particularly against other men. This is how they are "programmed" by evolution to acquire their unfair share of resources, including mates. Older men are known to make it especially difficult for younger men to come up in an organization—the age-old patriarchal fear of younger rivals.

The high-risk "venture capital" approach of men and the low-risk, "bank deposit" style of comparable women does get reflected in workplace in some shape or the other, Johnson says. And you find significant evidence of it in Fund Management. Some other studies have also shown that organizations with a masculinity culture are more risk taking.

Now all this is a tricky subject, a virtual minefield. Let alone feminist fervour, more and more women are taking up the challenges of higher positions in business and politics. And what about women like Mrs Thatcher or Indira Gandhi? What about the budding crop of women CEOs in major companies?

Yet what Johnson makes out cannot be simply brushed aside; it does focus attention on an intriguing gender aspect in business and management.

'Honorary' Man!

Linda McDowell, a Cambridge lecturer, has researched gender working in senior positions within the City's banking, London. Her book *Capital Culture: Gender at Work in the City* (Blackwell) brings out some of the dilemmas facing women in a largely masculine culture.

Our milieu is manifestly different, yet some of Linda's findings could be of interest to women working in upper rungs of the country's business and government; human behaviour is well-nigh the same everywhere.

One thing, Linda's interviewees commonly mentioned, was of being reminded everyday that they possessed a female body. They felt marked out and restricted to a small number of acceptable ways of presenting themselves at work. Many women argued that their femininity and sexuality was a constant issue at work, influencing everyday interactions with male colleagues.

Younger women believed that their age combined with their gender operated to double disadvantage, creating difficulties in being taken seriously. Being young and female means you have to really earn somebody's respect. "On the positive side, there's certainly the novelty aspect; that can work quite well for women but I really think it is outweighed by the fact that you are not taken seriously initially," says one.

And for younger women, there's the incidence of sexual harassment. Women in workplace are constantly reminded they are female and therefore sexually vulnerable; this vulnerability to sexual harassment is construed as if women, and not men, were responsible for it.

A respondent talks of her irritation when a man whom she was meeting for business kept letting his eyes drift to her chest, a reminder that "I'm thinking about your sex rather than your brains". In reverse, male colleagues can be seen making desperate efforts to avoid looking at your cleavage as they speak to you. "Some of my colleagues talk to me looking like this (*squinting sideways*), you know I think that's either because they've got something in their eye or they just have never seen a chest before. They are simply not comfortable with me and end up looking over my shoulder," comments a buxom banker.

Others speak of men—colleagues and clients—who let themselves get distracted because it is a woman speaking to them; they are just not listening to what you are saying.

Of the women Linda interviewed, all, without exception, raised the question of appearance. Their male colleagues frequently commented on women's clothes, hair and make-up in an intrusive way. "The minute you walk in they comment on your clothes. If you are wearing something slightly odd, they'll be rude about it. If you are wearing something slightly bright, they'll make a comment about it. A man can choose a style that will not attract attention or subject him to any particular interpretation, but a woman can't. Whatever she wears, she draws attention to herself," moans one. No wonder, for many a woman a compromise was a feminised version of the dark male suit.

Conversation, like clothes, operates under a similar logic. When men and women are in groups, women are likely to adapt their conversational style to become more masculinised—they raise their voices, interrupt and become more assertive. Some others become even more stereotypically female and are silenced, smile more than men and give non-verbal cues of assent or attentiveness to what others say, especially the men. Linda talks of ways in which women in general are disadvantaged, ranging from the pitch and tone of their voices which are associated with a lack of authority to the tendency to play "facilitative" rather than aggressive or confrontational roles in conversation in mixed groups.

One of the difficulties for women in male-dominated professional occupations is to figure out the image of a powerful woman that is not negative. There is a whole range of such stereotypes: schoolmarm, head nurse, headmistress, dragon lady, or governess. Mrs Thatcher was often compared with a governess, and Mrs Gandhi as "the only man" in her cabinet.

Indeed many women, to achieve success in masculinist organisations, adopt a workplace performance that constructs them as 'honorary' men. They behave as if gender is inconsequential to their careers. "For most of the time I am an honorary man. My male colleagues do treat me like an honorary male and that's what I prefer. I can even see the way they look at women," says one.

But many other respondents were sceptical of the success of this strategy. To them it was difficult, even demeaning to try to be "one of the boys".

There are problems involved in attempting to become an 'honorary' man. Women who attempt to behave like men are often distressed to find not only non-acceptance but distrust from their male peers. Men have a real problem with women who are unfeminine. "There's a certain female type in the City; trying to be men, wanting to show themselves as that much more aggressive. I find it quite sad really. It more often backfires with colleagues than helps," comments a male banker, responding to Linda's questioning.

But then men, especially younger men, also complain that femininity confers unfair advantage on women. Women, they make out, are good at getting on with people, and enjoy a natural advantage as the majority of clients are men. "There's a definite advantage to being a woman. Being feminine, even slightly sugar-coated can be a great advantage both within the organisation and with clients, because girls can manage to strike up an almost instant rapport, you know with their male bosses and their male clients," grumbles one.

So women seem to be in an impossible position, says Linda. As female bodies they are out of place at work, but should they manage to overcome the disadvantage of the masculinised environment and achieve success, this is put down to the advantages conferred by a set of naturalised female attributes.

It seems, most women have come to accept that becoming an 'honorary' man was not a viable strategy. "Why should I try to be a little man? I'm not a little man. It's not going to work. I'll never be a man as well as a man," says the woman director of a bank.

When Wife Outshines

Jyotish and Jaya have just celebrated their Silver Wedding Anniversary. Jyotish had wanted something modest and private; Jaya something classy, big and showy. Eventually it went Jaya's way.

Bagging a first in MA English literature, Jyotish took over as a lecturer in a top Delhi college. He nursed high hopes of professional success, let alone becoming an established writer, probably a novelist.

Tall, handsome, genial; at 27, he was rated a good catch.

Jaya held a second-class degree, and a diploma in textile designing. Not a beauty, but a fairly personable figure that came with a substantial dowry.

For the first ten years of marriage she busied herself with the household and bringing up two bright boys.

The marital equation clearly favoured Ravi. But by their Silver Wedding Anniversary, the situation stands reversed.

Jaya's boutique, opened 15 years back in a rented first-floor attic in Khan Market, has grown into a roaring business. She specializes in women's wear of salwar-kameez. And has blossomed into an established fashion designer.

By now she has her own impressive premises and showroom in South Extension, backed by a garment factory in Noida. Employs around a hundred people. A major part of her production is currently tied to export orders from UK, USA, Canada, Hong Kong, and East/South Africa for the Indian community there.

A happy combination of sustained strenuous work coupled with obsessive concern for detail and perfection, business acumen, and promotional drive has succeeded in making Jaya a known figure in her field, the ladies' suits. She has built numerous contacts in India and abroad. Travels oversees twice or thrice a year on business, let alone trips to metropolitan cities in the country.

Lately she has authored a book about her clothing designs; a pricey, heavily illustrated coffee-table tome that is selling well. That has given her a near celebrity status. It's another matter, Jyotish helped a lot with the language, format and editing.

Backed by rising income and heady sense of success, Jaya has retained her youngish looks. Goes for the best of beauty treatment—including plastic surgery on eyelids—skincare, and classy clothes. Tones up her figure with half-an-hour of Yoga in the morning. Doesn't look more than 33 for her 43 summers.

Jyotish had a better start at marriage. But he has fallen far behind his outshining wife. A professor, yes, but not even the head of the department; a senior fellow is blocking his promotion.

He has written two books, one a critical evaluation of Tennyson's poetry, and another *History of Indian Novel in English*. It took much pushing to get them published. And the books aren't selling; not even the first edition of 400 copies each.

For the last two years, Jyotish spends much of his time writing a novel; a story centred on his troubled boyhood. He has just finished the first draft of 1,00,000 words. And it has yet to evoke any interest in a reputed publisher. He's passing through a fairly frustrating phase of life.

Jyotish's only consolation, in fact, his pride: the two boys are doing brilliantly. The elder is in IIT Delhi and stays in a campus hostel. The younger has just joined Maulana Azad Medical College, and lives with the parents. While the elder one rides an imported BMW motorbike, the younger has a Santro. Both the boys are keen to study further in USA, and their mother has assured the financial support for it.

Jaya's successful business has upped family living standard. They have moved from Jyotish's official 2-bedroom flat to a bought-out spacious house in Sundar Nagar. Jaya goes about in a chauffeured Honda Accord. Jyotish is still sticking to his Maruti 800.

What's fascinating is the different ways the two have been reacting to their changing fortunes. When he was up, she seemed genuinely glad for him. Boasted to everyone how well he was doing in his teaching and writing.

Does Jyotish return the favour? He, actually, finds ways of countering anything uppity on her part. Often sulks, moves conversation away from her latest achievements to things like political corruption or American blunders in Iraq.

His negative feelings are particularly noticeable, say at a dinner where she's in the limelight, and he just the Husband. Invited to fashion parties he loses her within seconds. Usually finds himself alone clutching a drink. Dragged into a circle, he could suffer the mortification of watching the light go out of someone's eye when discovered that he wasn't one of the persons who mattered.

He's likely to whisper to Jaya as soon as the food finishes: "I'm going home. You can stay on if you want." That's his way of ruining her evening.

And, on reaching the privacy of their home, often accuses her of showing off, or boring others with her work.

At times, they end up having a row.

"You want everyone to see how grand your contribution is, while the lazy lout of a husband just hangs on to his silly work," says Jyotish with some bitterness.

"Don't you enjoy the benefits of the money I bring?"

"Oh yes, never let me forget about that, will you? You're the successful one, the famous one. I'm the boring old husband standing in the wings. You do make more money than me. But you love rubbing my nose in it."

"No, I don't," she remonstrates indignantly.

Jaya hadn't realized how much he resented her success. He might have liked living in a big and luxurious house but he wasn't really coping with the fact that her earnings had brought them there. Was he feeling emasculated by her success, she wonders?

To Jyotish, his wife is becoming too bossy as she outshines him more and more. Behaves more like a mother, though they have sex occasionally—-of late, very occasionally. A man evidently needs his ego to get the sex juices going.

The stark fact stares in his face that Jaya is now the principal breadwinner, not he. She incurs all the expenditure on food, servants' salaries, and sundry purchases. And these constitute the bulk. He mainly buys his own clothes and books, pays for his petrol, and settles outside payments like club bills. At times she even guiltily slips money to him under the restaurant table so that he can pretend to the guests, he's paying.

And the disparity in their styles of life manifests itself in trivial ways. For example, Jyotish is quite happy with an old suit, she forcing a replacement through gifting him an expensive one on his birthday; she wanting to go to Mauraya Sheraton for a marriage anniversary dinner, he advocating a cheaper meal at their club or a restaurant in Pandara Park. Jaya often tries to play down such differences, but to her money has become a luminous symbol of functionality and power. All this leaves Jyotish a bit confused and unsure of himself—not a promising scenario for marital harmony.

He's getting more and more conscious of his failure. And nothing adds quite so much to its sting as the proximity of dazzling success.

Failure not only corrodes the soul, its leaves its footprints on the skin. Jyotish has started looking older than he is. His wit and geniality is mostly gone.

His only hope of recognition lies in the novel he has drafted. Recently Jaya's publisher rang up—must be at the urging of his wife—to appraise the manuscript. A quick response has been promised. And it could well be favourable.

Now Jyotish-Jaya case isn't an isolated one. Husbands may make out that they are thrilled by their partners' achievements, but the truth is that many of them feel threatened by their more successful spouses. Husbands passively resist and emotionally withdraw from wives who have become too confident, apparently too independent. Being married to a powerful and successful man enormously enhances a woman's status. The reverse, however, isn't necessarily true.

Why is it somewhat hard for men to glorify genuinely in the achievements of their mates? Possibly it's a question of identity. So much of male self-esteem seems to be tied up in public acknowledgement of them as winners and leaders. If the woman they are married to has a more pronounced identity, they see themselves automatically diminished. The situation is all the more galling where the man is going through a bad patch in his own career.

Besides the hurt to the ego, what's at the root cause of men's antipathy towards outshining wives is their fear of abandonment. "She doesn't need my money. She isn't even keen to carry my name. She doesn't rely on me any more." It goes back to the basic fear of being abandoned by another female—his mother.

The psychological toughness of men—one of patriarchy's most powerful myths—may well be illusory. At the emotional level, men evidently need their wives in ways that their wives don't need them.

With husbands beginning to harbour the impression that their wives care more for their work than for them, it can produce a backlash. And this can take a few forms: criticism of her household running, sabotaging her professional aspirations, pushing childbirth on her when she's not ready for it, refusing to help in household chores, withholding affection, even sex, or an inordinate demand for it, and at its worst, having an affair with a passive woman.

Like most other changes, the process of accepting an outshining wife can be quite painful. And such situations could well be on the increase. Eventually one hopes, a new ideology of marriage will take shape where a successful wife isn't threatening to the male ego.

Women in Politics: the Biology Factor

Whereas the percentage of women legislators is around 15 percent in countries with elected legislatures, ours still hovers below 9 percent.

To remedy the situation, women's reservation bill was mooted. This was more in line with the earlier legislation prescribing a minimum percentage of seats for women in Panchayats and other local bodies.

From 1996 onwards, the charade of introducing the Bill has been played out. The Gujral Government did it. The Gowda Government did it. A repeat of the same by the Vajpayee Government. And possibly the Bill will meet the same fate with the current Congress-led government, though Sonia Gandhi has been advocating it.

The only positive aspect is that the issue now figures firmly on the national political agenda. Political parties know that sooner or later something will have to be done.

While major political parties find it politically expedient to voice support for the Bill, they aren't enthusiastic about binding themselves to it. Even the simpler suggestion of the Election Commission that political parties give a fixed percentage of tickets to women as an alternative to the 33 percent reservation provided in the Bill hasn't elicited encouraging response.

Critics dub it hypocrisy. Yet the parties' dilemma is obvious. Whatever may be the moral compulsions of having more women in legislatures, there is the ever intense pressure for party tickets from men. Another complicating factor: most current incumbents are men. And it isn't easy to reject their re-nomination, more so when incumbents claim to have better chances of success than fresh ones. Pushed too hard, political parties may get around by awarding tickets to women mostly from non-winnable constituencies.

Quite a few other proposals have been made, such as treating a third of seats as "Dual Membership Constituencies", and reserving the additionally created seats for women. This will mean that men retain all the seats they have now.

An argument is often advanced that the odds of a woman winning an elective office are generally lower than that of a man. Older voters, some say, grew up with the belief that women stayed at home to raise children. But then women voters may show a marked preference for a woman candidate.

A detailed study of women candidates to American state legislatures reveals that when women run, women win as often as men; the success rates almost identical in all comparisons. A striking similarity has been found between the percentage of female legislators and the percentage of women who were candidates. It's another matter that while American women have managed to notch over 20 percent of seats in state legislatures, their percentage in the powerful Senate and Congress stays dismally low.

The phenomenon of women not coming up to the level of men in politics should come as no surprise; the position is similar the world over. There were more women in the British cabinet in the 1930s than they are at present. Again there has been no significant increase in the number of female MPs over the past three decades—notwithstanding the momentous Mrs Thatcher era.

Many women in the last thirty or forty years have been brought up to believe that they are, or should be, "as good as the next man". They were led to believe that once they have shaken off the shackles of male prejudice and oppression—the supposed source of their second-class status—they would be on the way to achieving equality with men in diverse fields particularly politics. And are feeling quite frustrated because this has failed to materialize.

The real inhibiting factor, it seems, may be biology, not so much gender bias. Men and women are different, and the culture of politics as it currently obtains, affords a definite edge to "manly" characteristics.

Men and women do differ biologically, whatever the feminists may claim to the contrary. The main reason is that on average men produce more than ten times as much testosterone as women. And this chemical does affect profoundly the physique and behaviour, mood and temper—the biggest behavioural difference between men and women is the natural, innate aggression of men.

At conception, every embryo is female. But a surge of testosterone, coming around six weeks after conception, turns a little over half of the embryos into males, the rest remaining female. Earlier the assumption was that, in terms of our minds, we are born sexually neutral, our minds a blank slate on which our parents, our teachers, and the expectations our societies had of us would chalk their determinant messages. But recent advances in brain research make out that the brains of boys and girls are different from the foetus stage itself.

From the cradle, baby girls like to gurgle at humans. Boys are happier with looking at cot toys. There are discernible, measurable differences in behaviour between baby boys and girls, long before external influences have a chance to get to work. The brain biases persist and strengthen as children grow up, seeing life through that particular filter of the brain which they find easier, and more natural, to use. "The brain," according to a leading Canadian brain researcher, "is a sex organ".

The second major surge of testosterone comes to boys at puberty. Testosterone effects both the body and the mind. The body differences the chemical causes are obvious: the genitals, body hair, the ratio of muscle to fat, and so on. On the mental side, it engenders combativeness, an urge for dominance and power, even aggression. An overwhelming majority of those involved in rash or drunken driving, brawls and violent crimes are men. And this is largely attributed to their much higher levels of testosterone; it cannot be explained alone by social conditioning.

It is this sharp difference in the levels of testosterone between men and women that makes men take more to risky ventures than women. No wonder, activities such as military duty, boxing, wrestling, hazardous explorations, and gambling tend to be disproportionately male. Again male presence is pronounced in callings such as venture capitalism and playing the share market.

Politics is again a very combative calling, with its never-ending power struggles. It is saturated with ego, conflict and risk. To secure political power and to retain the same, practically no holds are barred—political morality assumed to be far more forgiving than general morality. No surprise, after a century of adult franchise where women form nearly half the electorate, the number of female politicians remains disappointingly small in most democracies.

Mahatma Gandhi had led a uniquely civilized campaign for country's independence, a campaign with no parallel in history for its humanity and transparency. This had encouraged many an Indian woman to enter the political arena. But the unrealistically high moral tone of politics could not be sustained for long. Indeed, our politics has been steadily degenerating, with growing incidence of criminality.

How well do women fit into this scenario? Can they match men in this sort of game? Or as in sports, have they to be organized in separate competition? Should women contribute their specific female gifts rather than waste their energies in the pursuit of a sort of surrogate masculinity. That's the dilemma many women face wanting to enter politics.

An obvious question arises. Are women legislators different from men? Admittedly this question ignores the rich diversity among women themselves. Women are, in many ways, as different from one another as they are from their male colleagues. Yet the short answer is, yes, women are systematically different from men.

Women legislators are generally seen to engage in a different mix of legislative activities. They concern themselves more intimately with the welfare of women and children, crime and other practical problems of everyday living. The qualities associated with low testosterone—sympathy, cooperation, conciliation, risk aversion—inform their outlook.

But then women have to climb the grisly ladder of politics, and here the average woman is handicapped biologically vis-à-vis her male counterparts. Women leaders like Mrs Indira Gandhi, Benazir Bhutto, Chandrika Kumaratunga, Megawati, Sonia Gandhi the Bangladesh Begums are different: they owe a great deal of their political prominence to their particular family background. Of course, there are always exceptions, such as Mayawati or Jayalalitha.

Admittedly, a low turnout of women into politics may not be endemic to it; the phenomenon has more to do with the culture of politics. In countries like Sweden or Iceland women's political participation is almost reaching parity levels. But that calls for a near transformation of the culture of politics. It's a hen-and-egg situation: larger women participation should usher a more forbearing politics but then you can't have larger participation without politics itself veering towards being benign.

10

Workplace Romance

More Than Friends, Less Than Lovers

As the workplace becomes increasingly open to women, the sexes are mingling more and more.

A question often pondered if not actually asked: Can men and women in workplace continue friends—without slipping into becoming lovers? Some pose even a more basic question: Can men and women be friends?

To Michael Monsour of the University of Colorado, and the author of *Women and Men as Friends: Relationships Across the Life Span in the 21st Century* (Lawrence Erlbaum, 2001), the answer is Yes. Platonic love does exist, he asserts.

Earlier in 1992, two management trainers, David R. Eyler and Andreas P. Baridon attempted a relationship model for the American workplace. It pictured a positive way for men and women to share intimate feelings outside of marriage or an illicit affair. And it rejected the traditional saint-or-sinner model of colleague relationship as too simplistic for modern life.

Yet social scientists concede that research on the subject is still in its infancy. Only now they are beginning to understand some basic truths about male-female friendship.

A new scenario is emerging at workplaces: women working side by side with men. This daily physical proximity between the sexes, more so when joined with the stimulation of shared work, brings with it the likelihood of sexual attraction. People usually go to office dressed in smart clothes and looking their best—unlike married people at home who see each other in various unglamorous shapes and situations.

Another factor favouring sexual attraction among colleagues is the fact of their being of the same age, similar education and socio-economic background, similar values and similar aspirations. And today's work in many offices and businesses can mean irregular hours, non-office settings, and the greater intimacy of business travel.

Already society is undergoing its awkward adjustment to the phenomenon of working wives. To it is added the complication of women interacting daylong with other men, which offers countless opportunities for work-related friendships to develop. "Even the most secure people in a strong marriage probably don't want a spouse to be establishing a new friendship, especially with someone who's very attractive," says Monsour.

Eyre and Baridon call this relationship non-sexual love. And find that women seem to have an intuitive grasp of the same. They're the ones who usually move to forge it, often out of the wreckage of a colleague's attempt at something sexual—the way some of our women are compelled to project a brother-sister set-up, often aided by rakhi-tying. Men usually have a difficult time adjusting to the idea. Men find it harder to give up the deeply ingrained macho model of a sexual conquest.

Admittedly sexual attraction among certain coworkers is inevitable. And some persons will pursue sexual attraction to have affairs or with a view to marriage. But the vast majority would neither be interested in a commitment like marriage, especially if already married, nor an affair that has the potential to disrupt their career or established relationships. For such persons Eyler and Baridon envisage a unique new relationship that is limited to sharing personal revelations and intimacy, but not sharing bodies; mutual respect and communication as an alternative to the old game of seduction and conquest.

The two trainers advocate this new sexual etiquette for those who wish to exploit the energy of workplace attraction without physical sex or falling in love, or the other extreme of avoiding each other altogether and pretending that the workplace is genderless. And they make a few suggestions that can pull off the new relationship—more than friends, less than lovers.

You have to establish boundaries and expectations for the right relationship. The parties are enjoined to discuss openly and decide what is and is not off-limits. Some boundaries, notably the sexual one, they agree never to cross. Similarly, neither physical contact nor the language of lovers has a place in the relationship, as these will only send wrong signals.

Without a conscious management of the proposed relationship, personal attraction can lead to destructive consequences. Differences have to be resolved openly, instead of letting them fester in ambiguity. Initially, it may be difficult to discuss emotional issues of the new relationship, but these should be brought into the open for honest discussion, when you sense some tension building up. Two people seldom approach a relationship with perfectly matched expectations. And so is the necessity to remove misunderstandings from time to time.

The workplace relationship has one advantage over marriage relationship: in the former you can have periods of cooling-off if things seem like going out of hand. And you are not obliged to take care of each other or to tolerate differences on daily basis as in marriage.

Where the new relationship succeeds, it can lead to much creativity in work. There's a magic between "Business Couples" that makes their work exciting. They do genuinely inspired work together; their creative energy flowing from a sexual attraction they've chosen not to indulge in physically or force into love.

According to Eyler and Baridon, the relationship advocated by them is largely workable. The days of insecure husbards who waited impatiently at home for a late-returning spouse have passed; part of the revolution sweeping women into jobs. Peers now understand peers. Colleagues may be sometimes tempted to become lovers, but many more may settle for being friends than lovers.

And the two trainers discuss a few myths of man-woman attraction. For example, it is believed that a full-blooded heterosexual male is incapable of spending long periods of time with an attractive woman worker without making sexual advances. That's why it's considered risky for men and women to work alone together after office hours. Yes, men admit that they can't control the feeling, but deny that it leads them to hit on every attractive female within their orbit.

Similarly it is commonly believed that if work partners are sexually attracted, they can't possibly do the job effectively—their minds will be on sex rather than work. That's why a management often feels obliged to break a team where it suspects sexual attraction. But then, sexual energy if kept within bounds, can stimulate creativity and work drive.

"The belief that men and women can't be friends comes from another era in which women were at home and men were in the workplace, and the only way they could get together was for romance," explains Linda Sapadin, Ph.D., a noted psychologist in New York. "Now they work together and have sports interests together and socialize together." Of course, it's tricky—society has long singled out romance as the prototypical male-female relationship. And the reality that physical attraction could suddenly enter the equation of cross-sex friendship uninvited is always lurking in the background.

The obstacles may seem numerous and formidable, yet male-female friendship is becoming not only a possibility but also a necessity. If men and women are to work, play and co-exist in modern society, researchers believe that men and women must learn to understand and communicate with each other. To Kathy Werking, author of *We're Just Good Friends* (Guilford, 1997), "of pairs that do face the question of lust, those who decide early on to bypass an uncertain romantic relationship are more likely to have an enduring friendship".

Happily men and women are also becoming more androgynous as their societal roles become more similar. Men are more willing to display feminine characteristics, and women are a lot more willing to admit to traditionally masculine characteristics, like assertiveness. Some studies show that men and women categorized as androgynous have twice the number of cross-sex friends.

Whatever the challenges of male-female friendship, researchers agree that to succeed as friends, both genders have to openly and honestly negotiate exactly what their relationship will mean. If sex is part of the problem, addressing it explicitly is deemed the best strategy.

How relevant is the "new relationship" to our conditions is hard to say. It could be made out that our social, cultural and work scenario isn't identical with the Western. Yet human beings everywhere are the same. With growing interaction between sexes in the country's modern workplaces, the phenomenon of male-female relationship therein calls for study and understanding; it would do no good to ignore it or push it under the carpet.

Workplace Romance

Workplace, they say, is the best venue to meet a life partner. You can get to know one another unobtrusively, observe each other under stress, and so gain a fairly good idea of a person's character.

In fact, some studies suggest that workplace is already becoming the prime meeting ground where people find their mates—next only to matrimonial ads and marriage websites. The trend towards later marriage has also meant more unmarried people in workplaces.

In one MSNBC.com Office Sex and Romantic Survey in USA, a 2002 online poll, two-thirds of over 30,000 respondents admitted to a lot of flirtation going on in their workplace. Married employees are as likely to flirt back as singles ones if they think it's all in fun.

In various surveys on this subject it came to light that people were more forthcoming on Web than on telephone, about their affairs in office, because the former mode offered greater anonymity. And it came out that there was a substantial element of underreporting, especially of embarrassing or incriminating behaviour such as sexual activity in office premises.

Of course, millions of workers don't seek or accept office romances; they do their work and go home.

Yet flirtation in office is now widely prevalent, and there are clear indications of this being on the rise. People take pains to look good at the workplace, more so women. For single employees workplace is the best—sometimes the only place—to dress attractively. And manners displayed in office between the sexes are usually one up on those displayed by marital partners.

The daily physical proximity between sexes in shared work can trigger sexual attraction. Gender segregation in offices is declining. Another factor favouring sexual attraction among colleagues is the fact of their being of the same age, similar socio-economic background, similar values and similar aspirations.

Many corporate managements, even government departments, frown upon office romance. And there are some valid reasons for it.

Office romances can lead to accusations of favouritism or retaliation in case of a breakup. Even otherwise affairs among staff breed unwelcome gossip and distraction from work.

Worker morale nosedives when bosses indulge in flagrant favouritism while enjoying sexual favours from subordinates. Women exploiting their sexuality for service gains reap particular resentment. In this game, some attractive women can also be falsely accused of sleeping their way up when it was their merit alone that earned them quicker promotion.

Despite the widespread prevalence of office romance and its potential damage to work and worker morale, very few companies are in a position to frame clear guidelines and policies to cover various aspects of this complex human phenomenon. At best they put out instructions that prohibit sexual relationships between supervisors and subordinates. There is the emerging consensus that dating up or down the reporting line—dating your boss or dating someone who reports to you—is a bad idea. There has been the recent known case of Boeing firing CEO Harry Stone when his affair with a subordinate embarrassed the firm.

Some companies operate what's called the 'the disclosure policy'. Persons involved in an office romance are required to disclose it to selected supervisors in secrecy.

The manager can then determine whether it's realistic to keep the involved individuals working closely together or whether it makes more sense to move them apart, or even ask one of them to seek job elsewhere.

But this disclosure policy has its own critics. People are not sure whether the person to whom the affair is disclosed will respect the confidence reposed in him or her. The disclosure obligation gets all the more complicated where individuals are engaged in extramarital affairs or homosexual or lesbian relationships. The crucial step is to establish a non-judgmental climate, where employees are guaranteed that their disclosure will be revealed only to the few with the need to know, who will again keep it in strict confidence.

With increasing number of women in our offices, the incidence of office romance is bound to rise, even when our social, cultural and work scenario isn't identical with the Western. Yet human beings everywhere are the same. The phenomenon of office romance would call for greater study and attention by our company managements, even government departments.

Working Women: Beauty a Boon or Bane

An German woman has complained in court that she was discriminated against on account of her beauty. She, a stunner in looks, was rejected for a managerial job in a major corporation. She alleges that the senior corporation executives interviewing her—a group of half a dozen men and women—harboured a prejudice about beautiful women that they couldn't be mentally sharp.

Is beauty becoming a handicap in workplace? One isn't sure whether the complainant will be able to prove her point, but her grievance is not as frivolous as it sounds.

The trouble starts with defining beauty itself. Is it something that only exists in the eye of the beholder? Is beauty all physical or a subtle mixture of the physical and mental? Will it be more appropriate to use the word "attractive" instead of "beautiful"?

In her bestselling book, *The Beauty Myth*, Naomi Wolf argues that there is no such thing as a quality called beauty that "objectively and universally exists". Anyway, previously it was the province of poets and writers to describe beauty. And of plastic surgeons and cosmetic companies to enhance it. But now scientists have joined in to answer the question: what constitutes beauty?

Donald Symons, an anthropologist, proposes that beauty is averageness—the average values of the features of faces in a human population. According to him, evolutionary pressures operate against the extremes of the population—say, persons with extra long noses or protruding chins. Thus there is selection pressure to find average features attractive.

Another research group—Perrett, May and Yoshikawa—is of the view that beauty is a combination of average facial features with certain distinctively attractive ones such as lighter-than-average unblemished skin and full lips, things that distinguish the owner from others.

Devendra Singh, a psychologist in Texas University, studied the waist-to-hip ratio of *Playboy* playmates and Miss America contest winners over the past 60 years. She found that both the playmates and Miss Americas had a constantly lower WHR (narrow waist, full hips) than average. She doesn't blame skin magazines for swaying male preference toward the more shapely of the feminine gender. Men, in fact, have been specially evolved to recognize the hourglss curves of a woman's waist and hips, as such a shape presents superior potential for bearing their progeny.

One has, however, to admit that notwithstanding the recent intervention of scientists, the concept of beauty continues to elude definition.

Coming back to working women, there are certain callings in which beauty is surely a boon, often an essential requisite. The obvious ones are those of film and theatre stars. And so also in various entertainment and service fields: singers, dancers, acrobats, air hostesses, receptionists, waitresses, call girls, and so on—an ever lengthening list. Even in sports and athletics, looks are a help. Sabitini drew more spectator cheers than Navratilova.

Yet a certain kind of beauty can have a curious impact, possibly prove a liability in work. Though many men are affected by female beauty in a positive way, some others may get disconcerted by it and react with hostility.

It surely affects women in an organization, who may see female beauty as threatening. An uncommonly beautiful woman is viewed with suspicion. Will she derive unfair advantage in the job by attracting the attention of men, who still, by and large, run the business of the world? Will her looks help her with the organization's clients or otherwise contribute to her success? Such a woman will be carefully watched. And anything on her part which could be construed as flirtation or even an indeterminate discouragement to male advances, would soon form the subject of office gossip.

In the workplace, more so in our conditions, there is also the side issue of beautiful women suffering greater sexual harassment than their less attractive sisters. And this can create its own stress and problems. That way, even beautiful boys encounter problems that their less endowed brethren don't.

A truly beautiful woman faces another handicap in work; she is often perceived as dumb. And this perception can be damaging for entry or promotion into high-class jobs. Apologists may make out that such an impression is not entirely off the mark. Stunningly beautiful women may not have been called upon to exert much to develop their skills or intellect; they are often able to get from men what they want—let alone getting married to rich or powerful men.

Of course, ugliness in women proves a far more serious handicap than in men. They have to work much harder to win approval or recognition. Surely there is a strong case for a reduction of this bias; something that feminists have been asking for years.

But, ironically enough, the work situation can be unfair to beautiful women too; they still tend to be treated superficially by men. Somehow men continue to think that brain and glamour do not mix well. No wonder, women in high places in politics and other public spheres are often underplaying their physical attractiveness to counter the prejudice. Hillary Rodham Clinton, for one, underplays her physical charm; she wants to be known as a woman with a social and political mission than the pretty wife of an ex-President.

Beauty in Workplace

Men stare in a way women do not. Men have the habit of looking from woman to woman, never satisfied, always seeking young, lovelier women.

Anthropologists believe that men's habit of looking comes from their ancestors, who squatted for hours behind the bush on the African veldt, watching an animal on its way to the watering hole. Some ethologists go as far as to surmise that the "copulatory gaze" men give may well be embedded in their evolutionary psyche.

On the other hand, feminists maintain that women are free to do whatever they want with their bodies and dress; men are forbidden to react. Whatever be the provocation of an eye-catching dress or makeup, a male co-worker responding in a manner that makes the woman uncomfortable is guilty of sexual harassment. It is one thing men looking lewdly at women on the street; one could always walk away. But office is a confined place where feelings get intensified by the compression of space. And always the apprehension that the look/words/touch could happen again tomorrow, the next week.

We have brought the jungle into a fluorescent-lit space, leaving human animals to work out the spectrum of male/female interaction.

"Beauty is a marketing tool for Mother Nature's most basic product—reproduction—which in turn depends upon sexual attraction and sexual success," says Lionel Tiger, a noted anthropologist. Beauty is power not only in the marriage market, it's deemed a distinct advantage in workplace.

Colleagues of the beautiful woman know that every male around, client or employee, is vulnerable to her. The male boss is likely to help her, to rescue her if she does fail. She could get used to getting protected, even having her way. Anyway she encounters little experience of being criticised.

The scenario, however, may be changing as women press deeper into the workplace and compete with both men and women for jobs. It's already happening in some countries and in some professions. With the influx of women into responsible positions, men could also be tempted to employ beauty power to further their careers. The contest for the admiring eyes of the world may no longer remain women's exclusive turf.

The power of beauty will always be a factor in workplace; of course, more for women than men.

Sexual Harassment at Workplace

On August 13, 97 a bench of the Supreme Court headed by the Chief Justice gave a landmark judgement, elaborating that fundamental rights encompassed gender equality, including prevention of sexual harassment or abuse. The court enjoined on employers, both government and private, to ensure that women do not work in "hostile" work environment, whether caused by employees or outsiders.

The court defined sexual harassment as "such unwelcome sexually determined behaviour (whether directly or by implication) as physical contact and advances, a demand or request for sexual favours, sexually coloured remarks, showing pornography and any other unwelcome physical, verbal or non-verbal conduct of sexual nature." And it laid down that until government came up with the requisite legislation, these directives of the court would be binding and enforceable in law. There's also a move for special legislation to curb sexual harassment in the workplace.

All this is in line with the law and standards developed in the United States over the last two decades. Sexual harassment at workplace, more so lately in the armed forces, continues to be the subject of intense debate in that country. Something like 1,000 studies are published each year in reputable journals alone.

Sexual harassment in itself is not new; women have been harassed at work ever since they worked alongside men. Traditionally it took the shape of employers/superiors giving or promising something in exchange for sexual favours. Or, in reverse, some service loss was inflicted or threatened for withholding sexual favours. And this kind of sexual harassment still figures widely.

However with more and more women coming into workforce, other forms of sexual harassment by colleagues, even juniors, is on the rise: lecherous looks—"eyes ever fixed at chest level", sexual jokes and innuendoes, touching and rubbing, asking questions of personal nature, and so on. Possibly nurses and policewomen fare worse than others.

Sexual harassment has been likened to "the dripping tap"—small, mundane, accumulating. Many a man indulging in it stays blissfully unaware of its harmful effects, treating it more as a form of fun.

During the 1980s and 1990s, a new legal concept of sexual harassment took shape: the concept of a "hostile" work environment. This is essentially an off-shoot of the full equality extended to women vis-a-vis men at the work place. Any sexual harassment that makes a women employee feel uncomfortable, lose her concentration, lower her self-confidence, and otherwise interfere with her efficient functioning becomes illegal.

American courts now lay down that an office environment to be judged hostile would be from the standards of "a reasonable woman", and not "a reasonable person". And the aggrieved has not to prove a psychological injury; merely feeling uncomfortable could be enough. Even a male colleague can complain, on the score of being offended by the vulgar comments or gestures of his fellow males towards women in the workplace.

Yet the most important development of all: courts have set out in unambiguous terms the obligation of an employer to provide working conditions free of sexual harassment. Employers have even been held liable for the behaviour of non-employees—the mailman, the copier repairman, or a client. A number of restaurant owners have been successfully sued for not providing requisite protection to their waitresses from abuse by patrons.

Even the failure of an employer to properly investigate a complaint of sexual harassment has been assumed as tacit support to gender discrimination. Ordinarily a complaint must be acted upon within twenty-four hours of its being received.

Suits on sexual harassment have multiplied. More money is reportedly paid, prompted by threats of sexual-harassment suits than actual awards by courts. Insurance companies have started offering insurance cover against such suits. Consultants are busy holding seminars on the subject, and training material is selling briskly.

At one time Europeans were rather amused at the emerging American scene. To many of them, Americans were carrying the matter too far. For example, American teachers tend to think twice before touching a student. Even in physical education classes, many teachers will no longer correct students through a physical touch, getting other students to do it. Critics feared that carried to excess, it could make men avoid friendly banter with women colleagues. And this could also hurt the chances of marriages coming through between people at the same work place. "How can a man get anywhere with a woman without harassing her," some ask.

By now, however, the countries of EEC and several others have enacted similar laws and codes. Firms are designating senior members of the staff as "advisors" (and giving them some training about it) to monitor sexual harassment and hear informal complaints. Major firms often issue a policy paper on the subject. Many corporate houses now see sexual harassment as bad for business. Some companies have stopped holding office Christmas parties—occasions notorious for bingeing and unwanted flirtations.

School boards and university authorities are designating senior faculty members to recognize acts of sexual harassment and take necessary action to ensure that such instances are addressed "quickly, fairly and effectively". Oxford University, for instance, has 267 "Sexual Harassment Advisors" (SHAs) for its 93 departments. Every SHA must fill out an annual form, listing the cases dealt with.

By and large, these moves to combat sexual harassment at workplaces seem to be succeeding. Not that sexual harassment has vanished, but the atmosphere in most work places is getting more congenial for women.

The Indian scene has still to be surveyed in depth but there is every indication that the incidence of sexual harassment at workplaces is quite high. And it may well be on the rise with more women coming into the workforce. Only the modalities of sexual harassment can be somewhat different from what obtains in the West.

Everywhere women sexually harassed at work are hesitant to complain about it. But in India particularly, most victims still prefer to bear it in silence than to make a complaint. Evidently this stems from the fear of losing the job itself, getting transferred, or inviting other reprisals. In any case, a complaint can bring much unwelcome notoriety, even blame for any possible encouragement in the first place.

Section 354 of the Indian Penal Code (outraging the modesty of a woman) and section 509 of IPC (insulting the modesty of a woman) do serve their purpose but are not designed to afford specific relief from invidious day-to-day sexual harassment which takes place at work places.

The latest judgement of the Supreme Court now provides the needed lead. The court has opted for an approach that has been fairly successful elsewhere. It is now for the government to legislate in detail.

Possibly a time has also come to set up a special agency to monitor sexual harassment in workplaces. Maybe we can model it on the Equal Employment Opportunity Commission (EEOC) of America. EEOC directly hears complaints as well as issues guidelines from time to time on the subject of sexual harassment. And its guidelines are deemed as binding.

Women Business Travellers: Still More Hassles Than Help

With rising number of women travellers, particularly business travellers, the hotel and allied travel industry is reorienting its attitudes and practices towards women travelling on their own. The proportion of such guests in many metropolitan cities, including ours, could go up to 20 percent in coming years.

As security is the primary concern for women travellers, moves are afoot to set up special hotels exclusively for them. Zurich, for example, now has one; "Hotel Lady's First", a hotel for female guests only. The Hotel has been specially planned for business women who want a relaxing stay in Zurich.

And there are clear indications that premier Indian hotels wouldn't be far behind in redressing the security concerns. Maurya Sheraton, Delhi, and Oberoi in Mumbai have entire floors exclusively reserved for women. Others like Mumbai's Leela Kempinsky plan to demarcate a women's wing. Taj Residency, Bangalore has taken a lead in installing cameras that let a guest see on a bedside screen an image of the person ringing the doorbell.

Women travelling on business have faced particular problems: harassment, humiliation, loneliness, discomfort, danger. And things haven't improved to the extent called for, despite promises and declarations by the travel trade—more lip service than real change.

This is borne out in a survey conducted recently by Total Research Corporation of Princeton, New Jersey, reflecting the views of 217 frequent women travellers in the United States and 136 in the United Kingdom. Even though women account for a growing proportion of business travellers—40 per cent in USA and over 20 per cent in UK—they say they are still not getting a fair deal. They continue to face indifference and disdain, if not rampant sexism, by airline, hotel and car-rental staff. Women believe they receive inferior service because of their gender.

Many choose room service in hotels because they feel intimidated. If a woman is brave enough to come down to the restaurant, she often gets shoved behind a pillar. Even in room service by male waiters, you have to be dressed up. The Oberoi, Mumbai is said to have introduced the innovation of sending female butlers for serving such orders.

Personal safety being an overriding concern, a majority of respondents laid emphasis on airlines to make more secure arrangements for women travellers when planes are delayed or arrive very late at night. And hotels to pay more attention to giving women more secure rooms away from stair-wells and elevators. And they want airports to provide a security presence at taxi stands late at night.

In hotels, room design should be more woman-friendly. For example, there should be a socket within hairdryer's reach of a mirror and proper ironing facilities. And preferably a toiletry kit that includes sanitary pads and basic cosmetics. Softer towels could be another amenity.

For more information on hotels for women travellers, refer to www.redcarnation hotels.com)

Here are a few suggestions offered by experts, based on experience and study of problems encountered by women travellers.

In choosing a hotel, smaller is better; you want the staff to be familiar with guests and with you. The smaller the lobby, the more noticeable the loiterers.

Ask for a room near the elevators and away from any renovation work. Anyway ask for a room as far as possible from emergency exits.

The Please Make Up the Room sign tells everyone you're not there. Better call housekeeping instead.

Have your room key ready when you leave the lift, instead of fumbling for it in your purse at the door.

Stand near the elevator buttons with your back to the wall.

Make sure your room door has double locks. For extra security, better bring along a rubber doorstop.

Put expensive clothing on hangers under other garments. Thieves usually take what they see.

Lock valuables in the front-desk safe.

In public lavatories, use the corner cubicle.

On overnight flights, take your purse with you when you go to the lavatory.

Don't exit a taxi until you're sure you've arrived at your destination. Pay while still in the vehicle so that you can be sure you've received the proper change.

Stay close to your valuables when passing through airport security.

If you place your carry-on bag on the floor when sitting in a restaurant or other public area, put your foot through the strap; don't leave it loose.

Rent a mobile phone or bring your own.

When possible, park your rented car so you won't have to back out. It makes for a speedier departure.

On flights to new places, talk to female attendants and passengers on the plane about the safety of your destination.

On the pavement, keep you handbag away from the street side, and on escalators, away from the opposite ramp.

Study your map before going out. Once on the street, use a pocket-sized guidebook to avoid looking like a tourist. Ask the concierge to mark any dangerous areas on your map.

Dress down. And avoid jewellery. Even a chain that's fake gold can be ripped off your neck.

Be wary when getting off a bus, a train, or an escalator; that's when pickpockets tend to strike.

Carry photocopies of important documents.

Divide money for small and larger purchases so you don't have to expose a wad of money. Become familiar with foreign currency before you have to use it.

Have tips ready for porters and doormen.

Should a car start to follow you, turn immediately and walk the other way.

Cross over the road to avoid anyone threatening or suspicious.

Ask directions from families or women with children.

To make an outside restaurant reservation, better ask your concierge to do so, and have him say "Please take care of our guest, she's coming alone and will need a taxi home."

Trust your instincts. If you have any doubts about getting into a car with someone or meeting him somewhere, don't do it. And don't feel bad about not turning up to a prearranged meeting if you've had second thoughts.

You may find it useful to wear a wedding ring, even if you're not married. Or carry photos of a scary-looking "boyfriend".

Avoid eye contact with strangers. Wearing sunglasses should do the trick.

Plan any journey in terms of daylight hours.

Be careful about disclosing where you are staying.

If groped on public transport, you may wish to draw attention of other passengers to the fact—loudly.

"The art of travelling is learning to behave like a chameleon," said a noted woman traveller. "Blending into the background is not only a prerequisite to understanding and observing a different culture, it also keeps you out of trouble."

For women, dress is the first line of defence and the most immediate symbol of respect. How you dress can be construed as camouflage or an invitation; it can make you one of the crowd or a moving target.

11

Working Women and Home

Working Women under Pressure of Time

Meera is a busy executive in a multinational pharmaceutica!company. She's a mother of two kids—a girl of 7 and a boy of S. Her husband is a high official in Delhi Administration.

Apparently Meera is hooked on a high-speed life-style. All day long, almost without pause, the slim 3S-year-old races through her crowded office assignments. She schedules herself to the maximum—sometimes right down to the quarter hour. And she's ever trying to accomplish more and more, with better efficiency and in less time.

And nearly the same way it continues when she's back home after a long, nerve-raking drive. At home she tries to do everything to perfection whether it's the care of children, relationship with her husband, and the upkeep of the house. It comes to looking after so many things big and small, let alone her own essential grooming to attend to.

All this means living in the fast lane; she's always short of time. Pushing her speedometer needle to the limit, often doing several tasks simultaneously. In fact she now finds it almost impossible to unwind—as slowing down leaves her somewhat bored, besides feeling guilty about chores lying unfinished. Even on vacation, she is seen keeping a checklist, and following a tight little schedule.

Psychologists are generally agreed that persons like Meera who are operating in overdrive and are under continued pressure of time, can develop dramatic mood swings and emotional difficulties such as anger and anxiety, and physical symptoms like constant fatigue, insomnia, and a sharp weight loss or gain. Some sufferers take to escapist drinking, over-dependence on nicotine or caffeine—the very things that are proven detrimental to the body's ability to adjust to stress. A working woman's never-ending tasks in pursuit of her career as well as keeping a perfect home can even kill the spontaneity of sex life. Years of continued stress, ever-hurrying to finish one's tasks, and the nagging anxiety of being found wanting can bring out a condition that's called burn-out.

And psychologists feel that it is harder for women to slow down than it is for men. Men often expect women to do more than them—and women expect themselves to do more too. Men with the hardest office jobs are often seen relaxed at home. This luxury is not easily available to their working wives. Even where the husband shares some household duties, the ultimate responsibility and coordination needed for running a home mostly falls on the wife.

What's then the way out for women like Meera with too much to do and never enough time? Such persons perforce must get better organized. They have to apply strategies that by saving time get them the control of the clock.

One basic time-management tool is to make To Do lists on paper rather than trying to keep them in one's head. A daily list can be an important instrument for keeping track of what is to be done or of what is to be got done. This lets the brain be free to be creative. And trivial tasks don't push out the worthwhile ones.

Another strategy is to make use of time "pockets". Things like phoning up the kids at home when you have a few moments break in office. Or, using bits of time when waiting for someone, for things like catching up on reading. And advance planning helps like making sure that the clothes you'll wear over the week are ready and ironed during the preceding weekend.

In actual life, a good deal of one's time is taken up by mundane matters. These have a tendency to take over, crowding out real priorities like fun time with children. Every time you begin a task, ask yourself: "How important is this?" Some may turn out to be of low priority but we keep on doing out of habit. Anyway you should be willing to let some things slide, even when you have the benefit of competent house help. For instance, you compromise a little on the quality of furniture dusting. The time saved could be diverted to talking to family members. A modern household—despite all its time-saving devices—throws up a lot of routine work.

Of course, the biggest potential time-waster is office chitchat. Such conversations could be kept short and sweet. While passing a colleague in the office corridor, a nice nod without stopping should often be enough. And if you keep a well-organized, uncluttered office, you save yourself much precious time lost in locating papers.

An important point to realize is that it's productive to relax. At least it rewards you with feeling refreshed. The idea is not to feel guilty if you aren't upholding your responsibilities round the clock. You need slowing down consciously to lend balance to your life. Here are a few tried tips to slow down.

Take your watch off on some weekends. Trick yourself into thinking there's no tyranny of time.

Once home from work, it helps to change your clothes; a symbolic act, signalling the close of the working day.

If you can manage, take a small nap after your midday meal. Even fifteen minutes of it can do you a world of good.

Caring for a pet can be quite calming—the time spent feeding it and playing with it.

Light exercise is a great relaxation and so also listening to music. Do something physical like taking a walk.

Give yourself a break even amidst your busiest days. A few moments of daydreaming now and then or occasionally looking out of the window.

Harden yourself to saying no sometimes. Acceding to the wishes of everybody around can knock away chunks of your time.

Same-Company or Rival-Company Couples

Vohras are working in the same software company as programmers. In fact Raj and Ritu were working in the very jobs before they got married. Now they form a same-company couple.

Of late there has been a rising curve in numbers of same-company couples. A firm initially recruiting a couple is uncommon but people working in the same place come together, fall in love, get married. And these marriages are mostly between persons holding equivalent positions, between persons having similar social and educational backgrounds.

Same-company couples could confer some advantages on the company: greater co-operation and work-sharing between them. Yet they also give rise to a few administrative complications for the management.

Take performance appraisal. Two employees joined in matrimony are rarely clones. One is generally more competent, more astute, more useful than the other. Appraisals, sensitive placings, and raises will be different for each.

But any differentiation at company level can make one partner disgruntled, more so if the person left behind is the husband. Even otherwise, one dissatisfied partner can sour the relations of both with the company.

Working in government is somewhat different. The employer is rather distant, impersonal, and bound by fairly rigid service rules. In companies, especially of medium size, the establishment's appraisal is much more sharply focussed.

There's the added complication if one partner has to submit work to the other. Managers are not sure—and co-workers have their own fears—whether the supervisory role of one partner over the other will be carried out without fear or favour. Even a meeting to clear the air doesn't often help.

Time was when employees, like soldiers, moved whenever and wherever the company wanted to send them. Getting someone to move anywhere these days is a formidable task. Even non-working-wife couples resist displacement. Those with children must seek out appropriate schools for them.

Transferring one half of a dual-career couple can meet with far greater resistance.

All office politics rests on the assumption that each person thinks and acts as an individual. What makes it difficult for couples is that they are often treated as one unit. This can be particularly frustrating for the pair when it comes to information gathering.

Co-workers are usually hesitant to tell one partner anything they don't want the other partner to know. The assumption is that at home all pillow talk is work-related. This is largely a false assumption; couples talk of other things most of the time.

There was this IAS couple of the same seniority serving the same state (quite a few IAS are now marrying batchmates). The wife happened to hold the post of Appointments Secretary. Colleagues couldn't help wondering whether her husband would come to know of various transfer proposals in advance, even learn about his Confidential Roll kept in her custody. In real life, his chances of becoming privy to his Roll through his wife were minimal. Yet the couple couldn't escape a suspicious air about it.

What causes this paranoia? Partly it is because of the fiercer competition among employees these days for promotions and places. People who used to ignore office politics 20 years back, now sift through every action of the management, looking for hidden meaning.

Couples working in rival companies face another set of problems. Luckily such pairing is still the exception.

Here are couples who stay in the same house, sleep in the same bed, eat at the same table, but go out every day to work for companies that are sworn and bitter enemies, such as Pepsi Cola and Coca Cola.

For some, especially those in higher positions, the situation can be quite stressful. So couples work out their own coping strategies.

Often a ground rule is operated that anything said within the house will be just between them. Banning all talk of work is simply impracticable; human beings are human beings. Something will slip, or they'll say something. There's no point their saying, "We're not going to talk of anything related to work." What they must agree is whatever they talk about has not to go outside the house.

You got a taste of this complex situation in *Santa Barbara* when Mason and Julia—a live-in couple—were representing contesting parties in court. Mason was the lawyer for the couple that wanted their child back from the surrogate mother, while Julia defended the paid mother for keeping the child herself.

The case gave rise to many a heated argument in the house. Mason even took an unfair advantage by glancing through Julia's defence papers left unattended in the living room.

No wonder, companies are a little chary of sharing all their secrets with an employee whose spouse is working with a rival company. This is something that doesn't do justice to rival-company couples but that's possibly the price they have to pay for the unusual situation in which they find themselves. They have to display extra loyalty and zest to win the trust of their employers.

One is again not sure whether work and living can be kept in watertight compartments. To that extent, marriage partners working at senior levels in feuding companies, run an added risk of strained relations. Anyway, it isn't a very promising situation for a harmonious marriage—unless leavened by a good sense of humour in both parties.

Wives of Successful Men

Kamla invariably experienced a feeling of rising unease and a wildly thumping heart whenever she was obliged to preside over some social function; her husband the Vice-Chairman of an automobile manufacturing company. And she bordered on panic when playing hostess to a group of his foreign business visitors.

Kamla dreaded the prospect of making the customary speech at any award presenting ceremony. And at business dinners, she worried no end about her inadequacy in making appropriate conversation. Now such occasions were getting more frequent with the opening up of the automobile industry and its growing globalization.

What to say of men, she found other wives often better informed about business matters, let alone those who had careers of their own. No wonder, Kamla hunted for excuses not to participate in corporate functions and was mercifully relieved if one of her ruses worked. "A child was ill." "I was too tired."

She was educated all right—a graduate. However, on marriage, she had principally concentrated on her home and bringing up the three children, while her ambitious husband Harish, was busily climbing up the corporate ladder.

Like many older wives, Kamla could have resigned herself to a quiet existence, allowing Harish to lead a separate, independent life outside the home. But such withdrawal, she felt, spelled defeat, a sure recipe for self-loathing. Wasn't it a sin to waste days of God's beautiful life in self-hate? And then the lurking fear, Harish may bring in a "trophy" wife—a smart young belle brimming with self-confidence and highly supportive of his career. This would sum up Kamla's fate in one phrase: *she didn't keep up.*

So, at forty, she took up the challenge of an executive wife. She began to study other people at all the social functions she attended. Watching and listening, she learned quite a few fascinating things. For example, she found that the best hostesses always appeared to be genuinely interested in their guests—all of them. They had a way of encouraging their guests to talk about themselves, and made mental notes regarding their guests' interests and comments. And then recalling those remarks during future meetings. It proved an instant conversation starter.

Life, it became apparent to her, was all about our approach to people—making friends, knowing business acquaintances and building business relationships. And here, some strategies worked surprisingly well: always a smile when being introduced, asking questions about others' lives and interests, and always listening intently to what was being said.

As Kamla gained in confidence as an executive wife—confidence breeding more confidence, she also sought professional advice on how to become the powerful influence behind her successful husband. She shed some weight and changed her hair style. Even started taking interest in the golf talk of her husband and his playing cronies. Her transformation within a few years from a diffident, poorly informed housewife to an effectively helpful mate in business surprised everybody, more so Harish.

Of course, if you happen to be married to a top man in business or administration or even politics, it is your choice as to how you are going to deal with it. Many wives have rejected the idea of being anything beyond housewives. A few others may be too busy pursuing their own careers. Some husbands actually want it that way while others accept the situation and endeavour to deal with all their official activities outside the home. Many couples have made this way of life work quite well, after having discussed the same fully between themselves.

No one can quantify the worth of a corporate wife. New style bosses believe the right wife creating the right ambience can genuinely oil the wheels of business. Whereas business deals were often clinched between men only, wives are now required to entertain and woo potential and existing clients. Cynics say the present trend to include wives is simply a way of keeping the ladies happy.

However, if you decide to become part of your husband's business life, then it is far better to make this decision early and to tackle the situation head-on. Nowadays, with a few exceptions, most well-known, high-flying executives have wives who back them all the way. They are well-presented, well informed and act as perfect hostesses. They could well miss a few desirable things such as a relaxed home life or some vocation of their own, but then the rewards of an executive wife are great. Being a corporate wife is wonderful! It can be exciting, alluring, glamorous, challenging, or powerful. There is travel, entertainment, and the excitement of meeting new people and solving novel problems.

In this age of fast-moving, complex business, it is difficult for many wives—especially those devoted primarily to raising children—to catch up with their husbands' work. They quickly get out of touch and this obviously results in the gap between them and their husbands becoming much wider—sometimes to the extent of couples drifting apart. Housewives married to top executives are waking up to the challenges they must face.

Her role is no longer merely ceremonial. She must be able to tell time in important world cities, have some idea of exchange rates, feel comfortable in foreign cultures and mix well with corporate hierarchy.

She is expected to know a good deal about her husband's company, even when she doesn't work alongside him. If called upon to entertain company's clients, she takes care to inform herself beforehand about their basic particulars. It has to be understood that no business-social function is for entertainment purposes alone. It is always a public relations exercise designed to promote goodwill, with the eventual aim of increasing business.

It must be said that a good percentage of younger wives are now taking the initiative and are going ahead with being a "good company wife". They realise that if they have not got the required skills already, these can be learned. Here professional help can minimize the travails of trial and error.

Has the "New Man" Arrived?

Has the "new man" arrived? Of late, the media has been talking a great deal about such a creature, or what it terms "complete man".

The idea is that, basically in response to the feminist movement, often coupled with a two-career marriage, men have changed. They have become more what women want them to be–more sensitive, more caring, more understanding, more intimate, more involved in household work and childcare.

Surely many men, by themselves or in groups, have started questioning the values they were brought up with. They are asking what it means to be a man and, more precisely, what kind of a man they want to be.

Yet it would be closer to the mark to say, not that the "new man" has arrived but rather that men today are struggling with a situation far more complex and confusing than it was for their fathers and grandfathers. Men are subject to new pressures and messages, many of which conflict with the traditional rules and values.

Yes, a man should still be strong, but this should be balanced with sensitivity. Too much show of strength would earn him the term *macho* (now used in a derogatory than an admiring sense). And a man has to be careful about the sensitivity part, as well. Too much of it can label him a weakling.

Yes, a man should be successful at work, but somehow also find time to relate to his mate and help a lot in household chores. Exactly where the time and energy will come from to carry out all these tasks is his headache.

Yes, a man should still be a forceful lover; women don't want a wimp in bed. But in addition, he should be tender and considerate, willing to do what is needed for her satisfaction.

Yes, a man should still take the sexual initiative, even persevere if he encounters some feigned resistance. But he should be awfully alert to a genuine rebuff. To take particular care, lest a sexual invitation he makes is construed as sexual harassment.

Today's man is caught in a peculiar bind because the very definition of familial love has changed. In the past, what husbands did—working to support the family, abstaining from chasing other women, helping at home in a few selected tasks commonly reserved for men—was accepted as showing their love. Now men are expected to show love the way women do, by sharing feelings and talking in a personal way.

Even the definition of sex is on its way of becoming feminized. Marital sex is no longer some impulsive, quick sex; it should be of adequate duration, with its component of foreplay and after-play.

This is not to say that men have a rougher time than women. Both sexes suffer in their own ways in today's world. Yet the modern man faces a unique new situation.

"Don't be a sissy", is the important socialization message boys receive from early years. To be *sissy* is deemed much worse for a boy than for a girl to be a *tomboy*. Since females of all ages are the softer ones—people who express feelings, who cry—boys do their best to do the reverse; they suppress their softer side. Indeed they learn to believe femaleness as something strange and inferior.

One result is the development of a habit of not taking women seriously. This inability to take women seriously can cause much friction in adult life, especially in marital life.

It is assumed that girls will grow up to be women simply by getting older. But boys need something special to become men. Manhood is conditional; having the right genitals is necessary but not sufficient. "No man was born man; you earned your manhood provided you were good enough, bold enough," says Norman Mailer.

For boys, combativeness rules their life, whether it's sports, fights, studies or sex, as if everywhere their masculinity is at stake.

Because of the emphasis on strength and self-reliance, men have trouble admitting to unresolved personal problems. If he acknowledges his confusion or fear and asks for help, it's taken as something wrong with him; he's not as tough as he ought to be.

No wonder, men avoid acknowledging their worries to their mates. They are slow to admit to illness and other physical problems, and even slower to admit to emotional distress. Quite a few choose to drown their feelings in alcohol.

One can see enough indications of the "new man" in the offing. Yet he's taking his own time to "arrive".

How Independent are Independent Women?

They can't possibly have all the prerogatives of being a woman and all the privileges of being a man at the same time.

—Mary McCarthy, the noted novelist

Roop Gupta, 42, heads a leading chartered accountancy firm in the capital. She had joined her father's company after being articled, and took over on his demise. Through sheer hard work and promotional skills, she has built a lucrative practice.

Roop is fully focussed on her career and wouldn't dream of giving it up for anything, and that goes for marriage, too. And she's well-nigh reconciled to missing the gratification of motherhood.

She has matured into a well-adjusted, strong-minded, independent woman. Seemingly her life is the model of today's female independence. She lives alone, pays her own bills, and runs a large establishment at office and at home.

Yet, behind this evident independence lurks a feminine yearning to be protected and provided for. Talking to her mother she admits to her fantasies of a strong man— superior in career and personality—to be around. Someone to take her out on holiday trips, and occasionally to a dinner where—in the old-fashioned feminine role—she can just relax. Someone to extend sympathy and support when things go wrong at work or elsewhere.

It's not a question of money—she has enough—but to have the reassuring feel of being protected and provided for. And in her mind, he has to be someone with a higher level of education and achievement.

Women like Roop want to be independent, and still find an element of eroticism in male dependence, as if they never really escaped the traditional female role. They want to be equal to men and yet crave for the protective presence of a "strong" man.

Take another situation, where a career woman happens to be married to a man manifestly less successful than her. In western countries such cases are numerous. And the trend is set to rise. Women are nearly matching men in higher education, even overtaking them in several specialties. Again the traditional areas of male employment—factories and manufacturing units—are shrinking, while new jobs are coming up in female-friendly fields such as information technology industries and services.

A similar pattern is likely to emerge in those developing, modernizing countries where women have access to higher education, careers, and jobs. And India is one such one.

Career women married to men much less successful are heir to their own emotional hang-ups. Most of them were brought up in homes where they saw their fathers at the helm of affairs. He was the one who paid for things, wrote cheques, and settled restaurant bills. He was the one relied upon to make major decisions. This model of masculinity could well be imprinted in their minds from early girlhood.

No wonder many a woman makes out, she wouldn't want to go out with a man who is palpably less successful than her because he would feel uncomfortable. But it's not only he who would feel uncomfortable; she herself would feel uncomfortable. Somewhere deep in the irrational layers of their psyche, they still think of the man as the prime breadwinner, the obvious one to pick up the tab. Indeed I know of a woman who guiltily slips money to her husband under the restaurant table so that he can pretend to pay for the dinner.

Aarti Bhan at 31 is a senior executive in an advertisement multinational. As a girl she couldn't have been luckier—the privileged member of a new generation. Affluent home, fond parents, an eye-catching Kashmiri complexion, 5-ft7 with stunning looks. Excellent education: Jesus and Mary Convent School, St Stephen College, a degree in commercial art from the famed Perkins School in New York. After a 5-year stint with a Manhattan advertisement company, she's hard at work at her Delhi job.

In her early 20s, the parents had been besieged by tempting marriage proposals. But Aarti was unwilling; her dream was not the romance of making a brilliant marriage, but the romance of making a brilliant career—the acquisition of an executive title and all that went with it.

At 33, Aarti sports a winsome figure. Attractive, high-profile men, both in business and social contacts, seek her company. But few of these men are looking for a lifelong mate;

in fact most of them are already married or dubbed as confirmed bachelors.

That way the marital scene changed adversely for Aarti in the last ten years, despite her remarkable gains in status, self-confidence, and poise. Men's feelings of beauty, it seems, are exceptionally well tuned to the age of fertility, and that for the human female peaks in the early 20s. No surprise, between 1953 and 1990, the average age of *Playboy* centrefold models—selected solely for sexual appeal—was 21.3 years. At 21, Aarti was a prized catch. At 33, successful men still seek her company but rarely for marriage. Aarti is looking for someone special. But to her dismay she finds that most high-profile men she comes across are nearly the same—the same self-centred blokes looking for a good time minus commitment.

At times, Aarti feels the unfairness of it all. By the time high-status single men and women reach their mid-thirties, their marriage prospects begin to diverge. Men's career achievements enhance their marriage market and increase the pool of prospective mates, because men tend to marry younger women of similar or lesser education, and here the supply is large. For women, opposite is the case: high-status women tend to seek husbands of higher levels of achievements, and this reduces the pool of eligible mates. For men, age is no barrier to attracting women. For women, age starts operating against them.

Of late, several books, both novels and self-help guides, have come out highlighting the downturn in marriage prospects of high-status American women in their thirties. These are mostly written by the women themselves: Amy Sohn's *Run Catch Kiss*, Kate Christensen's *In the Drink*, Laura Zigman's *Animal Husbandry*, and *The Girls' Guide to Hunting and Fishing.*

Girls graduating from elite colleges move into Manhattan seeking high-class careers. They go through a gruelling period of apprenticeship in order to establish themselves. Those lucky enough to succeed, often find to their dismay that their marriage prospects start shrinking steadily as they advance into their thirties.

12

Men and Women, How Alive, How Different

Men and Women: How Alike or Different!

Of all the things we do not know, possibly the most significant one: we do not know whether men and women are essentially different or fundamentally the same.

And this uncertainty persists despite all the research and writing, discussion and debate on the subject. With men's power over women deeply rooted and increasingly challenged, the intellectual activity generated by this gender issue has been furious. Still we do not know whether men and women are variations of a common category or very different creatures.

Some make out that sex is biological but gender is cultural: it's the upbringing that is responsible for accentuating the gender difference. "Once gender is ascribed," says Sandra Lipsitz Bem in *The lenses of Gender* (Yale University Press, 1994), "the social order constructs and holds individuals to strongly gendered norms and expectations." People come to live within their gendered roles; "the ultimate carrier of oppression is the psyche of the oppressed". Thus the subordination of women becomes an intrinsic part of the social order.

Indeed, some feminist writings delight in picturing a utopia where gender will wither away, the way state was to wither away in Marxism. A world where, "people of different sexes would no longer be culturally identified with different clothes, different social roles, different personalities or different sexual and affectional partners any more than people with different-coloured eyes or different-sized feet are now."

Whether a genderless world would be equally interesting is a matter of personal taste. Even some women who gain from gendered set-up may prefer the traditional order. Anyway, a world without gender markings can be a dull one; it would strip us of our ability to judge others by their identity signals.

The debate whether men and women are alike or different isn't merely an academic one or just amusing talk. Its outcome can yield a better understanding of many a socio-sexual phenomenon such as sexual harassment, marital violence, rape, infidelity, or women's share of prestigious jobs.

In this context, the role played by evolutionary psychology would be hard to ignore. We need some understanding of the psychological differences that evolved between men and women over the ages.

Take the sphere of status and hierarchy. During evolution, high male status seems to have expanded sexual access to females, as it does in many species of animals. Given this distinctively male link between social achievement and genetic proliferation, it is plausible to assume that millions of years of evolution would endow males with a distinctive thirst for power.

Or, take the "double standard", the much reviled male hypocrisy over promiscuity. This is not to say that the double standard is morally right or justified. But it appears to be a legacy of natural selection.

Males, in species after species, are almost always the wooers. Females—with the rarest of exceptions—are less eager than males. The female, who has to invest much time and energy in birthing and rearing of offspring, is sure to appraise carefully the quality of the aspiring mate.

In contrast, for a male reproduction can be frequent and low-cost affair. There is no reason for evolution to have instilled in the male mind an aversion to coerced sex with women. For sizing sheer sexual (not marital) opportunities, males are on average much less choosy; men are genetically primed to disseminate their sperm. As a general rule, the sex that can reproduce more often will typically be the randier sex. Contraceptives have surely short-cicuited this logic, but we are stuck with the minds the logic shaped.

Andrea Dworkin sums the situation in her own inimitable style. "A man wants what a woman has—sex. He can steal it (rape), persuade her to give it away (seduction), rent it (prostitution), lease it over long term (marriage in the United States), or own it outright (marriage in most societies)." While men may not be planning their pursuits in this conscious manner, the description is a fairly apt analysis of the emotions men feel.

Surely men are not beyond cultural improvement. Yet "men as a class are moral cretins"; evolution has bred in them things like lust and jealous rage.

A man's jealous rage at the promiscuity of his mate has an evolutionary logic. The more promiscuous the wife, the less likely that the children in which man invests his time and energy are in fact carrying his genes. The logic isn't the same for women, since the children they give birth to always carry their genes.

Men lust for loose women; these are easier to get. But men want to marry ones with good reputations—the women in

Penthouse aren't women a man would want to marry. No wonder, the average woman resists being labelled "easy" regardless of her actual degree of promiscuity. She takes extraordinary care to guard her reputation, as it's crucial to her marriage prospects.

Of course, anything "natural" doesn't mean it's unchangeable. Men in many cultures now don't murder or maim their mate for infidelity. We human beings are a malleable species.

How Men and Women Shop!

Do men and women shop differently?

The conventional wisdom on male shoppers is they don't fancy this activity, which is why they don't do much of it. And, even when they buy, they rarely shop. Women always shop when they buy, and are estimated to buy 80 percent of everything that is sold.

It's usually a struggle for a woman to get the husband as patient company when she shops. Most exchanges between men and women shopping together are more or less bad-tempered. No wonder, a husband often stands outside and prefers watching people passing by than goods in the shop. Big stores and shopping plazas are planning "creches—where men can be 'parked', have drinks, snacks and comfortable seats in front of a big-screen TV tuned to sports, while their women shop.

A recent field survey in UK indicates that shopping in crowded shopping stores raises stress levels of men to the point it's hazardous to their health.

"The peak levels were equivalent to emergency situations experienced by fighter pilots or policemen going into dangerous situations," says British psychologist David Lewis who made a study of men's stress levels at Christmas shopping.

Lewis sent three dozen men and women of different ages to stores with identical X-mas lists. Each shopper was accompanied by a researcher who kept recording the shopper's periodic blood pressure and heart rate. Even before they stepped out the front door, more than 70 percent of men started to show these symptoms. "For men even the thought of going shopping was enough to send stress levels soaring," concludes Lewis.

The stress levels for women who had brought their husbands along were much higher than those who went alone or with other female companions. Even those who brought their kids along recorded lower levels of stress than those accompanied by their husbands.

Women do have a greater affinity to what we think of as shopping—walking at a relaxed pace through stores, examining merchandise, comparing products and prices, interacting with sales staff, asking questions, trying things on, and ultimately making purchase. Even when shopping for the mundane, everyday necessities, where the shopping experience brings no particular pleasure, women tend to do it in a dependable, agreeable manner. Women take pride in their ability to shop prudently and well.

When a woman goes out shopping, she will buy something, usually for somebody else or for the "house". What makes women such heroic shoppers? The nature-over-nurture advocates make out that the prehistoric role of women as homebound gatherers of roots, nuts and berries, rather than roaming hunters of game, proves a biological inclination towards skillful shopping.

And when women weren't working outside, shopping gave them a good excuse to sally forth, to get away from the monotony and cares of housekeeping. With women increasingly joining the workforce, shopping is no longer the great escape. Indeed it's now something that must be crammed into tight spaces between job and commuting and home life.

Still shopping seems unchanged as a social, recreational activity for women. They like to shop with friends, egging each other on and saving each other from ill-advised purchases (one can't imagine two men setting off on a day hunting for the perfect bathing trunk). Studies show that when two women shop together, they often spend more time and money than women alone. They certainly out-shop and outspend women saddled with male companions, or even kids.

For many women there are psychological and emotional aspects of shopping that are just plain absent in men. Women tend to tally up coolly the pros and cons of every purchase. They can trudge from shop to shop looking for a bargain, placing little value on their time and energy. In fact they take pride in their ability to make the best possible purchase.

Possibly the ideal place to study female shopping behaviour is in front of the greeting cards rack. Women will devote quite a bit of time studying card after card—picking up, opening and reading—to find the one that speaks their hearts.

Shopping is actually exhausting work, but women are trained to it from infancy. Girls begin shopping before they have money to spend. Shopping is often presented to women as recreation and they fall for the cheat, Germaine Greer cautions.

Incidentally, any wife watching the family budget knows better than to send her husband to a shopping centre with kids. Men are particularly suggestible to the entreaties of children.

In buying clothes, women labour under a particular handicap vis-à-vis men. Men's clothing are designed to last a long time; women's clothing are almost obsolete from the time these are bought. And whereas few men are victims of fashion, all women are victims of it.

As shopping goes, men by comparison seem like loose cannons. They move appreciably faster than women through a store. Men spend less time looking, too. Often it's hard to get them to look at anything they hadn't intended to buy. They usually don't ask where things are, or any other questions, for that matter—they shop the way they drive.

You see a man impatiently move through a store to the section he wants, pick something up, and then almost abruptly, he's ready to buy. Men often forget their collar or waist size. Try to imagine a woman who doesn't know her brassier size. Impossible. And women generally don't buy lingerie without trying it on. But no man goes into a fitting room to try on underwear.

It's only at computer hardware and software purchasing that you see men spending time unhurriedly, or at music shops and stores dealing with car accessories, or at best bookshops.

Men and Women Laugh Differently

Men and women laugh differently. They laugh at different things, at different times, and even laugh at different elements in one joke.

While men excel in delivering punch lines, women's comic strength lies in telling humorous stories. Sometimes a woman telling a longish joke may even ask her husband to take over, to provide the punch line. And women are less likely than men to laugh at a situation where someone is hurt or embarrassed. To most women, humour occupies a different space emotionally and socially than it does for men.

The jollity and laughter of men gathered in select groups at bars and other congenial settings is proverbial; a sort of male bonding with people thumping backs and letting out guffaws. These guys tell jokes to amuse one another, but they also try to outdo one another. Not to come with another, better, dirtier joke is to these guys like not being able to come at all.

Laughter in the kitchen and girls' dorms is evidence of women's ability to joke and appreciate joking in an all-female group. Women even use comedy to narrate their experiences and so dilute the pain. And they commonly take to self-deprecating humour, instead of belittling someone else.

Women prefer to tell jokes to a group composed of other women—and often stop laughing when men join in. It is no surprise then, that men have thought women have very little sense of humour. They have certainly been privy to very little of it. Women could well tell smutty stories among themselves, but the sort of male competition for the sexually aggressive joke is absent.

In mixed-groups, it evolves into a more complex situation. "In cross-gender conversations, females laughed 126% more than their male counterparts, meaning that women tend to do most of the laughing while males tend to do most laugh-getting," says Robert R. Provine, a professor of psychology at the University of Maryland, Baltimore and author of the book *Laughter: A Scientific Investigation* (Viking Penguin, 2000). "Clearly women seek men who make them laugh, and men are eager to comply with this request . . . men were more interested in women who laughed heartily in their presence."

In the area of humour, as in many walks of life, women are expected to be passive and receptive than active and initiating. A woman is said to have a good sense of humour who laughs (but not too loudly) when a man makes a witticism or tells a good joke. Because of the power associated with the successful use of humour, the initiation of humour has become associated with other traditional masculine characteristics, such as aggressiveness, dominance and assertiveness. In fact it is deemed somewhat unfeminine for a girl to indulge overly in humour. "She's got a terrific sense of humour," has become a kind of shorthand for "physically unattractive".

One of the worst things that could be said about a girl is that she couldn't take a joke. But then what if a joke is in bad taste, sexually aggressive or plain "unfunny"? It may produce a nervous laugh—that particularly falsified response—to a non-laughable joke. Yet the joker tends to blame the non-laugher for making him uncomfortable.

Women also fake laughter for the same reason they sometimes fake orgasm—to make somebody else feel comfortable by pretending they're comfortable. The trouble is that it's nearly impossible to fake laughter convincingly, no matter how familiar we're with it through canned laughter on TV. Indeed it's easier to cry falsely than to laugh convincingly.

Another response commonly employed by women to a non-laughable male joke is to simply smile. In the general, all-purpose smile, you don't have to make direct eye contact with the speaker. In contrast, when you laugh with someone, the instinctive response is to look directly into the eyes of the person with whom you share that moment. You're connected.

The glazed smile is generic, the laugh is specific. You can smile at any time, keeping the expression in place under a number of circumstances. A good, hearty laugh is one of the most difficult things to manufacture if the genuine impulse is missing. A smile is much easier to manufacture because it is general, rather than specific, response.

A smile also remains ambiguous, and women have been taught to believe that there is strength in uncertainty. Mystery and elusiveness were all traditionally considered positive attributes of a woman. No wonder, the *Mona Lisa* with her elusive smile, is considered one of the greatest images of woman.

With the gains of feminism and increasing empowerment of women, things are also changing on the laughter front. The number of jokes at the expense of men has been burgeoning in recent years. Of course, women had been laughing at men for centuries, but only in private. Now women comics are doing it openly in talks and shows. And their women audiences are simply lapping it, splitting their sides laughing.

"I concentrate on men and what horrible bastards they are. I don't suppose I'll ever run out of material," says Jo Brand, a comedian in UK.

Again women high on the corporate ladder or public administration or politics are risking jokes in mixed-group settings. At one time it was the accepted wisdom that "wit and laughter in workplace can undermine a woman's career". That no longer holds good. Men and women in superior positions may well be converging in the area of laughter, but with women's humour still staying more playful than down-putting.

In a landmark study of the social functions of humour in the workplace, the psychologist Rose Laub Coser notes that jokes are told most frequently by those occupying a superior position in the hierarchy. These jokes are directed downward, made at the expense of those lower in status than the joker. The victims of these jokes do not respond by directing their own wit at those who had just kidded them, but they instead turn it either on those below them or interestingly, at themselves.

Do Men and Women Drive Differently?

Whether men and women act differently at workplace is being debated. But the two do act differently when at the wheel. Men and women seem to bring a differing perception to driving, even to the car itself. No wonder, if there's any time in married life when a couple are sure to have a row, it is with one of them driving and the other sitting alongside.

Possibly the best way to highlight the difference is to view the typical driving of one gender—particularly its failings—through the eyes of the other.

"My husband, otherwise a manageable man, turns a macho the moment he slides behind the wheel. To him, a car is a thrusting, aggressive tool for achieving road domination, cowing others into submission. Talks fondly of having a really powerful car someday.

Loves to overtake in daredevil manoeuvres. And takes it as a challenge if someone in front doesn't yield quickly enough. Mishaps are missed by inches, giving me a fright. But what worries me more; a hit may result in a fight. I'd be less tense if I sat in the back seat but he insists I sit in front—and witness his wizardly driving."

"Mine is all right except when he drives after an evening party. His sight, not too good at night, worsens with a few whiskies. I've actually to act as his co-pilot. Even tell him that the green light ahead was for the straight-going traffic, not for us turning right.

Any suggestion to hand over the wheel is simply brushed off. Men, it seems, harbour a deep feeling that the man must drive; it is genetic or something. In fact if they see a woman driving a man, they experience a sort of contempt for him. They don't understand how a man, a true man, can surrender the wheel to a woman."

"My husband rates himself as a very good driver—for that matter any man you talk to rates his driving as "above average". And he's terribly touchy about any suggestion or criticism about his driving—but himself can't resist doing "backseat driving", more so when I'm at the wheel.

He never admits to driving at the wrong speed. Anyone whom he overtakes is termed a road hog. Anyone who overtakes him is a speed maniac. He curses every erring motorist in sight. Even gestures excitedly when angry at someone. At times he's so preoccupied ranting in his road rage, he forgets to watch what's in front—till alerted by me."

"Mine has this infuriating habit of not asking for directions till he has completely lost his way. I urge him to seek help from outsiders but obviously it hurts his ego to admit failure. Once we became so argumentative over it, we gave up the search for the dinner-party venue and ended eating an omelette at home in stony silence."

"Women drivers are no good at reversing. Maybe, because women rarely do a reverse in life," says a wit. "And women drivers are no equal to men in fitting cars into tight parking places. Recently a woman psychologist has advanced the theory that men develop better spatial-awareness skills because as boys they learn to pee accurately into a receptacle while standing up."

"When we wanted to buy a new car, I spent innumerable hours comparing cars for their acceleration and pickup. The good wife was merely interested in something that looked nice and roomy to ride. Women, it seems, don't concern themselves overtly with horsepower and speed but view the car as a practical means of locomotion; something that aids their liberation and self-fulfillment. And at best, makes a style statement."

"During 40 years of married life, I was involved in half a dozen auto accidents, while the wife managed without one. Of course, I drive ten times more than she does, still her record of [illegible]ty is not to be sneezed at. Insurance companies are [illegible] in grading women as safer drivers than men. [illegible]nce of drunken driving among women is negligible as compared to men, and that is true without exception of every country and culture.

But that doesn't prove women are better drivers. On average, they drive slower than men. Indeed it is at times this dawdling between the lines and clogging up the right of way that causes accidents. I would say that the speed at which many women are seen driving seems to have scant relationship with road conditions or what the rest of traffic is doing; it's governed by some inner logic of its own. And this can be quite frustrating to men drivers."

"After 30 years of marriage, I and my wife still drive each other crazy. Literally. As it happens, I get behind the wheel (she dislikes driving), while she gets in the front passenger seat. She starts giving "helpful" suggestions as we pick our way on Delhi's roads. "That was a risky overtaking. Slow down," she says. "We're already late for the film show," I mutter, as if to remind her that she initially caused the delay in starting. "Will you get ahead of that monster belching black smoke," she says. I'm not amused; I had been trying to overtake the blasted lorry for the last five minutes. At times I wish we had a car fitted with dual controls, the sort used by driving schools. "Better do it yourself," "I'd say, and take my hands off the wheel and feet off the pedals."

No wonder, if there's any time in married life when couples are apt to have a row, it is while driving in cars. "The small enclosed space of a car is a powerful symbol that you're together," says Dr Isaiah Zimmerman, an American couple therapist. And space in cars is commonly small.

Complicating the balance of power between couples is the fact that within the confines of a car, the person behind the wheel has the upper hand. This usually arouses the other sitting alongside to redress the imbalance by making "helpful" suggestions in driving.

"Mind the scooter on the left." "Watch that fool wobbling on his bicycle." "Give way to the fellow hooting behind."

And the situation turns trickier when a wife is driving and the husband is "idly" sitting by.

Men driving are often faulted for losing their way because they are hesitant to ask for directions from outsiders.

Recently, Thomas Bever, a psychology professor at Rochester University, carried out an elaborate experiment about how differently men and women find their way. Over a large maze in a college basement, male and female students, wearing blinders that enabled them to see only a part of the floor, were asked to find their way. The women, he observed, relied on recognition of specific landmarks—peeling paint, a stain on the floor, a crack in the baseboard. When these cues were removed, they did poorly.

Men, on the other hand, depended on the primitive sense of motion and direction—estimates of direction, speed, and time. And they did rather well.

Bever explains the fascinating difference like this. Males in the hunting stage had to rely on a good sense of direction. Those who possessed it brought more meat. Those who lacked it ended up with less meat—or were themselves turned into meat.

Females busied themselves in locating edible roots and fruits in the complex forest terrain. They developed a special memory for the kind of subtle clues that would guide them to the sources of natural foods.

Bever concludes by saying that neither gender's style was superior, that both navigated with equal efficiency, and neither got lost more than the other.

Margaret Mead, the noted anthropologist, when asked whether men and women drive differently, wasn't too sure about it. "In the long run, wherever men and women drive the same kinds of cars, under the same conditions, with equal frequency and for the same general purpose, I think one is unlikely to find sex-determined differences in styles of driving," says she.

Indeed she makes fun of the male tendency to pick on women drivers. "Women drivers, as the most readily identifiable and frequently encountered on the road, get a tremendous share of men's explosive criticisms."

And whatever quarrels cars may generate among couples, an automobile can also create a cocoon of intimacy. "I love taking long drives with Ravi," says his wife, "We put on music, make rambling conversation and feel like we're newly married." Ravi, on his part, finds the rolling of wheels on the asphalt soothing. "It's much easier for me to open up when we're on the road. Maybe it's because part of my brain is occupied with driving, but things come out of my mouth that I could never say across the table." Of course, all this assumes fairly fine driving conditions.

And couples can be happy driving in silence. "Couples are sometimes appalled that they're totally silent during a long drive," says Dr Zimmerman. "You don't have to converse to prove you're a happy couple. Sometimes you just want to daydream or watch the scenery."

Men, Women Watching TV!

Men and women watch television differently. And some of these differences are surprisingly universal; common to men and women in diverse cultures and countries.

This is not to suggest that the man-woman differences in TV viewing are attributes of their essential biological characteristics. The phenomenon may have more to do with cultural conditioning and social roles within families.

Men tend to watch television more attentively, in relative silence, and without interruption, as if they don't want to miss anything. You see them showing annoyance at people talking or boisterous kids causing disturbance.

Ads intervals, of course, are altogether different. Indeed with ads intermissions getting longer and more frequent, differences between men and women watching TV are narrowing down.

To most women, just sitting and totally watching TV in silence doesn't make much sense. They usually combine it with chores such as ironing, sewing, knitting, or supervising children's homework. And they aren't averse to bits of casual conversation.

Presumably it all stems from a basic difference in approach. Men tend to view home as a site of leisure, as distinct from their workplace. To women, even to those with outside jobs, home is primarily a place of work. The result: while men watch TV rather wholeheartedly, women seem to do so distractedly, guiltily. Many women stay somewhat uncomfortable just watching TV when there are always domestic tasks to attend to. Even women having household help aren't fully free from this feeling of guilt.

No wonder, while men watch TV comfortably stretched on sofas or beds, women mostly sit on the edge of a settee or sofa; they may be required to get up for some household chore.

Surely when women feel free enough of their domestic responsibilities, they may "indulge" themselves fully in seeing a favourite serial or video film, alone or in company. But then this comes in the category of a treat than routine TV viewing.

Men, on the whole, are seen to plan their evening's viewing, through checking in papers or TV magazines. Women rely on knowing which evenings and timings their favourite serials are on.

In family viewing, the remote control is ordinarily in possession of the dad. And in the absence of dad, it's often the older son who commandeers the control device—a highly visible symbol of power relations. Of late, women have been gaining greater control over the remote, unless a cricket match is on.

Women commonly complain that the wielders of remote device flick channels too fast, too frequently, with scant regard for the other viewers. "It is aggravating, because I can be watching something and all of a sudden he turns it over to see the progress of a sporting event," says an irritated wife. Men do admit to using remote control rather liberally, what's called "channel surfing", but justify it on grounds of searching for the best available show (as per their taste) at any given time.

What about programme preferences of the two sexes? Worldwide, without exception, men show far greater preference for action, that's sports. And that includes men who stopped playing active sports years back. Indeed millions of men are said to have grown obsessive about watching sports; some even coming home early to watch a particular sporting event. Surely women are increasingly participating in all sorts of sports but their TV watching still remains largely confined to a few sports like like tennis, gymnastics, cricket, or golf for women golfers. Sustained female viewing is mostly missing from the sports heavily patronized by men viewers, such as football, boxing, wrestling, and auto racing.

Men also show a strong preference for "factual" programmes (news, current affairs, crime, adventure, documentaries especially on science and technology), while women display a marked preference for fictional programmes (soap operas, romances—called "tear-jerkers", full-length films). And this feature is seen to operate with remarkable consistency the world over.

It is commonly assumed that women are heavier viewers of television than men as many women don't go out to work. Several actual studies have revealed that in a lot of families, the husband watches far more TV than his wife. Women may be exposed for longer time to the small screen, their attentive viewing mostly works out lower than that of men's.

It's another matter that women indulge more in TV-related talk than men. Commenting on characters in popular soap operas or chatting about particular happenings therein is fairly common among women friends and neighbours. Men are less inclined to talk to other men about what they see on TV, except in the field of sports. As a general rule, they are less willing to project themselves as avid consumers of fictional programmes.

Television producers claim that the whole of their industry now revolves round selling products. No wonder the prime time TV shows are largely designed keeping women watchers in view; these are meant to sell mostly women's products.

Do Men and Women View Time Differently?

A situation that's likely to bring on a marital tiff; when a couple is getting ready to go out to a party.

Early in the day, Rajesh and Renu had decided they would leave the house for their friend's dinner by 8. Allowing an hour for driving time, they could make it by 9—nowhere late by Delhi norms.

By 7.50 Rajesh is all ready, shaved, bathed, dressed; he's attuned to be ready a little before time through years of attending official engagements. Again is his boyhood, his fearsome father had drilled punctuality into him.

Now he is pacing up and down the bedroom where Renu has just emerged from the adjoining bathroom.

"We've to leave by 8. You better hurry up," he says.

"You seem to suffer from 'hurry sickness'. Why don't you go out in the lawn; you make me nervous with this pacing up and down."

"Too hot outside. The sweat will spoil my shirt, my best party shirt. This is the only room with the AC on."

"Oh God. Why don't you go into your study? Put the AC on. I shall be ready in good time."

"All right, I'll look in after 15 minutes," says Rajesh and moves out.

Now he knows his wife will take a minimum of 30 minutes to do the make-up, and another 10 minutes to get into her meticulously assembled garb. So they are already late by nearly half an hour. Not that he's enamoured of the dinner party but he just hates to be late anywhere.

Men and women, it seems, do not view time the same way. In general, women think there is more time than men do.

It's 8.30. Rajesh can't wait any longer. He barges into the bedroom. Renu is still giving finishing touches to her make-up, wrapped in her housecoat. Yet he knows from past experience that any criticism about delay could result in a row. So he simply makes his presence felt as a reminder.

Even this proves provocative; the good wife doesn't fancy his staring impatiently when she's dressing. So he sits with his back to her; he has switched on the TV to take his mind off his unrest.

Eventually she's up and ready by 8.50. Forth with he proceeds to the car. He could save a few precious moments by starting the engine and AC, adjusting the rear view mirror, and unlocking the front passenger door.

No sign of her for five long minutes. He is sorely tempted to honk but a similar action sometimes back had made her flare up.

So he waits listening to music on the tape. He's getting more restive minute by minute. In fact he's about to climb out and call for her, when she appears.

"I've been waiting all this time in the car," he says with a hint of exasperation.

"But I'd some essentials to attend to: last-minute instructions to the maid, locking a pantry shelf, switching off some lights. I don't have your luxury of sitting straightway in the car."

By the time the couple leaves the house at 9.05, the situation in the car is well-nigh inflammable. And it can grow uglier if he happens to lose his way to the host's house.

Men and Women Stay Different

Rajan and Mala are happily married for twenty years. It was a love marriage between two graduates of IIMA Ahmedabad. Rajan is now managing an industrial firm while Mala operates her own advertising agency. They have no kids; earlier they didn't want any, now they aren't getting any.

In the beginning Rajan and Mala were fascinated at how similar they were. Both were avid readers. Both played tennis. Both were fond of movies and loved listening to ghazals. Both liked hot food and disfavoured alcohol. Both were cheerful, easygoing.

Some common interests persist. Yet over years of marriage the two have come to notice how different they actually are.

Rajan likes to sleep early and get up early while Mala likes to stay up late and rise late. Rajan is for saving money, Mala is for spending. Rajan is taken up with high-tech gadgetry, Mala has her flower pots. Rajan likes staying in posh hotels, Mala prefers her home comforts. While Mala holds to old relationships, Rajan quickly moves on. And Rajan now downs a stiff Scotch every evening while Mala shows no inclination to imbibe alcohol.

Then there are the usual gender differences. Whereas Rajan is reserved and detached, Mala is communicative and emotional.

The two are increasingly aware that they are different, and that the difference adds to their mutual attraction. This has also freed them from the tendency to try and change each other. What they are aiming at is to apply advanced relationship skills to manage the difference.

Men and women evolved different through millenniums of differing roles and activities. Men, working outside, learnt to cope with strong emotions through silently solving problems. Women, keeping home, most efficiently sort out their thoughts and feelings by talking. Men thrive on appreciation, especially female appreciation; women yearn for communication, more so with their near ones.

However the traditional marital pattern is getting replaced with working couples. Wives work on similar jobs as their men, at times doing more important or more paying work. Wives are often performing what were essentially masculine jobs while husbands are increasingly called upon to help at home, the female preserve. In some cases it has come down to a complete role reversal.

This emerging marital pattern is giving rise to a host of novel complications, which in turn are exacerbating marriage tensions, even causing marriage break-ups.

How to promote harmonious relationship in a working couple? How masculine should men behave and how feminine the women? Should men develop their feminine side and women their masculine side?

It's almost agreed in all quarters that to sustain passion and romance in marriage, men need to retain their maleness and women their femaleness. The question: how to nurture this maleness and femaleness in the midst of contrary pulls and pressures?

Every man has a female side and this side has legitimate needs. He needs his wife's sympathy and support in his work. But if he panders to it excessively by burdening her all the time with his troubles, big and small, it will tend to push his mate into the masculine mode. She could even begin mothering him. Or she gradually pulls away.

Failure is indeed deadly for a man and his marriage. A "failed" man copes with his pain by, either immersing himself into more work, or taking to drink, or withdrawing himself into a shell—all these unwelcome to his partner. Or, he swings to his female side and unloads his mood and misery on his mate. The latter course may afford some temporary relief, but ultimately weakens his male side.

Women want strong sensitive men, not the whining ones who can't manage their own pressures. She actually wants someone who listens to her feelings, someone sensitive to her needs. If her husband is all the time ventilating his own grievances, she finds that much harder to get support for her female side. When a man is emotionally too demanding, a woman apprehends she can't trust him to hear her feelings correctly.

A woman feels most nurtured when her female side is supported. Accordingly, the best option for men—in line with their maleness—is to solve their problems mainly by themselves or seek emotional support from male friends. If a man is upset, he better stay silent; at least keep an appearance of inner strength.

Wife, on her part, can help a stressed husband by showing appreciation for every little thing he does. This repeated appreciation from her boosts his self-esteem. And she can further improve matters by staying as cheerful as possible.

On the other hand, if a woman is upset, what her female side craves most is sympathetic listening. When a woman is convinced that she is not alone coping with life's problems, she feels deeply comforted. Working women particularly have more need of talk at home as the working world usually prevents them from nurturing their female side.

Men and women are different. And they should not let their masculinity and femininity go out of balance, by men behaving over-feminine or women behaving over-masculine. Without the sexual polarity, the attraction between partners tends to dissipates.

13

Man-Woman Equation

Man-Woman Equation Through the Ages

One basic factor has governed man-woman equation through the ages: men are simply bigger and stronger than women. In an argument between them which cannot be resolved verbally, the man usually wins when he takes recourse to the option of physical violence.

Since the dawn of history, women have had to protect themselves against men's physical aggression. The male-female size difference among early humans was at least as great as it is today, if not greater. And the societal protection to women against aggressive males was mostly missing.

Practically the same situation obtains in the animal kingdom. For example, studies of lions in the wild show that females are good hunters—at least as fast as the males. Working as a team, it is often the female that will single out a herd animal and kill it. But immediately thereafter she retreats from the kill, even if she has not eaten for days. Only when the mature males of the pride have eaten their fill will the weaker females approach. Any earlier attempt could provoke a nasty swipe from an upset male lion.

Studies of monkeys yield a similar picture. If a female monkey intrudes uninvited into the social space of a senior male, she is at high risk of being attacked. But there are occasions when this intrusion is essential such as reclaiming a wandering infant. Confronted with an angry male bearing down on her, the smaller female has three options. She can run away; this will work as long as the male chooses not to pursue her, which is usually the case. Or, she can physically confront the male, which is virtually self-destructive. Or, she can present herself sexually to him, thereby distracting him from his aggressive behaviour.

It is highly probable that, when retreat or avoidance was impossible or ineffective, the early woman presented herself sexually to a male aggressor. The tactic also had the effect of creating a bond between particular males and females. The human female is unique among primates and other higher mammals that she is sexually attractive and responsive at almost all times, and can become pregnant during most of her menstrual cycle.

In those early times, women were often the sexual initiators, because being sexually active, preferably with a range of different sexual partners, increased their chances of survival. If men are biologically unsuited to monogamy, as is commonly said, the same could be true of women too. But men, through their superior physical force, did manage over centuries to impose monogamy on women. This was indeed fundamental to the development of patriarchy.

In the beginning, childbirth was considered something magical, and thought to be an entirely female event. No wonder most of the deities were women then. Goddesses were worshipped because they symbolized fertility.

The relationship between sexual intercourse and pregnancy was not understood, at least by men. Men had little chance to observe the relationship between a specific sexual encounter and the birth, nine months later, of a child—nine months was a very long time in the Stone Age. Women were more likely to remember a particular sexual act and its context; and they noticed the first signs of pregnancy long before men did.

Eventually, of course, men learned the truth. They learned that they played a fundamental part in the creation of babies. At this point began the long struggle by men to gain control of the fertility process.

With the advent of settled agriculture and acquisition of property, power and influence could only be maintained through male children—physical strength was needed to safeguard one's property and status. How could a man be sure that the children borne by his official wife or wives were his own?

The only way to guarantee paternity was to exercise total control over women's fertility. This meant controlling female sexuality. Patriarchal societies evolved elaborate ways of controlling the sexual activities of women. That meant not only physical curbs over their movements and regulation of their behaviour but more important, the psychological indoctrination that sexual fidelity to their man was absolutely necessary and proper.

To achieve all this, it also became necessary to reduce women's social status. Married women especially were enjoined by most cultures to stay subservient to their husbands and obey their wishes. Women who didn't fall in line were often declared witches and tormented mercilessly, if not killed. Witch hunting was mainly an exercise to get rid of women who refused to conform to the rules of patriarchal society.

The economic power of women was still considerable in pre-industrial societies. Women worked equally along with their men at agricultural operations and at cottage crafts. Consequently they shared a good deal in decision-making about the family business.

The coming of industrialization and urbanization wrought a profound change in all this. Men went outside for paid work while women mostly stayed home looking after the children and household. Women lost their economic clout, when man became the sole bread winner. The overall effect on women's status was well-nigh devastating. In fact, the Industrial Revolution did unintentionally what religion and society was yet to achieve; it permitted the psychological subjugation of women.

On top women, more so middle-class women, were increasingly conditioned to live up to the men's unrealistic ideal image of them that required them to be perfect models of tact, charm, morality and general "goodness" and "caring". For men, one of the best status symbols became a beautiful, well-dressed wife. And women obliged by spending disproportionately long time over cultivating the same.

By identifying with their husbands, most married women achieved a measure of psychological well-being. Yet there was a high price to pay for the marital identity; they had to live by proxy, through their husbands and male offspring. They could experience the world outside their homes—the world of men—only at second hand.

Man-made Myths About Women

Gordon Wilson in *The Third Sex* (Taprobane) has written a highly provocative book on the gender of the human species. Here's a run-down of some things he says on man-made myths about women. You may disagree with him, even violently, but you can't help conceding he makes an interesting presentation.

The great mythical beauty of the female body is a product of male invention. Art is distinguished for the pretence that art is something to do with women's bodies. Nudes are always female, the sex interest respectabilised by avoiding the term "naked". Photographers borrowed the idea from artists and are presenting female nakedness as "art".

A male flasher is rated as disgusting. Yet no one would say the same for a female flasher—if at all, she would be surrounded by art-admirers.

To woman's own amusement, males have glorified her body into a mythical marvel. Male poets wrote fantasies about the body and painters transformed it into visual myths, when to the woman herself, her body presents perennial problems.

The average male's conditioned belief that the female body beneath all that elaborate packaging of clothes and cosmetics is even more beautiful than the packaging itself, is a measure of the success of myth-making. Some female bodies may be beautiful, but it's absurd to suggest that millions of highly-diverse women's shapes are all beautiful, unless one is simply equating feminity with "beauty".

The normal female body is hardly the ideal idol for eulogising and romanticising. Compared to a male body, it's rather short, fat and disproportionate, and any beauty it holds is more transient. Woman herself has never had any illusions about her body, and condemns herself to a lifetime of endless investment in time, money and laborious effort to escape from its reality. Every woman is all too aware that, far from man's perception of it as glamorous, her body is a little more than a collection of lumps of fat, flesh and bone which she is forced to carry about.

Female beauty is not only not an objective concept, it is essentially a derivative of the male sex instinct, a fundamentally male viewpoint. A particular woman's lips are deemed as divine. The similarly-shaped lips of a man do not elicit rave eulogies from poets and artists. Men's interest in breasts and bottoms is primarily a part of their sex-drive, and not so much about the aesthetics of these parts. "Beauty" then, is a male concept—the beholder must be male—and is, simply, a manner of perceiving particular features of the female.

No wonder we have so many statues, drawings and photographs of nude and semi-nude females in erotic poses, while men's bodies are mostly shown covered. You see breasts erected with artificial supports but it is against law in almost every country to show a naturally erect penis, as being obscene. This means that every man, every day, is guilty of obscenity.

Another myth perpetrated about women is that they are weak and helpless. This is not only to be compensated by extra male help and attention, but even meriting male deference if not deification. The ultimate apotheosis of this code manifested itself when the *Titanic* sank in 1912. 1,513 people died, all men. Conditioned to view women as weak, the men assiduously put all women and children in available boats, and themselves went down to their watery grave.

For the ancients, men and women were equal as human beings, and no favours or gestures were due from one to the other on the basis of gender. Women did, and were expected to do hard work little different from men. Like men, they were valued for their output. Even today this position obtains in rural areas and amongst the poor. Poverty has no time for garnishes.

Things however started changing in the last two hundred years or so, especially in Europe. The ascendancy of women owed much to the burgeoning middle classes whose increasing wealth exempted woman from her traditional duties as a housewife. Servants now performed her functions leaving her with little to do other than dress up in expensive clothes and jewellery, coupled with pastimes like music or painting.

An elaborate edifice of customs and practices was invented—collectively called "good manners". Men with good manners always stood up when a woman entered the room, opened doors for her, drew chairs for her, carried her luggage for her, surrendered their seats in buses, and settled the restaurant bills. The level of conditioning is such that if a woman is carrying even a small bag, a man walking besides her feels obliged to offer to carry it for her—as if she is not strong enough to carry it.

Men change wheels on motorways while women look on, pretending to be incapable. Grown healthy woman are helped into cars by their male escorts. And when a man stops his car, the good-mannered one hastily clambers out and rushes right round the car to the woman's side to open her door and help her out. She, on her part, waits motionless and immobilised as if unable to open the door herself.

In polite society, a man is expected to stand deferentially behind a woman, and he allows her to walk, talk and be served first. Indeed, in day to day life, women are conditioned not to even stand up when shaking hands with a man—as would be expected of, or appropriate for, an Equal.

Traditionally in every language, there's always a reference to man before the woman because of his pre-eminent position; "male and female", "man and woman". This then got reversed, and the new address system is "ladies and gentlemen". The modern buzzword is "lady". While "gentleman" is hardly used outside a few limited situations, almost every woman has been elevated to the status of a "lady". And any kind of insult is permissible against men, but women are sacrosanct. A joke at their expense is simply an exhibition of awful manners.

Both in the prologue and epilogue, Wilson makes out that his book is not an attack on women. He says, his sole object is to observe various phenomena and present his comments on their implications and effects.

Is a Matrilinear Millennium in the Making?

Men have been winners throughout recorded history. Is it something preordained by nature? Is the pattern set to last all time?

The way things have been shaping in the last quarter of the twentieth century, men don't look like staying winners for very long. Men, on top since *Homo* became *sapiens*, are slumping. To this extent, the year 2000 may mark a watershed in the affairs of mankind.

The feminist movement—possibly the most potentially explosive of all human movements—has wrought a radical change in gender equation. Sufficiently oppressed women acted, and the result has been an unprecedented speed of change in the heartland of human life, which is male-female relationships.

Pointers to the transformation are plenty; the more advanced a society, the more the obvious signs. In fact a society's advancement in these times can well be gauged from the degree of women's participation in various walks of life.

Incidentally it's very doubtful whether there would ever be a masculinist movement. Men will never get together against female oppression. Individual men don't want to offend individual women. Anyway men are too competitive with other men ever to pull together.

Girls are doing better at school—even in such traditionally male subjects as math and the sciences. They gain better qualifications, and find it easier to get jobs.

In the new technological society, women's smaller size does not handicap them, as machines are there to do the heavy work. And female fingers are nimbler on the computer.

Well, women are better at living without men than men are to live without women. "Who needs men?" is a common feminist quip.

Women are increasingly coming into the job market. And this pace is set to accelerate. Employers find female workers cheaper, make fewer demands for perks, and pose less of a challenge to management. Besides being customer-friendly, women are better prepared to accept part-time or short-term jobs.

Women are infiltrating into the exclusive male bastions of military and church. Some have even taken to wrestling and boxing, the essentially male violence sports. "The Millionaire Baby" which won an Oscar is about a female boxer.

Of course, the movement towards women's equality and liberation is far from uniform over the globe. You still have the Iranian mullahs and the Saudi orthodoxy. You still have honour-killing of women and dowry deaths. And there's still an awful lot of female infanticide, sexual exploitation, rape, and marital violence.

The female rise—some say, a long overdue ascension—is surely a welcome development. Yet it often gets associated with the decline of males. Lionel Tiger in his contentious new book *The Decline of Males* (Golden, 1999) sees the world—at least with regard to gender—as a zero-sum game. Citing income data, educational data, and health data, he gives voice to fears that most males are fast becoming unnecessary, both as workers and domestic partners. The shift, he says, is already having profound effects on family life, human relations, the workplace, and Corporate America.

It is a gender battle without a declared war, says he. Only in most wars the combatants retire to their homelands, after the battle. But men and women have to live together—by and large they want to.

Once there was relatively little gender competition in the workforce. Now men and women compete for places in desirable schools and then for jobs. Parents are striving to provide often very costly education for their daughters, as they deem it hazardous for any woman to depend entirely on a husband for a lifetime of affection and support.

What worries Lionel Tiger is that males in the lower income group are finding it increasingly hard to get jobs in competition with females. "Where are the guys?" he asks in anguish. As the birth rate declines women will spend more time at work and less at home. This will eventually mean more and more women having more earning power than men.

And with men losing their place as the primary breadwinners, it could signal the demise of the patriarchal system, a system to which human beings had been biologically attuned for aeons. The traditional male commitment to rear a family, wife and children, would be in jeopardy. Already the dad's home image has taken a battering.

Men are said to be losing on sperm count, too. Several surveys have revealed that the average man produces half the sperm his grandfather did in his prime. This is blamed on pollutants in air, water and food. Some blame it on higher levels of estrogen in childbearing women, possibly from birth-control pills.

All in all, male anxiety and vulnerability is markedly on the rise. He dies earlier than his mate. He has more health problems: smoking, drinking, a worse diet, and the prostate. And he could be occupying an inordinate amount of his time watching sports and pornography.

Besides the known body changes, the male levels of testosterone engender combativeness, a spirit of competitiveness and challenge, even aggression. It makes men prone to risky enterprises, even fool-hardy ventures. No wonder men have a disproportionately large presence in hazardous explorations, or for that matter in gambling. An overwhelming majority of those involved in rash diving, brawls, and violent crimes are men. And this is largely attributed to their much higher levels of testosterone.

However, the most crucial area of gender inequality is politics, a sphere of activity that continues to retain paramount importance. Politics is a very combative calling, with its ever-present power struggles. It is saturated with ego, conflict, and risk. To secure political power and to retain it, few holds are barred. Little wonder, after a century of adult franchise where women form half the electorate, the number of female politicians remains pathetically small in most democracies.

How well do women fit in this scenario? Can they match men in this sort of game?

Not that women are not good at governance. The qualities associated with low testosterone—empathy, cooperation, conciliation, risk-aversion—boost good governance. But then women have to climb the grisly ladder of politics, and here the average woman is handicapped vis-à-vis her male counterpart.

The culture of politics will have to undergo a transformation that could enable women to come into it in increasing numbers.

Indeed, a matrilinear millennium is hard to envisage till women manage a dominant role in politics.

Women Out-performing Men in Some Sports!

Would women out-perform men in some sports? As the traditional ideas about the physical limitations of women are undergoing a change, the question isn't as absurd as it sounds.

After a particularly late start (while the modern Olympics began in 1896, women were admitted only in 1924), women have made dramatic improvements in performance in almost every competitive sport, more so in the last two decades. Women are now besting world records held by men 10-15 years back. Whereas it took men 75 years to knock 25 minutes off the marathon record, women have done it in 15 years.

Admittedly women out-performing men is unlikely in most present-day Olympic events. Equestrian is the only Olympic sport in which men and women compete head to head. Shooting could be another.

There is a major physiological difference between the sexes; men (besides being bigger and taller on average) have more muscle while women have more body fat. Speed and strength require muscle power, and the male sex hormone testosterone increases muscle mass. Conversely, female sex hormones increase body fat, and fat to an athlete is excess baggage.

Yet fat can come in useful in sports needing endurance than speed. And it could play a crucial role in what are called ultra-endurance events, such as the longer triathlon: 3.8-km swim, followed by a 180-km cycle ride and then a 42-km run (included in the Sydney Olympics for the first time). Here male and female athletes are known to have recorded identical times for the marathon (42 km), and women even out-performed men with the race extended to 90 km.

In long-distance swimming, extra body fat is a distinct advantage, providing both extra buoyancy and insulation. The English channel crossing record for both men and women, is held by a woman swimmer, Alison Streeter.

At one time women were considered to be physically incapable of running long-distance events, such as a marathon. No wonder, the first women's Olympic marathon was not held until 1984. But women's potential in such events came as something of a surprise. Experts had erred in comparing the physiological characteristics of sedentary women to those of athletic men, for the simple reason that there were relatively few highly trained female athletes available for study.

During endurance races, an athlete uses both fat and glycogen (carbohydrate) to fuel the muscles. By using more fat to provide this fuel, athletes preserve their glycogen stores and so continue longer. It's only when glycogen runs out that an athlete reaches the limit of his or her endurance. Women's extra fat, it was suggested, might mean that they are less reliant on glycogen metabolism, making better use of fat metabolism.

This theory has its critics, some even scoffing that this should make fat men do better than leaner men. Yet recent researches show that there are gender differences in the way muscles are fueled, for example, over very long-distance running. And this difference could confer an advantage on women in high-endurance sports.

Women's sport has now fully come of age. It's a long way from the ancient Greek Olympics where stark-naked male athletes competed before a mainly male audience (women forbidden not only to participate but even to watch the Games; exceptions sometimes made for unmarried girls in the company of male relatives). Women, however, held a quadrennial event of their own, called Heraea, again in the nude.

Among the 11,000 athletes at the Athens Olympics, nearly 4,500 were women. The number of girls participating world over in school and college sports is escalating fast. More and more girls are beginning their athletic careers at the same age as boys. And the new generation of parents is highly supportive of girls in sports. In popular mind, sports are deemed good for character building and better health. And if you develop into a star athlete, you now earn huge sums and celebrity status.

The traditional myth that women aren't interested in sports stands more or less demolished, with the possible exception of a few Islamic countries. With women coming into top sports in a big way, the traditional ideal of a woman's body may well be in for a change. A new model of feminine beauty may be emerging.

While men, following the Greek tradition, have always been shown in statues and paintings as muscular, women were enveloped in a blanket of fat—ample thighs, full bosoms.

Then there's the modern fashion model. These girls mostly stay skinny through a strict control of diet. Tall and fit, but with a captivating feminine air.

The athletic body is different, both from the classical ideal of beauty and today's fashion models. Through much exercise and hard training, it's become increasingly streamlined. Hips have been largely eliminated—the equipment with which nature outfits women for motherhood. And the body stripped of anything extraneous—any padding, any surplus flesh. Highly competitive runners can't afford to carry an ounce of excess baggage.

The image of a muscular woman can evoke some uneasy emotions deep down in males, as if she was a trying to become a man or pose intimidating.

In her book *The Frailty Myth* Colette Dowling talks of the scenario where women fight for the freedom to enjoy the strength and power of their bodies whether around the playground or striding down the sidewalk.

The athletic woman exudes a certain charm and confidence. There's nothing apologetic about her hard-earned muscles, something that her mother never had. And these impart the owner a sense of self-possession. In star athletes, tennis greats, beachball beauties, we recognize women who own their bodies, inhabiting every inch of them, and the sight of it is exhilarating.

An athletic body can also be quite sexy. Take the shapely Sharapova stretching for her tennis strokes. Our Sania Mirza is another example.

Maybe, another ideal of feminine beauty would also emerge, the athletic female body.

Women Often Ageing Better than Men

Poonam is sixty. She looks fifty. Feels more like forty.

Mother of a thirty-five-year old son living in USA, and a granny too, Poonam runs a bustling boutique. Fortnightly she visits a beauty parlour for things such as facials, pedicure, manicure, waxing, hairdo. And she plays 9 holes of golf twice a week. Hers is a regulated diet, sparing in sugar, salt and fats. And she has chosen to go on estrogen/progesterone supplements since the last four years.

Health-wise, her husband isn't doing too badly at sixty-five. Yet the toll of years is telling on him, compounded by occasional excesses in eating and drinking. Mohan, once a cheery, fun-loving chap stays somewhat depressed. After retirement from the Administrative Service, he could only land a low-profile consultancy job while quite a few of his former colleagues hold on to prestigious positions.

Poonam, in contrast, stands transformed during the last 20 years from a mere housewife into a busy business woman. She's already earning three times what Mohan did. Her business and housework just leave her no time to feel dispirited, even if she had a cause.

Among upwardly-mobile middle class women in their fifties and sixties, Poonam's case is becoming more typical than an exception. This category has experienced dramatic changes in the last two decades, and more could be in the offing.

For ageing women, one traditional loss was that of youthful looks. Women as sex objects had to be young; whereas men matured, women got old. The fear of this loss is diminishing with women's heightened self-worth through other accomplishments.

And many now succeed in retaining a trim figure and attractive appearance far into their middle years. Germaine Greer, the noted feminist writer, when complimented on her youthful appearance at her sixtieth birthday quipped, "That's what a woman of sixty would look like". Some older women are even accepting their age with pride; a departure from the age-old pattern where women persistently, almost pathetically, lied about their age.

Yet the greatest gains in the last few decades have been in the area of psychological health. Earlier the incidence of impairment in mental health increased as women slid into their thirties and forties. Psychiatrists mostly blamed it on women enjoying much less control over their lives than their male counterparts. Now this percentage is markedly down for educated middle-aged women; not only for those who combine outside jobs with housework, but also with full-time housewives.

It has been the accepted wisdom that menopause was a critical event in the life of a woman. The ending of her reproductive life was deemed a major threat to her adjustment. Evidence is accumulating that a large majority of present-day women really suffer no psychological problems, and little physical discomfort except occasional hot flashes. Menopause is more of a bugbear than a stressful experience. Some even report a positive improvement in their physical and emotional health, and the event no way affecting their sexual activity. In fact, to a lot of women, the cessation of their fertility comes more as a relief.

Widowhood is the ultimate tragedy; women often fear it more than their own death through illness. There is the loss of identity as someone's wife, a horrid feeling of incompleteness and incompetence, an ugly void in social life, and a host of other problems and complications.

Yet some recent surveys have thrown up a different picture. An overwhelming majority of widows—after they got over the initial grief—became more independent and competent than while their husbands were living. They managed to develop more rounded personalities as a consequence of being left on their own.

New research reveals that older women "adjust" to the death of a spouse and, with whatever pain or grief, move on to new strengths afterward, with less apparent difficulty than younger women—and than men at any age. If an older man's wife died, he is more likely to become sick and die within the next 2 years, than other men of comparable age. The vulnerability disappears if he remarries—or after he survives five years alone. No such drastic toll on women's life takes place with widowhood.

Another traumatic event is retirement: the loss of identity, status, satisfying work, peer support, let alone reduced finances and increased hassles in everyday living. Previously women only coped with their husbands' retirement.

Men, compared to women, seemed more deficient in basic strength to survive retirement. Women, of course, have this advantage; they never retire from housework. To that extent, retired women's lives stay fuller than those of retired men.

Some psychologists make out that women develop a greater capacity to meet "discontinuities" than men, because they encounter more of these in their lives. From a girl-child playing freely with boys, she abruptly changes at puberty into one demure and self-protective. She takes a job or prepares herself for one, but often gives it up with marriage and children. And then suddenly at forty-five this role is over: menopause, the "empty nest". Women thus grow better accustomed to change and impermanence than men.

From adolescence through their forties, women become increasingly feminine and men increasingly masculine. But by fifty, each is seen allowing qualities conventionally assigned to the opposite sex to emerge. Women become more assertive with age, men more giving. Women who had been constricted by the conventional values to attract and please men begin to express their feelings in all sorts of new and different ways; they grow more self-confident. At midlife, there possibly occurs a male-female "crossover".

And the same finds reflection in the sexual sphere. The husband's sexual drive diminishes (a biological phenomenon related to age) whilst the wife's remains unchanged or may even increase (there's no such direct link with age). Indeed, women usually ceased sexual activity mainly as a result of their mate's lack of libido or his demise.

On average, women live longer than men.

Looking around the globe, we find that longevity difference between men and women varies; being 6-8 years in western Europe, North America and Australia, 3-5 years in much of Africa and Latin America, and zero or even negative in the Indian subcontinent. This suggests at once the importance of social factors; how differences in the treatment of young girls and boys might explain the absence of any female advantage in expectation of life in India.

14

Unfair to Women

Suffering is Mostly for Women

Out of over eight million sterilisations carried out every year over the country, men now figure no more than one percent.

Obviously our couples when they decide to control births through surgical intervention are mostly opting out for the more complicated operation for the wife than the far simpler one for the husband.

What could be the rationale behind such a seemingly weird choice?

It is usually explained on the male apprehensions of an impotency or some loss of virility. Others are said to be held back for the fear, if their wife died or got divorced—the latter event less likely in our conditions—they won't be in a position to produce an issue with the next wife. Or is it simply a case of escaping contact with a surgeon's knife when the object can be achieved by shifting the onus on to one's wife?

After all she is well acclimatized to pain, discomfort and bleeding through years of menstruation (human female is the only mammal that menstruates monthly, she ovulates throughout the year and not at particular seasons like other animals), burdensome periods of pregnancy and the childbirths. In the context of putting up with physical pain and discomfort, women seem to be the stronger sex.

Are these factors enough to produce the alarming imbalance between the number of tubal ligations and vasectomies performed in the country? Or is it all due to the greater motivation of women to avoid unwanted births? "Men never think, at least seldom think, what a hard task it is for us women to go through childbirths very often," rued Queen Victoria.

Some say it is to be blamed on the basic selfishness of men (this expression is being used for want of a better one) or their enhanced perception of what happens to them? Men would like to do without "the spoilsport" condoms in marital sex, though the condoms have vastly improved; these are thinner, lubricated, even perfumed and coloured. So it often means the wife taking to birth-control pills with all the attendant risks that go with interference with the natural body processes. Or have an intrauterine device (IUD) fitted in, and become "the (grumbling loop wife" with chances of pelvic inflammation. And finally she gets pushed into the more difficult and dangerous operation of tubectomy instead of his undergoing vasectomy. And mind you, all this in a field of activity which is patently more pleasurable to men—at least more sought after by men-than their spouses.

In men's defence perhaps it can be argued that vasectomy and tubectomy are nearly the same thing. In vasectomy, the vas deferens, the duct passing sperm from the testes to the prostrate and the penis is severed. In tubectomy again, the uterine tubes (commonly called fallopian tubes after the name of Dr. Gabriel Fallopius, the great Italian anatomist, who is also credited with the invention of a linen condom for the prevention of venereal disease) that carry ova from the ovaries to the uterus are blocked.

But there the similarity ends. Vasectomy is a quick, simple operation normally carried out under local anesthesia, and in a doctor's clinic. The vas deferens duct is easily accessible in the exposed scrotum (nature hung the testes out to keep the sperm cooler than the body temperature). Normal work can be resumed soon after the operation. No long-term adverse effects have been demonstrated in men. Vasectomy leaves the bulk of seminal fluid intact unlike castration.

On the other hand, fallopian tubes lie buried deeply in the female pelvis. To perform sterilisation a surgeon must either open the abdomen, in a procedure called laparotomy, and close the tubes under direct vision, or insert an optical instrument (laparoscope) to view the tubes so that a clip, ring or electrocautery can be applied. The operation is best performed under regular surgical conditions, and often requires a day or two of hospitalisation for recuperation and observation.

Surgical reversal is again easier for male sterilisation than female sterilisation; the success rate in the former is over 50 percent. And this is poised to improve with advances in microsurgical techniques.

One is not sure whether much can be done to change men's perceptions in this field. Yet it may be a good idea to keep on highlighting the difference between the two operations in a popular media like TV. A better appreciation of the same may generate higher sensitivity on the subject. Admittedly fewer male sterilisations than female sterilisations have been performed worldwide, but the ratio is something like 1 to 2, not 1 to 100.

It Works out Unfair to Women

Many things work out unfair to women: things like property rights, promotions to high places, or even conditions at work. But while these wrongs provoke protests, another one that works out unfairly stays largely ignored.

And this is the unfairness of waiting much longer than men in toilet queues. Take the toilet queues at cinemas or theatres at intermission, or at stadiums or conference halls at a break in play or session. And because most public restrooms are built on the principle of adjoining plumbing, the two lines of men and women, are seen stretched in proximity.

Half through the intermission or break, the men's line is gone; they are all out in the lobby or back in their seats. But the women's line is still moving at snail's pace. Some of those standing far behind are anxiously looking at their watches, wondering if they're ever going to make it. People waiting like this can't be harbouring much sisterly feelings towards all the sisterhood ranged in front. A few bolder spirits even talk of temporarily taking over the men's empty wing.

A couple of recent studies carried out in USA have shown that women take nearly twice as long in the restrooms as men. One study found that men took between 84 and 118 seconds while women took between 153 and 175 seconds. And it was noted that the longer time was caused not just by women taking excessive time in front of the mirror. Men did that too, and they also washed their hands.

Women take longer for some obvious reasons, like the way their bodies are designed and the way their clothes are designed. And women are the ones who usually have to take small children to the toilets.

Men's toilets have another advantage; they provide more urinals in the same space, with no time lost in closing doors and opening.

The situation is working out so unfair to women that there are moves afoot in USA to change the plumbing code that could increase by 50 percent the number of women's toilets in new theatres and sports arenas. The present regulations requiring an equal number of toilets in men's and women's restrooms is deemed out of date. The move should be welcome to men too; they often have to wait restlessly for their female companions.

Elderly Women: Up against Ageism and Sexism

Satya Sobti is seventy-five. She's at age that marks her transition from the "young elderly" to the "elderly".

Satya Sobti—now more Satya than Sobti; Amar Sobti has been dead for two decades—is seen as not doing badly. She lives in her own spacious house in South Delhi, with the rented upper floor fetching her a tidy income. No serious health complaints except arthritic knees, coupled with problems of overweight.

Her only son and his wife stay solicitous but are too busy with their own life in Mumbai. To them all her needs are comfortably met. But Satya's greatest need is to be cherished by her progeny, not its money.

Married to a high government official, she had enjoyed a busy, almost an envious social life. And there was plenty of travel, tennis and bridge. But over years as a widow, she is left with few intimate friends, mostly women of her age. And her main pastime now is playing bridge every afternoon.

Satya no longer feels at ease in the company of her husband's former friends, colleagues and subordinates. They do extend to her ritualistic deference but otherwise tend to avoid her—"the leprosy of old age". At times she thinks it may be widowhood *per se* which has thrust her prematurely into the life pattern of old age.

Never before have so many people reached into their seventies and eighties, and women now predominate in this group. Yet feminist movement has shown scant interest in elderly women. Historically the feminist focus was on younger women's concerns and priorities: safe contraception, legal abortion, equality at work, protection from marital violence and sexual harassment. Young feminists may have even felt that older women generally shared some responsibility for their repression and holding back women's liberation. Literature has again neglected the old and their emotions.

Research on older women may increase as feminine sociologists themselves experience the effects of ageing. Betty Friedan (65), for example, is developing ideas about elderly liberation, adding ageing consciousness to feminine consciousness. An interesting book on the subject is *Growing Old Disgracefully* (The Hen Co-op, 1993). Six British women, aged between 60 and 75, talk of the cultural restraints on the lives of older women.

Over centuries elderly women have been the victims of popular prejudices, even of witchcraft. Scientific and social progress has surely ushered in an era of humane enlightenment, yet dismissive, patronizing, contemptuous and hostile attitudes towards elderly women persist. They are commonly characterized as slow, clumsy, inept, stupid, unhealthy, and unattractive.

Women as they age have to contend both with ageism and sexism. These prejudices, in combination, create a double standard of ageing, in which growing older has a different significance for women and men.

Male chronology hinges on work and job but a woman's age status gets defined more in terms of her reproductive cycle and sexual attractiveness. Because a woman's value is sexualized, positively in the first half of life, negatively in the second, it hinges a lot on youthful appearance. The discrepancy between the societal ideal of female attractiveness and their actual appearance widens with age, whereas signs of ageing in men are not considered so material.

Aware that loss of youthful appearance brings social devaluation, women are vulnerable to immense pressure to ward off signs of ageing with an armoury of cosmetic aids, including surgery. Thanks to higher health standards and better grooming, more and more women are managing to retain their youthful appearance into their forties and fifties, some into their sixties.

Yet psychic penalties are inherent in the double standard of ageing. Indeed it would be surprising if cultural denigration or invisibility has no effect on women's own perception of their ageing selves. Some women try to counter it by imagining that the elderly image befalls other people; for themselves they construct and maintain a false sense of self which rests precariously on the avoidance of any sign of ageing. They internalize what they "should" be like at certain ages. Such a denial of ageing could well alienate an elderly woman from her true identity, and from others like herself.

The negative stereotype of the elderly woman considerably varies with her class and background. It's more pronounced in families where men reflect sexist assumptions about women's role and capabilities. The negativeness looms less among women with higher socio-economic status, higher educational levels, and greater commitment to employment.

Women whose earlier lives conformed more closely to the homemaking model tended to internalize themselves as useless in old age. Such women often described their lives as unimportant, although they were full of activity and interests. Low self-esteem in later life, it seems, is related to the completeness of socialization into femininity.

On the other hand, women whose lives were less home-centred maintained a more positive self-identity. Several studies confirm the importance of employment in a desired occupation for the maintenance of positive identity by women in later life.

The less completely a woman has conformed to the conventional ideal of domestic femininity, the more likely she is to age with pride and independence.

Another potentially damaging aspect of the stereotyped elderly woman is her assumed mental decline, including inability to make decisions. But now an increasing number of women are not adopting these negative views of themselves; they see themselves as active participants in society, showing a lively understanding of topical issues.

In some societies, including ours, where tradition remained strong, the possession of experience often made older women take on high status roles in the extended family and in religious rites. But this may be fast changing, especially among the urban elite. Pace of technological innovation is one factor that makes the accumulated skills and knowledge of older people redundant. Grandmother's knowledge of pre-natal and post-natal care, bringing up of children, even her traditional cooking skills may appear somewhat outmoded to younger mothers and wives with college degrees and familiarity with all sorts of kitchen gadgetry and processed foods.

Ageism is a particular form of social oppression—a process of systematic stereotyping of people because they are old. Even toasts at their birthday parties are rather jocular, at times caustic. And so also the greeting cards for their birthdays. Hospital staff, even when kindly, tend to treat them more as children.

Ageism worsens when combined with sexism—a prejudice on grounds of sex. Older women expect more filial support than older men, but often actually get less.

Another disquieting feature is the increasing abuse of the elderly, especially of the frail elderly women. Old women's dependence on others leaves them open to neglect and to financial, mental and physical abuse. Faced with the prospect of alienating a relative whom they depended on for help, many victims are reluctant to complain or seek outside help.

Sexism in Sport

To be a girl at the turn of the 21st century is clearly better than it has ever been before. She'll sail through school, beating boys in most subjects. And with superior results in schools, she'll skip easily over further education, and later a job. She'll use her money as she pleases. Marriage, if she wants. Children, if she's ready. Today's woman, assertive and independent, never had it so good. Unless she's born into our underclass, in which case it's all a life of malnutrition, unwanted pregnancies, unending household chores, low jobs, and every sort of exploitation.

How well women may be doing in other spheres, men manage an edge in the prestigious field of sports. Take cricket, our ruling national obsession. It is played by and supported by men. Yes, we have female cricketers, but can you name any? Yes, we have female cricket supporters, but it's mainly men who play, coach, manage, and analyze the game. Leaving aside tennis and athletics which throw up noted women champions that interest the media, elsewhere it's men who grab popular attention.

Sexism in sport remains a reality. The physicality of male body represents power and dominance, whereas the physicality of the female body represents frailty and weakness. Perhaps more than any other social institution, sport—grown into a powerful institution because of its status and economic clout—perpetuates male superiority over female inferiority. Men grow up believing that sport is the inherent birthright of being male, and that women need to earn the right to play.

Of course, the earlier debate regarding women's participation in sports has been rendered irrelevant in most cultures. Yet women using their bodies for "masculine" sports like football are hardly favourites. And media practices are not gender neutral. In tennis, for example, women players are more commented upon their youth, their clothes, the showing of cleavage and hips than their game.

Take the Olympics. Women have been conspicuous by their absence from the administrative hierarchy of the International Olympic Committee right till 1981. While the number of females participating in the Olympic Games has steadily risen (nearly 4,000 out of 10,300 athletes at the Athens Olympics) there was little evidence of a corresponding increase in the proportion of female officials at important positions.

Majority of members on sport governing bodies in various countries tend to be men. And, whatever female officials are present, they mostly fulfill stereotyped role such as physiotherapist, masseuse, and hostess. Even in a game like badminton where female participation nearly equals that of males, women still form a small minority among its senior administrators.

At a more fundamental level there is much evidence to suggest that within society in general there is a perception that being a woman and being an athlete are incompatible. This is complemented by a perception within sport that to be a woman is to be an inadequate athlete and to be a successful woman athlete is to be an inadequate woman. For men participation in sport confirms and enhances their sexuality but for women participation undermines and questions their sexuality.

Culturally, women labour under a certain compulsion to demonstrate at large that their interest in sport does not detract from their commitment to heterosexual relationships, marriage, children, and family life.

Women's actual performance in sport, however, is on the way to closing the gender gap considerably. They are reaching world records held by men 10-15 years back. If Maurice Greene, the fastest man en earth, does 100 metres in 9.79 seconds, Marion Jones, the fastest woman on earth, does it in 10.75 seconds—a difference of less then one second. Whereas it took men 75 years to knock 25 minutes off the marathon record, women have done it in 15 years.

Surveys have indicated that around the age of 14, girls' interest and participation in school sport declines rapidly. The reasons for this are complex but boil down to a fear of being deemed unattractive and uncool. The astounding success of women athletes in recent times is, however, changing this scenario. In the minds of teenage girls looking for models of what they might become, "elite sportswoman" is now a new possibility. The current generation of parents is also getting fairly supportive of girls in sports.

Women and Depression

"You have only a limited number of days on this earth; the fewer spent wishing you weren't, the better off you are."

—Andrew Solomon in *The Noonday Demon* (2001)

Simi often stays depressed. There are days when depression brings on deadening lethargy or bouts of self-loathing. These spells of despondency interfere with her appetite and sleep, perhaps her sexual drive, too.

Simi and her architect husband Mohan, live in a well-appointed flat of their own. They have two kids, a girl of three and a baby boy 2 months old. To their relatives and friends, Mohans are a happily married couple, enjoying good income, and with no particular worry in the world.

Simi isn't exactly sure what makes her so depressed? Is it because she has put on hold a promising career in textile designing to rear a family? Is she envious of her counterparts working at interesting jobs? Or, was she getting jealous of

Mohan himself—smartly groomed every morning and busily driving away to work, while she in her nightclothes was left changing nappies and dusting sofas? Or, is it something genetic—her mother was definitely depressive?

Simi, sharp and sensitive, would love to shake off this shadow of sadness. She has tried more of reading novels, more of serial watching, and more of elaborate cooking. Yet the depression descends on her whenever she's free from work.

Simi's dilemma: should she call attention to her mental unrest or should she simply soldier on in silence? She doesn't seem inclined to seek professional help.

Depression is defined as an emotional state marked by melancholy, inactivity, and self-deprecation. The depression may be fleeting or chronic, mild or severe. What is central to depression is the element of self-loathing, a sense of one's worthlessness or abject failure. Sometimes these feelings are strong enough to produce suicidal urges. This self-denigration, psychiatrists say, often stems from a sub-conscious disappointment or anger or hatred towards another person or even a circumstance.

And, unlike the demons of hunger and want, the demon of depression largely dwells among the affluent and the sophisticated sections of a populace. With rising living standards and competitive pressures, depression has become a common scourge in advanced societies, afflicting an estimated one in ten.

Happily for the depressives, medical science is fast coming up with a number of effective anti-depressant drugs. Whereas a mild depression may respond to talking therapy alone, most cases call for a combination of drugs and psychotherapy.

One thing that has helped the treatment of depression is the new-fledged openness on the subject. Those who have sampled depression's dark offerings are speaking out and seeking help. Styron's book *Darkness Visible* where he mostly discusses his own ordeal of depression has become an important landmark. In Styron's case, the depression lifted, burned off by drugs and psychotherapy, and stay in a hospital. However people who come out of it have to watch against a recurrence of the same—the way reformed alcoholics do.

The new generation of drugs allows a sophistication and flexibility in treatment that was not possible in the past. And, of all these drugs, Prozac retains its premier position.

What's so different in Prozac from the other anti-depressants used for years? The basic principle of all is the same: to bolster the action of serotonin, one crucial chemical that transmits impulses between nerve cells. Shortage of serotonin, scientists believe, is a major cause of depression.

The traditional anti-depressants did the job in a scattered fashion, thus needing larger doses and causing serious side effects like dizziness, blurred vision, constipation and weight gain. They even caused low blood pressure and heart disturbances—real hazards for the elderly. Prozac is more narrowly focussed; it manages to maintain higher levels of serotonin, but with low toxicity. The unprecedented success of Prozac has given rise to several similar formulations, such as Wellbutrin and Anafranil. And many more are on the way.

The new drugs have fewer side effects. Yet they are not perfect, and do have some side effects such as constipation and dry mouth. Medicines can't gift happiness to mankind without exacting some price. The sorrow of a broken love affair, the death of a dear one, or the loss of a job or money or position can't be simply overcome by medicines.

One important development in dealing with depression is the emergence of gender-sensitive psychology. It is being increasingly recognized that women require different medication and behavioural therapy than men because of their different hormonal surges, especially progesterone's ebb and flow with the menstrual cycle. Many women also fall prey to postpartum depression, a minor or major depression that overcomes them in the weeks after a childbirth; sometimes lasting as much as a year. The same can be occasioned by hormonal changes as well as the added stress of a newborn child. With quite a few women, the birth of a child also marks the start of marital violence.

"It's a common misconception among psychiatrists and psychologists that the risks and causes of depression in men and women are the same, so treatment should be the same," says Ellen McGrath, chairwoman of the 30-member US expert panel on female depression and disorders. 'But none of that's true. Paying attention to gender differences is an essential part of therapy for depression." Besides biology, men and women are brought up differently.

The expert panel found that the incidence of depression showed up twice as often in women as in men, and for a far wider variety of causes, including violence and sexual abuse against them, excessive focussing on depressed feelings, hormonal effects of the menstrual cycle, birth control pills and childbirth, body dissatisfactions, marriage strains, pressure of parenting, and weaker economic position.

Psychotherapists are therefore counselled to look carefully for those underlying factors to choose from an array of therapy approaches that are especially effective with women's problems. For example, group therapy is considered more useful for women than men. The latter tend to lack confidants, while women open up more easily to close friends.

What about the children off depressed women? A barrage of recent studies conclusively proves what was suspected: the children of depressed parents particularly mothers—like the children of alcoholics—can suffer significant psychological damage. Their emotional scars, starting as early as the first few months of infancy, can last deep into adolescence and possibly beyond. Many deficits and disturbances have been observed in these children such as low birth weight and excessive crying in newborn babies whose mothers were depressed during pregnancy (detailed in the book *Gloom in the Womb*; inability to smile starting at 3 months of age; lower concentration in school; hostile behaviour or a withdrawal in adolescence; and increased depression as time goes on.

Depressed mothers are emotionally "flattened" and are thus able to give less encouragement and affection to their children. At some moments she may be sharp and angry at being bothered, at others she may become intrusively involved in her kids. An "overcontrolling" depressive mother might sit for hours clutching and stroking a four-year-old. Middle-class mothers with postpartum depression may even tend to display far more irritability and volatility with their infants during the first six months than non-depressed mothers. Their infants in turn often become withdrawn, refusing even to look at them, what to say of smiling at them. For a child, the first six months are crucial for learning social interactions, and the same get retarded in these kids.

In adolescence, the troubles of children with depressed parents mount up. Either the child becomes wild, out-of-control, or overtly obedient and sensitive. These are the strategies a growing child usually adopts to gain the attention of the preoccupied depressed parent. In both ways it hurts the adolescent's personality.

The point of all the current research on parental depression isn't to aim an accusing finger at the parents for their children's problems. The basic aim is to help depressed parents, particularly mothers. She has to examine the hard facts of her life to identify the cause of her depression, whether it's from being deprived of the satisfaction of an outside job or from a destructive marriage.

Meanwhile experts offer a few tips to depressed mothers when dealing with their children.

Avoid talking your problems to your children; it will only undermine their sense of security. Instead, talk to your spouse, a friend, a therapist.

Never criticize your child; only criticize specific behaviour. Say "That was selfish," not "You're a selfish girl".

Don't malign your parenting skills to your children. Learn these skills if you are deficient.

15

General

What Women Want of Newspapers!

Every newspaper wants more women readers. The reason is simple. Advertisers are convinced that married women make most of consumer decisions in households. They decide what foods to buy, and so also kitchen gadgets, crockery and cutlery. Women choose the clothing for themselves and their children; even have a say in their husbands' clothes. And single working women—their numbers on the rise—purchase everything for themselves, including cars and TV sets.

Goods and services purchased by women are still most effectively advertised through newspapers and magazines. After all, you can't tear an ad out of a TV screen. Women find it rather convenient to have a cut-out ad handy while out shopping.

How to attract more women readers? Newspaper editors and their staff hold frequent discussions on the subject, but often end up with no clear answers. The old-style women's sections, with their tight focus on food and fashion, haven't been a roaring success. And attempts to renovate the women's section into women's pages that reflect current realities—such as women working outside, women struggling between the demands of homes and bosses—have fared somewhat better in certain papers. But then there are all those women's magazines with their space and pictorials to compete against.

Indeed, the urgent task of all newspaper editors is to make the whole paper more meaningful to more women.

Women care deeply about certain issues. Most important of all is education. They want to know more about schools—the qualifications of teachers, the facilities on offer, the school transport. They want to know whether the schools are safe from hoodlums or tottering from shoddy construction and maintenance. They want to know what percentage of the city's budget is devoted to education. They want hard, verified information, not the usual press releases issued by officials or politicians.

After education, women are concerned about the environment. A rapid decline in tiger population may be alarming, but women are more interested to know of practical matters, things like whether the tap water is safe. They want to know whether their children are more likely to develop asthma in certain areas of the city. They want assurances that someone is inspecting meat and fish they are buying in the market. And so also about the authenticity of everyday medicines and allied preparations.

They want solid information about health; not only of disease, but prevention. That includes health and exercise. It's the obligation of a responsible paper to examine any fad diet thoroughly, consulting reputable nutritionists, before putting it out. Similarly a newspaper should resist publishing a scare story on health, without professional verification.

And it's naïve to think that women don't care about the rest of the paper. They care about things like taxes, inefficient government bureaucracies. They want solid information about the state of economy, and how it will affect their lives. If criminals are roaming the streets of their neighbourhood or selling drugs, they want newspapers to highlight the issue, so that an indifferent police force is compelled to act. They walk those streets. Their children play in those streets.

Even the sports section is no longer a closed shop for men. Millions of younger women now play in organized sports; they understand the language of sports, the rules, the nuances.

Possibly the most important measure that can make a newspaper more meaningful to more women is the involvement of professional women journalists at all levels of the editorial process. They must be among the top editors at every newspaper, and not as tokens. They must share the power to decide what stories are to be covered and how. And now women can easily be found to fill such positions out of the fairly large available pool of women journalists.

At the reporting level, the contribution of women journalists is already considerable. But at editorial policy levels, newspapers are still not taking enough of talented women. Again women staff members could be encouraged to write critical memos to editors. And their opinions should be respected in the best possible way; by being put into effect.

Women and Porn

Traditionally men had a near monopoly over the production and consumption of pornography. Women largely left it alone. And often chose to overlook their menfolk's occasional indulgence in it. This pattern held good over centuries.

However the last three decades have been witnessing significant changes in the otherwise static relationship between women and porn. The definition of what constitutes porn is itself changing. There are shifting standards. Things that used to be pornography no longer are.

Surely many women are plainly alarmed at the expanding coverage and scope of the porn industry worldwide.

Feminist groups oppose porn as being dangerous to women. To Catharine MacKinnon, dubbed "the anti-porn star", pornography is the mainspring of sexual violence against women—almost akin to rape. A few recent scientific experiments do corroborate that men massively exposed to pornography of violent imagery tend to make less of the suffering undergone by victims of rape or sexual assault.

Feminists also denounce porn as degrading to women; even women acting in porn films are often made to act against their will. And feminists oppose pornography as a form of women hatred, the male power at its worst.

Bizarre though it may sound, throughout its long history, pornography—as an instrument of sexual arousal—has been shaped by technology. It was oral jokes till printed word came in. Photography and motion pictures ushered in porn magazines and porn films.

Pornography has taken the most dramatic turn with the coming of VCRs and video cassettes. People can buy or rent video cassettes and watch them in the privacy and comfort of their homes. That way VCR has put porn where it belongs: in people's bedrooms. And cable TV has pitched in with soft-porn pay channels, such as the Playboy channel in USA. Now it is a common practice in hotels to offer paid porn viewing on their room TVs.

The phenomenon of wives watching porn along with their husbands has strong implications for the porn industry. It has to have it act cleaned up a bit to melt down the traditional female repugnance to porn. Not that pornographers have suffered a change of heart; they are simply interested in expanding their market. So some semblance of a story before the clothes come off. An injection of romance, with the settings more glamorous than a mere bed in a room.

Another technological development is the computer. Computer discs can carry pornographic words, pictures and sounds. And now Cyberporn on the Internet—people sending pornographic messages and the emergence of porn websites. Keeping control over porn on the Internet is proving more problematic than monitoring it on TV and video cassettes.

In the light of these technological advances, women may well be watching porn in increasing numbers. Sallie Tisdale, writing in Harper's Magazine (Feb, 1992), details her growing taste for pornography. And narrates her experiences of going unescorted into "Sex Shops" to browse through the displayed magazines and buy video cassettes.

We also see the start of a phenomenon where women themselves have taken to pornographic writing, even directing porn films. Of late, there's a spate of steamy novels—could be categorized hard porn—coming from known women writers.

The British writer Maureen Freely, eight months pregnant, retired to bed and wrote a novella *Under the Vulcania.* The story is set in a health spa where middle-class women have their sexual wishes catered to by muscular, medically screened young male attendants. The language of sex used in the book is as explicit and graphic as you find in any standard work of pornography. And the book is published by no specialist porn press but by Bloomsbury, a respected London publishing house.

The mainstream publishing firm, Picador, has brought out *Launch*, written by a New Yorker writer, Karen Moline. Her book is again full of passionate sex, with numerous sexual descriptions that leave little to imagination.

And Macmillan has published *Every Woman Deserves an Adventure*, by former *Observer* journalist Yvonne Roberts. "Women are only just beginning to learn how to write about sex on their own terms, in their own language," says she.

Linda Grant, author of *Sexing The Millennium*, argues in favour of women writing on sex, "It's liberating and empowering and helps women to get in touch with how they really feel sexually, instead of internalising the objectified images of themselves that they get from films made by men."

Yet possibly the most daring venture has been a new book of photographs of naked men by women artists, entitled *What She Wants,* published by Verso. The book, according to its editor, Naomi Salaman, allows women to explore responses to erotic images they previously refused to acknowledge.

The book, based on exhibitions of women's works, has a bewildering variety of images. There are men masturbating, men tied up, close-ups of genitals and bottoms.

And you have films like "Urban Heat" (a film by Femme Productions, women producers of porn) that is clearly hard-core porn. As expected, these pornographic writings and productions by women have been attracting much feminist criticism who are frankly dismayed at the entry of women into the production of erotica. Others seek consolation in the thought that this may be a passing fancy and that women indulging in it would soon get browned off.

Women's interaction with porn, it seems, is entering a more complex phase. A majority will retain its distaste against hard porn, especially porn which shows women in degrading positions. Yet an increasing number of women may not be put off by erotica.

Another current development in pornography is its entry into the academic world. Today, porn studies are taught at Berkley, N.Y.U., Columbia, and Northwestern among other American universities. Porn stars lecture on campus. Professors do porn courses and bring our serious treatises on the subject. Indeed there is a growing shelf of academic books devoted to pornography. The main debate is about the nature of visual pleasure generated by pornography.

Linda Williams, a professor of film studies at the University of California teaches a graduate course on porn. She is also the author of a book *Power, Pleasure, and the Frenzy of the Visible*, which has gained wide readership among academics.

Laura Kipnis, a tenured professor at Northwester, is known for her pioneering study in this field, *Bound and Gagged: Pornography and the Politics of Pornography in America*. Chris Straayer, of the New York University, has authored the book *Deviant Eyes, Deviant Bodies: Sexual Reoreintation in Film and Video*. Joanna Frueh, an art historian at the University of Nevada, has written a book *Erotic Faculties* in which she includes nude photographs of herself. And Amy Flowers, who not only conducted interviews with phone-sex workers but got a job as a 900 operator herself, has a book published by the University of Pennsylvani entitled The Fantasy Factory: An Insider's View of the Phone Sex Industry.

Curiously, nearly all the leading figures in the field of porn studies are women. "It's easier for women to have a legitimate voice," says one.

Evidently, our scene is different from what obtains in some other countries. Lewedness in films and magazines does provoke popular protests from women groups. And watching of porn by women, let alone writing of porn material by them or pursuing academic studies on the subject, is still insignificant.

Yet, whether we like it or not, ideas, attitudes and happenings elsewhere are bound to have their impact here. We are living in an age of massive international travel and an entertainment media that has a global reach. The relationship between women and porn won't stay static for long.

Are Men and Women Getting Mismatched?

Andrew Hacker, a professor at Queens College, New York has recently written a book *Mismatch: The Growing Gulf Between Women and Men*. The distinguished political and social scientist interprets the gender scene as is evolving in USA. Yet the same may have some relevance to other societies as well, including ours.

Admittedly, men and women are known to behave differently. They talk differently, they shop differently, they drive differently, they watch TV differently. Their approach to money, sports, politics is different, and so also to personal relationships.

According to Hacker, women and men are moving further apart in virtually every sphere. And he marshalls a wealth of statistics and surveys in support of the proposition. The proverbial war between the sexes, he says, has intensified, and shows few signs of abating.

Nowadays women not only expect "full equality", more and more of them are competing against men. Women reaching parity with men has given rise to quite a few tensions and unresolved issues.

To Hacker, the current high divorce rate (as high as 50 percent in USA) may be the evidence of this estrangement, which transcends the difficulties of individual couples. It's becoming increasingly difficult to describe today's couples as a natural match, the way it was in their grandparents' day, when a natural complementarity between men and women was simply assumed. Men and women were then married to the family, and their marriage reinforced by society, by religion, and so on. There may not have been great sex or continued romance, but the couples learned to live together.

Surely, men and women still live together. But now there's more of a psychological separation. A separation, not just of opinions on various issues, such as crime, schooling, warfare, but also of deeply-held values. Women have a growing consciousness of being their own person.

Hacker attributes the changing gender equation mainly to education; more and more girls going for higher education, and for professions like law and journalism. Men still want to be doctors, but more women are being accepted in medical colleges because they have better records.

Women are often outnumbering men in institutes of higher learning. Some universities in USA, alarmed at the trend, started giving male applicants extra points to keep gender parity. The practice has been struck down by courts. Yet many schools, even prestigious ones such as Harvard, Yale, Princeton are said to be letting in men who have lesser records than women, so that they can stay at 50/50.

Many of these women, unwilling to marry down, will have difficulty finding suitable mates.

Based on actual experiments, Hacker finds his girl students more reflective than boys. When asked whether United States was unquestionably the best country in the world, 90 percent of the boys forthwith said, yes. Only about 60 percent of girls gave that answer. The rest wanted time to reflect about it.

Similarly, as an exercise in personal relationships, he gave his class, boys and girls, two hours to write down everything they knew about their girlfriend or boyfriend. Twenty minutes later, boys started leaving after having written a couple of pages. Girls were still at it for two hours. Having filled the first book, they were asking for the second.

The odds of a young woman finding Mr. Right or a young man finding Ms. Right are much longer these days, because people have much higher expectations of mates. If not exactly picky, people are getting more selective.

Is the gulf growing between men and women?

Some would accuse Hacker of drawing too flattering a picture of women vis-à-vis men. Men are still staying tops in the corporate world and in politics—the two most competitive areas of human endeavour. They still retain a distinct lead in the money market and the sports field. But then women are progressively closing on the male lead in athletics and sports. Money management is made out to be a mystery—a fertile field for sharpies, when it is something that can easily be learned by anybody with a modest education, if so inclined. Politics, however, needs to be cleaned up a bit before women can participate in requisite numbers.

Men have to watch their image, especially in the marital arena, if the mismatch is not to grow more ominous. Educated, earning wives, with all the feel of equality, will be harbouring high expectations of their marriage. Hacker is sounding a note of caution to American men, more so American husbands, about the growing gulf between men and women. And this may well apply to men in other countries, including ours.

Staying Single

Renu Misra, an executive with a clothing company, lives on her own. She did her Masters in Commerce and topped it with a diploma in visual arts from the famous Parson's School of Arts, New York. When free from her busy work schedule, she plays at the piano—an imposing one gifted by her parents.

Her parents had actually wanted her to join the family's burgeoning pharmaceutical business at Delhi and were keen in getting her married. She chose instead to work and live on her own in Mumbai. And she's in no sort of panic to "settle down" as she turns 30. Indeed she likes living alone. "You are free to make your own mistakes when you're single," she declares. Only mealtimes pose a problem. She feels lonely eating by herself at home, and find it awkward to go to a restaurant and sit on a table by herself. She's wanting to talk to someone after a hard day's work, but there's none at home.

Renu is evidently a part of metropolitan India's gathering trend towards single living, at least postponing marriage from year to year. Single by choice, not by accident or *kismet.*

Another group that's often staying single is of the divorcees; the one's whose marriage went awry. Many of them have developed a horror of marriage, while others are wont to be doubly careful about their next choice. With divorce rates going up, the number of singles in this category is registering a rapid rise.

People living single is good for the economy, say some economists. It means more of houses and flats, with the usual separate complement of refrigerators, air conditioners, TVs, music systems and furniture.

This trend towards staying single seems to be worldwide. In America, millions are adopting the solitary lifestyle. *Bowling Alone*, a recently published best-seller by Harvard professor Robert Putnam, draws on the dramatic picture of someone bowling alone, rather than with a group of friends. Putnam argues that the post-war generation brought up on shared values and community service has been supplanted by crude individualism—the picture of a "de-socializing" society. Even today's adolescents spend much time closeted in their rooms with the Internet or watching TV or playing video games instead of participating in team sports. Voter turn-out in elections is falling and so also Sunday church attendance. And more people are spending more of their lives single than ever before.

And surprisingly, women are showing a greater inclination towards staying single. They still feel pressure to marry by the time they enter early thirties—more to do with their biological clocks. But career women no longer need a husband to provide the traditional supports: housing, financial stability, social status or social life. Some, in fact, treasure the personal space a single state affords them, coupled with those "long, peaceful periods of silence". Others are put off marriage, apprehending too much sharing, too many arguments.

Rima Gupta, 28, a textile designer, lives with her rich business parents in a posh Delhi locality. She has stunning looks and a lively mind. No wonder her parents get plenty of marriage proposals. Yet Rima seems in no hurry to marry. She doesn't feel the absence of Mr Right: she has a career, her family and friends. "When I meet the right person, I will spend the rest of my life with him," says she. "But I don't need a man for his money. I want someone who will challenge and motivate me."

Many modern singles would rather accept occasional loneliness to preserve their freedom. "I love being on my own," says another female executive in her middle thirties. "I would like at some time to have a deep relationship, but I am not in a hurry to get there."

Times have really changed. Being single used to be viewed by many as an empty life. Nowadays, a growing number think it can mean a fuller one. Particularly the divorced women, disenchanted with an earlier marriage, are rather wary of entering into fresh commitment.

The result is that a new community has emerged that is unlike any that has come before; a strong, growing community with many shared understandings and values. Singles are evolving their own strategies to combat loneliness, especially social strategies devoted to non-romantic relationships. They keep busy making connections through various organizations and societies, social activities and sports, friends and relatives.

Of course, there are no guarantees that life alone will be fulfilling for everyone as it is for some. In fact, some research suggests exactly the opposite. One recent study showed that 61 percent of single Canadians consider themselves "happy more than unhappy", significantly lower than the 73 per cent for married people.

Single women in societies like ours, except for the few in sheltered top positions in metropolitan areas, are still heir to certain special disadvantages. They are prone to feel somewhat insecure, vulnerable; the social acceptance of single women being far from complete. People around tend to exploit them, and married women shun them socially, fearing their husbands could be led astray. For the younger ones particularly, staying single is often a tightrope walk.

Just Like a Virgin!

In quite a few cultures, a woman's future can hang, literally, by a membrane; the translucent tissue partially covering the vaginal opening. The hymen is there in most females until it is ruptured, usually by sexual activity.

An intact hymen is accordingly taken as proof of virginity. Various cultures set varying value on it for the prospective bride.

This demand for an intact hymen has given rise to surgical procedures that can stitch or re-attach a ruptured one. The surgery is called hymen restoration.

One of the leading surgeons in the field is Robert Stubbs, based in Toronto. "The hymen's a delicate membrane that separates girls from women," says he. The Canadian plastic surgeon, also known for his technique to lengthen penises, reconstructs hymen in two ways. He either stitches the membrane back in place if it is not too damaged, or he attaches a flap of skin from the vaginal wall across the opening.

The process takes one to two hours, and patients can return to normal work the next day. And it costs around US $2,000. He gets patients from all over the world, especially richer ones from the Middle East.

Stubbs has also specialized in what he terms, vaginal rejuvenation or tightening, mostly using absorbable sutures.

The Chinese are known to set a high store on intact hymen. No wonder, a Chinese company is now marketing a hymen-repair kit, called the "Jade Lady Membrane Man-Made Hymen".

Here are extracts from the instruction manual accompanying the kit.

For the female sex, the value of the hymen cannot be overestimated. But the rapid rise in modern women's social status combined with the relentless increase in the pace of our daily lives means that more and more hymens are accidentally damaged or even broken by vigorous activity. These can cast a heavy shadow over a woman's preparations for entry into the blissful state of matrimony and can cause unbearable emotional stress for a newly married couple. Thus, many women are willing to spend thousands of yuan on hymen-repair surgery, thereby placing a burden on both their bodies and their finances.

Through high-tech expert research, Wan Li Hong Corporation has brought its "Man-Made Hymen" products to the market.

PRODUCT DESCRIPTION

A colorless, transparent outer wrapper, with blood-colored powder inside. The device may be folded up to form a plug and may be used to repair a broken hymen. It will also kill bacteria and eliminate infections. This device is safe and reliable. It will not stain clothing.

INSTRUCTIONS FOR USE

The device should be inserted into the vagina. Secretions will cause it to dissolve into an adhesive substance that will then proceed to seal up the mouth of the vagina. When the male member enters and spreads apart the sealed edges of the vagina, the blood-colored ingredients will be released and will quickly mix with natural fluids, creating a liquid that resembles blood. Because the woman will experience no pain when this device is used, it is recommended that she increase the product's efficacy by accompanying its rupture with the moans and groans that typically accompany the rupture of a real hymen. The sexual act may begin 20-30 minutes after this device has been inserted. If the device does not break on its own the woman may discreetly use her finger to break it open.

Men and Women in Conversation

Once people realize that their partners have different conversational styles. they are inclined to accept differences without blaming themselves, their partners, or their relationships. The biggest mistake is believing that there is one right way to listen, to talk, to have conversation... Understanding the other's way of talking is a giant leap across the communication gap between men and women, and a giant step towards opening lines of communication.

That's Deborah Tannen, a professor of linguistics at Georgetown University, in her pioneering book "You Just Don't Understand", (Ballantine Books). Tannen has written a refreshing and readable account of the complexities of conversation between men and women.

Tannen explains that male-female conversation is cross-cultural communication; they are said to speak different "genderlects". If women speak a language of connection and intimacy, men speak and hear a language of status and independence.

Even as boys and girls who grow up in the same locality or house, or as brothers and sisters in the same family, they grow up in different worlds of words. Others talk to them differently and expect and accept different ways of talking from them. Even when they are together, boys and girls spend most of their time playing in the same-sex groups. Their favourite games are different, and their ways of using language in their games are separated by a world of difference.

Boys tend to play outside, in large groups, with every group having a leader who tells others what to do. He mostly uses the language of command. Boys' games have winners and losers and elaborate systems of rules.

Girls often play in small groups or in pairs. Within the group intimacy is key. In games like jump rope and hopscotch, everyone gets a turn. Many of these games have no winners or losers. Girls' talk is mostly concerned with getting cooperation from their playmates than obedience.

And these differences in conversational styles engendered in early childhood persist over a lifetime.

Recriminations between women and their men are a common occurrence when women relate their troubles. Women want the gift of understanding, but men give the gift of advice. Men see themselves as problem solvers. Any complaint is a challenge to their ability to think of a solution, just as they would like to fix a broken kitchen machine or stalled car presented by a woman. But whereas many women appreciate help in fixing mechanical equipment, few are inclined to appreciate help in "fixing" their emotional troubles. A wife bothered by a bodily defect is often looking for her husband's understanding and sympathy in her trouble, not merely advice. On the other hand, men are frustrated when their sincere attempts to help a woman solve her problems are not met with gratitude but with disapproval.

The book also discusses the stereotyped image of women as great talkers. There's that classic home scene of a silent man and his talking woman. The simple explanation that the man may not want to talk because he is tired when he comes home from work, is not convincing enough. Women who work come home tired too, and yet they are eager to tell their partners what happened during the day. It seems that for women, gossip as an exchange of confidences and bits of information, is an important means of getting closer. The difference shows up most when parents talk to their college-gone children on telephone. Most of the conversation takes place with mothers. Fathers typically join in only when they have a business matter to discuss or report. Clearly women are much better at making small talk than men.

Men make out that they remain silent because there is nothing important to say. To women the very process of conversation with their partners or others boosts rapport. And so they harbour dissatisfaction with men's silence at home, or with their men engrossed in paper or absorbed in watching sports on TV to the exclusion of conversation.

A wife lamenting, "He seems to have everything to say to everyone else, and nothing to say to me." Incidentally men are also accused of occasionally using silence as a weapon or a means of power against their womenfolk. Denying information to the partner which she is wanting it, or just keeping mum or staying monosyllabic when she is expecting a proper reply.

Actually men talk more than women, says Tannen, and has expert support for it. In conferences and meetings, in outside gatherings, even cocktails, men are holding the floor more often than women.

What is the solution, then, if men and women talk at cross-purposes? To Tannen, both men and women should try to take each other on their own terms rather than try to change the other to their standard of talk and behaviour. Habitual ways of talking are hard to change. Learning to respect other's way of talking may be a bit easier, says she. Men should accept that many women regard exchanging details about personal lives as a basic ingredient of intimacy, and women should accept that many men do not share this view.

Connected to talking is the phenomenon of listening. Tannen finds that women listen more to men than men to women. And while at it, women give more listening signals, like asking questions or giving more listening responses. Men listen rather silently, and go for making statements than asking questions. This different pattern of gender-listening creates its own problems. Sometimes women may get the impression that men aren't listening when they really are. Of course, some men really don't want to listen at length because they feel it puts them into a subordinate role.

Allied to listening is this phenomenon of interrupting. In contradiction to the stereotype image of women interrupting men, research findings indicate that men interrupt women more, says Tannen. And in this context it's the nature of the interruption that is important. Is it intrusive or an attempt to dominate—a kind of conversational bullying? Or is it just a cooperative support to what is being talked? Women often interrupt as cooperative overlappers and not for dominance, says Tannen, and such overlapping speech is not destructive. Again to many women, talking together is often valued in casual conversation. It's another matter that many men find this spectacle of women talking simultaneously among themselves rather funny.

Men and women are observed even aligning their bodies differently when talking. At every age, girls and women sit closer to each other and look at each other directly. At every age, boys and men sit at angles to each other, sometimes even parallel. Girls and women are seen anchoring their gaze on each other's faces, occasionally glancing away, while boys and men are anchoring their gaze elsewhere around, occasionally glancing at each other.

Tannen's book "You Just Don't Understand' can be considered a notable and timely contribution to improving relationships between men and women, through a better understanding of the way men and women converse.

Index